The Complete ACOA Sourcebook

The Complete ACOA Sourcebook

Adult Children of Alcoholics at Home, at Work and in Love

Janet G. Woititz, Ed.D.

Health Communications, Inc.
Deerfield Beach, Florida

www.hcibooks.com

Library of Congress Cataloging-in-Publication Data

Woititz, Janet Geringer.
The complete ACOA sourcebook : adult children of alcoholics at home, at work
   and in love / Janet G. Woititz.
         p.   cm.
      Includes bibliographical references.
      ISBN-13: 978-1-55874-960-3 (tp)
      ISBN-10: 1-55874-960-8 (tp)
      1. Adult children of alcoholics—Psychology. 2 Interpersonal relations. I. Title.

HV5132 .W63 2002
362.292'4—dc21

                                                                              2001052762

Publisher: Health Communications, Inc.
              3201 S.W. 15th Street
              Deerfield Beach, FL 33442-8190

R-07-07

Cover redesign by Lawna Patterson Oldfield
Inside formatting by Lawna Patterson Oldfield

A NOTE FROM THE PUBLISHER

The following material from the late Dr. Janet Woititz originally appeared as three separate books: *Adult Children of Alcoholics*, published in 1983; *The Self-Sabotage Syndrome*, published in 1987; and *Struggle for Intimacy*, published in 1990.

We have combined the main body of these three books into one complete volume, in their entirety, with each book appearing as a part of the whole work *The Complete ACOA Sourcebook*. Although some material may be repeated, we felt it important to preserve the integrity of Dr. Woititz's work by maintaining the books' original content.

CONTENTS

PART THREE

At Work: The Self-Sabotage Syndrome

Section One: ACOAs on the Job

FOREWORD

I am honored to write the foreword for these three very important works of Dr. Janet Woititz. For many years I had the privilege of knowing Jan. We shared much. There was work, countless speaking engagements, books to be written, stories to be told, laughter to be heard, interviews to be given, thousands of people who wanted someone to listen, and most importantly—friendship. In 1994, after a gallant battle against cancer, Jan died. I miss her.

In June 1994, I was participating in a conference sponsored by the *U.S. Journal* in Philadelphia as both a speaker and as conference chair. Jan was going to be a speaker at the conference and, as usual, I was looking forward to seeing her and to introducing her to the audience. When I arrived I was informed that, due to illness, Jan had to cancel. I knew that she must have been very sick not to show up. On the evening of the second day, just as I was preparing to deliver my presentation, I was informed that Jan had died. It was decided by the conference sponsors that I should be the one to break the news that evening to the audience. It was a painful task and a difficult night. We had a lost a good friend. So many people had been touched by Jan's work and life. There was not much to say, but there was a lot to be felt.

Now, years later, I am being asked to introduce Jan again by writing the foreword for some of her works. This feels right for two old friends.

In 1983, Jan wrote a book about adults who as children grew up in alcoholic families. She titled her book *Adult Children of Alcoholics*. Prior to that, in 1978, I wrote a book about children living in alcoholic families. I titled the book *Children of Alcoholics*. Obviously, we were both very creative with our book titles! But maybe that was the point. We took feelings of self-doubt, feelings of shame, feelings of being different and behaviors of denial, covering up, and pretending to be normal and gave them a name. We named the condition for what it was—children and adult children of alcoholics. Straight to the point. Straight to the heart. No more denial, no more misdiagnosis, no more lack of intervention and no more excuses for not recognizing the impact of parental alcoholism on children.

During those years there were approximately 28.6 million children of alcoholics in the United States. Of those, about 22 million were adults. For them childhood was over, but not the impact. They were now adults and Jan's work was not only a breath of fresh air, but also for many, it was the story of their lives written by someone who understood. Her work offered hope to the many victims of alcoholic families who believed that their lives were different and that surely something was wrong with them. Now, years later, their numbers continue to grow.

The three works that are contained in this book have helped millions of adult children of alcoholics to realize that there are reasons for the way that they think, believe and feel about themselves. There are reasons that adult children of alcoholics have often felt isolated, have had difficulty in relationships, at work or feeling good about themselves.

If you are an adult child of an alcoholic and you are reading this book, you will find out that many of your feelings, behaviors and thoughts are normal. Perhaps, more than anything else, Jan helped adult children not only to gain insight into themselves, but also to feel normal for the first time in their lives. And her work reveals that just because you are an adult child of an alcoholic does not mean that something is wrong with you. She tried to tell us that how you felt growing up with all of the limitations, fears, isolation and self-condemnation is not how you have to live as an adult today. As an adult child of an alcoholic you have something today that you did not have as a child. You have a choice. You can change. You can break the legacy of addictive families. Jan knew this, and it is the core of her writings.

Combining these three works into a single volume makes a lot of sense. This new work talks about adult children at home, in love and at work. In each of these areas, we find that the experiences of growing up in an alcoholic family are apparent. In *Adult Children of Alcoholics*, Jan helps us to understand ourselves by examining many of the thoughts and behaviors shared by many adult children. She offers insights and strategies for overcoming childhood trauma and hope for our futures.

In *Struggle for Intimacy*, we find the core of most problems for adult children—how to develop healthy relationships. She shows us that all the ingredients of being truly intimate, such as being vulnerable, allowing others to get close and liking ourselves, are the exact opposite of the survival skills developed by most adult children of alcoholics while they were growing up. She also shows us that just as we learned to protect ourselves from emotional pain while growing up, we can now learn the necessary skills to improve our relationships.

Finally in *The Self-Sabotage Syndrome*, we find that the very characteristics and behaviors that often make adult children very successful occupationally can be the very same characteristics and behaviors that put us at such a high risk for professional burnout. We might make great employees because of our workaholism, perfectionism and willingness to accept responsibility, but without self-care we are in danger of self-destructing.

I cannot speak for Jan, but whether you are an adult child or you are trying to help one, I hope that this book helps you. It is obvious by the tributes to Jan and the many bestseller lists for her books that she has helped millions. Her message has stood the test of time and it has always remained clear. It will never be dated. We do have a choice about how we live. And I thank Jan for reminding us of that.

—*Robert J. Ackerman, Ph.D.*

ACKNOWLEDGMENTS

Part One

I want to thank those many people who helped to make this book possible. They are the children of alcoholic parents of all ages, and the children of nonalcoholic parents of all ages.

To Diane DuCharme, who convinced me to write this book.

To Sue Nobleman, Debby Parsons, Tom Perrin and Rob, for their tireless devotion to the project.

To Lisa, Danny and Dave.

To Kerry C., Jeff R., Irene G., Eleanor Q., Barbara P., Martha C., Loren S., my students at Montclair State, my students at Rutgers University Summer School for Alcohol Studies, my students in the Advanced Techniques in Family Therapy Course (Westchester Council on Alcoholism), Sharon Stone, Harvey Moscowitz, Linda Rudin, Eileen Patterson, Bernard Zweben and James F. Emmert.

Part Two

To Dave, Lisa and Danny for their specialness. To my Monday Night Group—Dr. Don Gregg, Ken Kirkland, Andrea Becker, Bonnie White, Eileen Lindsay, Claudia O'Brien, Ed Ellis, Miriam Sender, Sue Falan and Bernie Zweben for their help.

To the "Super Brats" from my Adult Children of Alcoholics course at Rutgers Summer School for Alcohol Studies for their validation.

Part Three

The impact of growing up in a dysfunctional family is experienced in every aspect of adult life. The workplace is no exception.

In order to demonstrate the ways in which the work environment becomes a home away from home, I drew on both my own clinical experience and that of a number of colleagues. I acknowledge the assistance of the following consultants:

Chapters 9 and 10 draw heavily on conversations with Mel Sandler, M.S.W. Mel is Managing Director of the Institute for Counseling and Training, West Caldwell, New Jersey. His career includes extensive involvement in workplace settings, counseling employees and training management personnel to deal with employees with personal problems. Settings in which he has worked include United Airlines; the American Federation of State, County, and Municipal Employees; and the International Ladies' Garment Workers' Union. He currently acts as a consultant in corporate workplace settings.

Other chapters benefited from the input of:

Administrative

Gyni Garner, M.S.W.—Charlotte, North Carolina
Bob Lynn, N.C.C., C.A.C.—Piscataway, New Jersey
Kerry Peltier, M.A., C.A.C.—Verona, New Jersey

Professional

Pat Clyne, B.A., R.N.—Astoria, New York
Kathi Goode, M.A.—Montclair, New Jersey
Rev. James Mahoney, Ph.D.—Chatham, New Jersey
Audrey Roberts, M.A.—Montclair, New Jersey

Clinical

George Brines, A.A.S., C.A.C.—Lafayette, Indiana
Dana Finnegan, Ph.D.—South Orange, New Jersey
Emily McNally, M.A.—New York, New York
Martha Moore-Russell, Ph.D.—Princeton, New Jersey
Amy Stromsten, C.A.C.—Cambridge, Massachusetts
Bick Wanck, M.D.—Conifer Park, New York

Research

Coleen Peruo, B.A.—East Rutherford, New Jersey
Patrick Peruo, Ph.D.—East Rutherford, New Jersey

General

Jackson Braider, M.A.—New York, New York
Ed Gogek, M.D.—Providence, Rhode Island
Matt Johnson, B.S.W.—Anchorage, Alaska
Marilyn Stager—Hawthorne, New Jersey
Lisa Woititz, B.A.—Montclair, New Jersey

Employee Assistance Programs

Debby Bem, M.S.W.—New Rochelle, New York

Leighton Clark, M.S.W.—Chicago, Illinois

Betty-Ann Weinstein, M.S.W.—Washington, D.C.

PART ONE

At Home:
Adult Children
of Alcoholics

A Message from
DR. JANET WOITITZ

Preface

Ten years ago when I began to explore the possibility of writing a book about what happened to children of alcoholics when they grew up, I had no idea what the impact of such a book would be.

It has long been my belief that anyone who sees the world in a slightly different way from others has a responsibility to publish and make those perspectives available to others. It was with this in mind that I began working on the project. My friends and colleagues shrugged their shoulders. I was, once again, making a mountain out of what others considered a molehill—or less. Since it was a familiar position for me to be in, I was not discouraged.

I had done my doctoral dissertation, *Self-Esteem in Children of Alcoholics*, in the middle 1970s. At that time, the only other work in this area was Margaret Cork's *The Forgotten Children*. There appeared to be very little interest in this topic. The prevailing thinking in the alcoholism field was that if the alcoholic got well, the family would get well. So attention was focused on the alcoholic. After all, most folks find the person with the lampshade on his or her head more interesting than the partner cowering in the

3

corner. This was not true for me; I have always been more fascinated by the reactors than the actors.

The '70s, when I was doing my research, was an era of great individual exploration. It was a time of encounter groups, drug exploration and sexual freedom. It was a time of I—I—I. So the idea that there were millions of people being profoundly impacted by the behaviors and attitudes of others and who had no self to indulge ran contrary to the flow of the time.

I had been outspoken against the Vietnam War when John Kennedy was in office. I had argued for civil rights before the sit-ins. Since I was acutely aware of the overwhelming impact of my husband's alcoholism on me and my children, it was only natural that I call it the way that I saw it. It also was not surprising that my point of view was not shared.

My continuing interest in what happens to the family led to my writing *Marriage on the Rocks*. I had found that if I gave my clients a talk about what other folks I knew felt about living with alcoholism, it would cut down their denial. When I told them before they told me, they were amazed and relieved. This led me to believe that if someone saw their feelings and experiences in print, it would validate them even more strongly and be helpful in the therapeutic process. Someone needed to bring this reality out of the closet. This information had to be shared.

When *Marriage on the Rocks* was published, I went on a book promotion tour that covered all the major markets in this country. The idea of the influence of what we now call "codependency" was not of general interest. Although the need was great, the denial was clearly greater.

Ironically enough, almost every radio and television station I visited greeted me with an apology because my book had been stolen. I knew what that meant. Someone living with alcoholism was too embarrassed to ask to borrow the book. I also found that I was invited not because it was a "hot topic" but because a reporter or producer had the problem and wanted a private session with someone who "understood."

The Al-Anon program was and continues to be a primary resource for family members. I will always be grateful for the personal support and professional encouragement I received in those rooms. It was the one place where folks believed that the family could get well regardless of what the alcoholic did. Since the program is designed primarily to serve the newest member living with an active problem, and rightly so, others who are in different life circumstances have to do some translating in order to relate what is being said to their own lives and to gain the benefit. So adult children, although equally needy, don't quite connect. The development of much-needed support groups specifically for ACOAs fills that gap.

In 1979 I was invited to participate in a symposium in Washington, D.C., on services to children of alcoholics. It was sponsored by the National Institute for Alcoholism and Alcohol Abuse (NIAAA). Twelve of us were invited, and we were told that they only had twenty-four people in the country to choose from. For the first time I felt that I was among other professionals who appreciated the importance of the work.

In 1980 I was invited to design and teach a course on counseling children of alcoholics at Rutgers University Summer School of Alcohol Studies. It was then—and to the best of my knowledge still is—the only course of its type in the world. It is a great credit to Rutgers and the willingness of those involved in the summer school that they were educational leaders. That course set the spark. And it was so wonderful to be validated and supported. Soon there was much interest within the alcohol treatment community, and I received invitations from all over the country to address and train professionals.

At about the same time the adolescents whom I had known through friends in Al-Anon and through my clinical practice were growing up. It was clear to me that the struggles of those who were affected by an alcoholic parent were somewhat different from others of the same age whom I knew and with whom I worked. One day when I was giving a lecture on children of alcoholics, I happened to say, "The child of an alcoholic has no age. The same things hold true if you are five or fifty-five." I am convinced that it was from that moment on that people started listening differently. I was no longer talking about "the children." I was talking about them.

I made the decision to form a group that focused on the problems of being an ACOA, to work in this area with individual cases and to test my findings nationally. For the next two years I did precisely that. No matter where I went in this country or abroad, the response was the same: "You are describing me and my life." "At long last I feel validated." "I am not crazy." From those findings, I wrote the book *Adult Children of Alcoholics*.

Adult Children of Alcoholics was not designed as a clinical book. It was not a scientific report of my research. It was rather a sharing of my observations and of the consensus of self-understandings of the hundreds of adult children of alcoholics with whom I came in contact. In describing the characteristics of ACOAs, I was not discussing character defects. I was sharing my awareness. It is my belief that knowledge is freedom and that those who identified could now have new choices. They could decide to work on changing aspects of themselves that cause them difficulty, or they could choose not to do so. In either event they had greater self-knowledge, which leads to greater self-understanding, which helps in the development of a sense of self. It was a win-win situation.

Adult Children of Alcoholics was not an immediate bestseller. It was turned down by many publishers. Once again I was told that I was making a big deal about a little problem. Perhaps it was worth a pamphlet but not a book. I had met Gary Seidler of the *U.S. Journal* at a National Council on Alcoholism conference, and someone who was familiar with my work suggested that I show him the manuscript. We are both glad I did.

The book was first published in 1983 and was sold primarily by mail order. The bookstores were not interested. ACOAs who read it told each other about it and started buying copies for all the members of their families. The word was getting out. Bookstores began to carry it because of the demand, but for the most part they kept it hidden in the back of the store. People who wanted it had to ask for it. They could not just take it off the shelf. This created discomfort for folks who had been taught to keep their family business a secret. They were forced to ask a stranger for a book the mere title of which would tell all. The need overcame the embarrassment.

By 1987 sales swelled and *Adult Children of Alcoholics* hit *The New York Times* bestseller list and stayed there for close to a year. The book had not been promoted nor had it been marketed. Even when it was on the list, it was not placed, for the most part, with the other bestsellers. The demand was truly grassroots. The people who believed it would be useful demanded the right to read it.

At this writing, *Adult Children of Alcoholics* has sold close to 2 million copies in the United States, Canada, England, Australia and New Zealand. It has been translated into Norwegian, Finnish, Danish and German, and will be translated into Russian. There is the beginning of international recognition that the impact of alcoholism on children is similar regardless of culture, race, national origin, religion or economics. It is truly a pandemic. The language of suffering is universal.

It also has become clear that the impact of other troubled systems is similar, and that the alcoholic family system is a model for many other troubled families as well.

Since part of the recovery process from alcohol is to give up "the secrets," folks involved in overcoming this disease have nothing left to hide. They are wonderful about letting us study and learn from them. They benefit and we benefit and others who identify also benefit.

Adult Children of Alcoholics was originally written with only children of alcoholics in mind. Since its first publication, we have learned that the material discussed applies to other types of dysfunctional families as well. If you did not grow up with alcoholism but lived, for example, with other compulsive behaviors such as gambling, drug abuse or overeating, or you experienced chronic illness or profound religious attitudes, or you were adopted, lived in foster care or in other potentially dysfunctional systems, you may find that you identify with the characteristics described here. It appears that much of what is true for the children of alcoholics is also true for others and that this understanding can help reduce the isolation of countless persons who also thought they were "different" because of their life experience. Welcome.

Five years ago I founded with the assistance of several talented colleagues the Institute for Counseling and Training in Verona, New Jersey. Now in West Caldwell, the institute is designed to provide excellence of outpatient care and education to individuals and to families who identify with the problems found in the alcoholic family system. Another purpose of the institute is to provide a research base to add to the knowledge in the field. This has led to several other published works that take a deeper look at aspects discussed in general terms in *Adult Children of Alcoholics*.

Struggle for Intimacy was written as a direct response to the desire that our clients have to develop healthy intimate relationships and to identify the pain involved in that process. It is important to be clear as to the nature of the struggle in order to be able to make desired changes.

My desire for those working in employee assistance programs to understand the value of and the conflicts experienced by the ACOA led to my writing *Home Away from Home*. It was an attempt to make clear to the employer the value of the adult child in the work force and the risk of burnout if that value is exploited. Later, an edition designed for the general consumer was published as *The Self-Sabotage Syndrome*. The point made in both editions is that when folks do not address the characteristics of ACOAs, the workplace becomes a replica of the home and the adult child can once again feel victimized.

We are seeing more and more men and women who suffer from traumas related to sexual and sexuality abuse, and who need to heal from that abuse. Their experiences inhibit their ability to appreciate their worth either individually or in relationships. That prompted my writing *Healing Your Sexual Self*.

Adult Children of Alcoholics was largely based on the premise that for the ACOA there is a lack of database: ACOAs do not learn what other children learn in the process of growing up. Although they do wonderfully well in crisis, they do not learn the day-to-day process of "doing life." So when Alan Garner suggested we do a book together—*Life Skills for Adult Children*—it seemed like a logical next step. It was a return to basics. Insight and adjustment will only take you so far. The next step is to "live it" and to be educated as to "how to do it."

When Peter Vegso approached me about revising *Adult Children of Alcoholics*, it was a curious thought. After all, what was true then is true now. Why fix what is working? As I thought more about it, I realized that there was a section missing—a section on recovery. When I first wrote the book, there were no recovery programs for ACOAs. The idea that calling yourself an ACOA had validity was being debated, and many folks had difficulty accepting the idea that one could recover from the experience. At about the time the book came out, support groups were starting in different parts of the country. As support groups developed, so did recovery programs, and more people began working and writing in the field. Within the last few years, many more therapists have specialized in working with ACOAs, and books, workshops and conferences have proliferated. Public awareness has grown and the recovery industry has been born.

At one point, there was shame involved in admitting to being a child from a dysfunctional family; now it is okay. At one point the isolation involved in this life experience was profound; now one can have a sense of being a part of the whole human family. Because of these developments, recovery now has a special meaning for ACOAs. Therefore a basic book about what it means to be an ACOA needs a section on recovery hints to help keep the recovering ACOA on track. So a new chapter has been added, as well as this limited history of "the ACOA book" and the subsequent "ACOA movement" according to "Jan."

It is heartwarming to feel heard, at last.

Introduction

During the last several years, more and more research has been done on alcoholism in this society. Although figures vary, there is general agreement that there are upwards of 10 million alcoholics in this country.

These people, as well as being victims themselves, have an adverse impact on those with whom they associate. Employers, relatives, friends and families of alcoholics suffer from the effects of alcoholism. Many person-hours of work are lost because of absenteeism and inefficiency due to alcoholism. Relatives and friends are manipulated into making excuses for and covering up for the alco-holic. The promises of reform, although short-lived, are believed because those who care want to believe them, and, as a result, they unknowingly become part of the disease pattern.

Those who are the closest suffer most of all. The family is affected when the employer has to terminate the alcoholic's services. The family is affected when the relatives and friends can no longer toler-ate the consequences of alcoholism and avoid the alcoholic and his/her family. The family is also directly affected by the alcoholic's behavior. Unable, without help, to counteract this, the family mem-bers get caught up in the consequences of the illness and become emotionally ill themselves.

The bulk of popular interest has been with alcoholism, alcohol abuse and alcoholics. Less attention has been paid to the family, and, more specifically, to the children living in alcoholic homes.

There is little question that there are large numbers of children affected by living in alcoholic homes. Identification of these chil-dren has been difficult for several reasons, including embarrassment, ignorance about alcoholism as a disease, denial and protection of children from unpleasant realities.

Although the suffering manifests itself behaviorally in different ways, children of alcoholics seem to have in common a low self-esteem. This is not surprising, since the literature indicates that the conditions which lead an individual to value himself or to regard herself as a person of worth can be briefly summarized by the terms "Parental warmth," "clearly defined limits" and "respectful treatment."[1]

There is considerable literature in which it is argued that these conditions are absent or inconsistently present in the alcoholic

[1] S. Coopersmith, "Self-Concept Research Implications for Education." Paper presented to the American Education Research Association, Los Angeles, Calif., 6 February 1969.

home.[2] The alcoholic parent's behavior is affected by the chemicals within, and the nonalcoholic parent's behavior is affected by reaction to the alcoholic. Little emotional energy remains to consistently fulfill the many needs of children who become victims to the family illness.

Parents are models whether they want to be or not. According to Margaret Cork, it is in the give-and-take of relationships with parents and others that the child finds a sense of security and self-esteem and an ability to deal with complex inner problems.[3]

Coopersmith's study with adolescent boys indicates that children develop self-trust, adventuresomeness and the ability to deal with adversity if they are treated with respect and are provided with well-defined standards of values, demands for competence and guidance toward solutions of problems. The development of individual self-reliance is fostered by a well-structured, demanding environment, rather than by largely unlimited permissiveness and freedom to explore in an unfocused way.

The research of both Stanley Coopersmith and Morris Rosenberg has led them to believe that pupils with high self-esteem perceive themselves as successful. They are relatively free of anxiety and psychosomatic symptoms, and can realistically assess their abilities. They are confident that their efforts will meet with success, while being fully aware of their limitations. Persons with high self-esteem are outgoing and socially successful and expect to be well received. They accept others and others tend to accept them.

---

[2] M. B. Bailey, "Alcoholism and Family Casework (New York National Council on Alcoholism, New York City Affiliate Inc., 1968). M. Hecht, "Children of Alcoholics Are Children at Risk." American Journal of Nursing 73 (10) October 1973: 1764-1767.

[3] Margaret Cook, The Forgotten Children (Toronto: Alcohol and Drug Addiction Research Foundation, 1969), 36.

On the other hand, according to Coopersmith and Rosenberg, pupils with low self-esteem are easily discouraged and sometimes depressed. They feel isolated, unloved and unlovable. They seem incapable of expressing themselves or defending their inadequacies. They are so preoccupied with their self-consciousness and anxiety that their capacity for self-fulfillment can be easily destroyed.[4]

My own research for *Self-Esteem in Children of Alcoholics*[5] showed that children of alcoholic parents have lower self-esteem than those who do not come from homes where alcohol is abused. This was expected. Since self-esteem is based most importantly on the amount of respectful, accepting and concerned treatment from significant others, it is logical to assume that the inconsistency of the presence of these conditions in an alcoholic home would negatively influence one's ability to feel good about herself.

Interestingly enough, a variable such as the age of the subject was insignificant as a determinant of self-esteem.[6] Eighteen-year-olds and twelve-year-olds saw themselves in essentially the same way. They may behave differently, but they don't have different self-feelings. This points up the fact that self-perceptions do not change over time without some form of intervention. The way the self-attitude manifests itself will change, but not the self-perception.

If this is true, and research tends to support this concept, then an important population to pay attention to are the adult children of alcoholics.

---

[4] S. Coopersmith, The Antecedents of Self-Esteem (*San Francisco: W. H. Freeman and Co.*, 1967). Morris Rosenberg, Society and the Adolescent Self-Image (*Princeton, N.J.: Princeton University Press, 1965*).

[5] J. Woititz, Doctoral Dissertation, New Brunswick, New Jersey, May 1976.

[6] *Variables such as sex, religion, occupation and sibling order also proved to have no statistical significance.*

We have not ignored this population. We have simply not labeled them fully. We have called them alcoholics. We have called them spouses of alcoholics. We have not given them acknowledgment of the full measure of their exposure. It is time to identify them further. It is time to call them ACOAs. It is important to recognize this factor because there are very profound implications for treatment if we do so. The adult child of an alcoholic has been affected and has reacted in ways that those who are not adult children of alcoholics may not have. This book will profile for you the adult child of the alcoholic, what it means and what the implications are.

It will discuss how poor self-image shows itself and will offer very specific suggestions as to ways to change, if that is desirable.

I have been working with groups of adult children of alcoholics. We are taking an in-depth look at their thoughts, attitudes, reactions and feelings, and the powerful influence of alcohol in their lives.

Half of the group members are recovering alcoholics, the other half are not. Half are men. Half are women. The youngest member is twenty-three. Some are married, some single. Some have children, some do not. All are committed to self-growth.

There are certain generalizations that recur in one form or another at virtually every meeting. These perceptions are worthy of careful examination and discussion.

1. Adult children of alcoholics guess at what normal behavior is.
2. Adult children of alcoholics have difficulty following a project through from beginning to end.
3. Adult children of alcoholics lie when it would be just as easy to tell the truth.
4. Adult children of alcoholics judge themselves without mercy.
5. Adult children of alcoholics have difficulty having fun.
6. Adult children of alcoholics take themselves very seriously.

7. Adult children of alcoholics have difficulty with intimate relationships.

8. Adult children of alcoholics overreact to changes over which they have no control.

9. Adult children of alcoholics constantly seek approval and affirmation.

10. Adult children of alcoholics usually feel that they are different from other people.

11. Adult children of alcoholics are super responsible or super irresponsible.

12. Adult children of alcoholics are extremely loyal, even in the face of evidence that the loyalty is undeserved.

13. Adult children of alcoholics are impulsive. They tend to lock themselves into a course of action without giving serious consideration to alternative behaviors or possible consequences. This impulsivity leads to confusion, self-loathing and loss of control over their environment. In addition, they spend an excessive amount of energy cleaning up the mess.

This book is written to and for adult children of alcoholics. It is also my hope that counselors and other interested persons will find it to be of value.

It can be useful in a number of ways: (1) To gain greater knowledge and understanding of what it means to be the child of an alcoholic, and how this process evolves over time; (2) To use as a self-help or clinical guide in working toward individual growth; and (3) As a basis for discussion groups of adult children of alcoholics.

I have had many requests from all over the country as to how to go about setting up groups for adult children of alcoholics, how to meet their special needs, and yet remain true to the principles of AA and Al-Anon. This book provides an answer to these questions.

1

What Happened
to You As a Child?

When is a child not a child? When the child lives with alcoholism. But, more correctly, when is a child not childlike? You certainly looked like a child and dressed like a child. Other people saw you as a child, unless they got close enough to that edge of sadness in your eyes or that worried look on your brow. You behaved much like a child, but you were not really frolicking, you were more just going along. You didn't have the same spontaneity that the other kids had. But no one really noticed that. That is, unless they got very close, and even if they did, they probably didn't understand what it meant.

Whatever others saw and said, the fact remains that you didn't really feel like a child. You didn't even have a sense of what it's like to have a child's feelings. A child is very much like a puppy . . . offering and receiving love freely and easily, scampering, somewhat mischievous, playful, doing work for approval or a reward, but doing as little as possible. Most important, being carefree. If a child is like a puppy, you were not a child.

Others could describe you in a very simple sentence, probably related to the role you adopted in the family. Children who live in

17

alcoholic homes take on roles similar to those taken on in other dys-functional families. But in this kind of family, we see it very clearly. Others are aware of it, too, only they don't recognize it for what it is.

For example, "Look at Emily, isn't she remarkable? She's the most responsible child I have ever seen. I wish I had one like that at home." If you were Emily, you smiled, felt good and enjoyed getting the praise. You probably didn't allow yourself to think, "I wish I could be good enough for them." And you certainly didn't allow yourself to think, "I wish my parents thought I was terrific. I wish I could be good enough for them," or "Well, if I didn't do it, who would?"

To an outsider looking in, you were simply a remarkable little child. And the truth of the matter is, you were. They just didn't see the whole picture.

You might have taken on another role in the family. You might have been the scapegoat, the one in trouble all the time. You were the family's way of not looking at what was really happening. People said, "Would you look at that Tommy, he's always in trouble. Boys will be boys. I was the same way when I was his age."

If you were Tommy, what did you feel? You might not allow your-self to feel. You'd just look at the person and you'd know that they really *weren't* like you when they were your age. If they were, they wouldn't be so flip about it. Yet, you couldn't allow yourself to say, and probably wouldn't even allow yourself to wonder, "What do I have to do in order to get them to pay attention to me? Why does it have to be this way?"

You might have been more like Barbara and become the class clown. "Gee, she should really be a comedienne when she grows up. How clever, how funny, how witty!" And if you were Barbara, you might smile, but underneath you wondered, "Do they know how I really feel? Life really isn't that funny. I seem to have fooled them. I can't let them know."

And then there's little Margaret, or is it Joan? Somehow I can never really get the name straight. That little child off in the corner. That withdrawn child—the one who never gives anyone any trouble. And the little child wonders, "Am I invisible?" That child doesn't really want to be invisible but hides in a shell, hoping to be noticed, powerless to do anything about it.

You looked like a child, you dressed like a child, to some degree you behaved like a child, but you sure as hell didn't feel like a child. Let's take a look at what it was like at home.

Home Life

Children of alcoholics grow up in similar environments. The cast of characters may be different, but what happens in each alcoholic home is not a whole lot different. The specific happenings may vary but, in general, one alcoholic home environment is like another. The undercurrent of tension and anxiety is ever present. What happens with it in particular may vary, but the resulting pain and remorse predictably follow. The differences exist more in the way you reacted to your experiences than to the experiences themselves.

You internalized what happened differently and, as a result, behaved differently. But most of you felt pretty much the same inside.

Remember what it was like at home? You can visualize what it looked like, but do you remember what it felt like? What did you expect when you walked in the door? You hoped that everything would be fine, but you never really knew for sure. The only thing you were sure of was that you never knew what you would find or what was going to happen. And somehow, no matter how many times things went awry, as soon as you walked in the door, you were never prepared.

If your father was the alcoholic, sometimes he was loving and warm. He was everything you wanted a father to be: caring, interested, involved, promising all the things that a child wants. And you knew he loved you, too.

But other times he wasn't that way. Those were the times he was drunk. When he didn't come home at all, you worried and waited. At home, he passed out, got into big fights with your mother, even came at you, which was really scary. Sometimes you got in the middle, trying to keep the peace. Never knowing what was going to happen, you always felt somewhat desperate. And then the drunk father forgot all those promises he made the day before. That felt strange, because you knew he meant it when he promised them. You thought, *Why doesn't it ever happen? Why doesn't he ever do what he says he is going to do? It really isn't fair.*

And then there was your mother. In a very funny kind of way, even with all of his problems you may have preferred your father. Because she was grouchy and irritable, acting as if she had the weight of the world upon her shoulders, and tired all the time, you felt like you were in the way. Even though she told you that you were not in the way, you couldn't help feeling it.

She may have gone off to work. Your father may not have had a job. You couldn't help feeling that if you weren't in the picture, there wouldn't be all this trouble. Your mother wouldn't be fighting with your father. She wouldn't be tense all the time; she wouldn't be screaming; she wouldn't be so short-tempered. Life could be a whole lot easier if you simply weren't there. And you felt very guilty. Somehow your very existence caused this: If you were a better kid, there would be fewer problems. It was all your fault, but there didn't seem to be anything you could do to make life better.

If your mother was the alcoholic, chances are your father had already left or was staying pretty late at the office. He didn't want to be around. Or perhaps he came home at lunchtime to do your mother's work. He sewed the buttons on your clothes and made your lunch. That may have happened for a while. But you felt peculiar about it, because you knew it wasn't his job and he was doing it to make up for the fact that your mother was drunk.

In the end, you probably took over the things that mothers usually do. You learned pretty fast how to cook, clean and shop. In addition to taking over the care of younger brothers and sisters, in a very real way you may have become a mother to your mother. You may have helped her to eat and clean herself up, even helped her up to bed so the younger kids wouldn't see her passed out. You took care of the whole family.

In her sober moments, your mother tried to make up for what she lacked, and guilt overwhelmed you. There might have been long periods of time when she delayed her drinking to try and keep the home in order. How painful for you to be aware of her struggle. How grateful, but how guilty, you felt as you got more and more confused. Just what was your role?

If both your parents were alcoholic, life was even less predictable, except they took turns getting worse. Being home was like being in hell. The tension was so thick that you could cut it with a knife. That nervous, angry feeling was in the air. Nobody had to say a word, as everybody could feel it. It was extremely tense and uncomfortable. Yet there was no way to get away from it, no place to hide and you wondered, *Will it ever end?*

You probably had fantasies about leaving home, about running away, about having it over with, about your alcoholic parent becoming sober and life being fine and beautiful. You began to live in a fairy-tale world, with fantasy and in dreams. You lived a lot on hope, because you didn't want to believe what was happening. You knew that you couldn't talk about it with your friends or adults outside your family. Because you believed you had to keep these feelings to yourself, you learned to keep most of your other feelings to yourself. You couldn't let the rest of the world know what was going on in your home. Who would believe you, anyway?

You saw your mother covering up for your father. You heard her making excuses about how he was too sick to go to work. Even if you said something to her about your father, she pretended that it wasn't true. She said, "Oh, nonsense, don't worry about it. Eat your cereal." You learned quickly to keep your father's drinking to yourself, as your stomach churned, you felt tight inside, you cried into the night—if you could still cry.

Your fantasies about leaving home or living with a family that was like *The Brady Bunch* you knew would never happen. It was very difficult for you to go away from home, even for a weekend. If you left overnight, you worried about what was going on at home: *If I am away from home, I am like a rat leaving a sinking ship. How will they get along without me? They need me.* In a very real way, they did need you. Without you, the family would have to relate to each other. There was no escape.

You were trapped. You were trapped physically and trapped emotionally. These feelings are expressed by Gloria in the following dream:

> *The following is a description of a dream that I had when I was about eight years old. That was nearly fifteen years ago; it remains to date the most vivid and most frightening dream I can remember. It took place during a period of my life when my mother's drinking problem started getting "serious."*
>
> *The dream was in black and white. A transparent, hazy mist surrounded everything. It was strange to me because I was not only in the dream, but observing myself in the dream. I could see myself as one might see oneself on TV or film.*

My mother and I were in a very dark and gloomy place; it resembled a dungeon. We were both behind bars in what seemed to be a cage or jail. The place had no walls, no floor, no ceiling; only the cage, my mother and myself, and the black void. I remember pacing back and forth; I was restless but not frightened. Then, out of nowhere, there appeared a guard, a woman in uniform. She walked up to the cage, unlocked the door and released my mother. She took my mother by the arm and led her away. I was left behind. And so I waited, patiently, certain that in due time the guard would return and release me also. I waited and waited for what seemed to be an eternity. Finally, something appeared out of the dark. I thought it was the guard coming for me. Instead, it was a strange, inhuman thing, which very slowly passed by the cage and then disappeared out of sight. It vanished into the void, and I was left alone. The thought hit me that no one was going to release me. I was alone. I became panic-stricken.

I awoke terrified. I was beyond reason. I remember sitting up in bed and screaming. At least I thought I was screaming. I forced the air from my lungs, but no sound came from my throat. So, I took another huge, deep breath, and still there was no sound. I had lost my voice.

I was trying to call for my mother. I wanted her beside me so badly, but she had no way of hearing me. So I slid back under the covers and prayed that in the morning my voice would return. And then I went to sleep.

Gloria felt trapped. Gloria was trapped. She was alone with her pain. She told no one, and every day after school she would come straight home and take care of her mother. As painful as that was, it was easier than being at school and worrying. Nobody noticed.

Nobody saw. Gloria was a good little girl who did as she was told and gave nobody any trouble.

School

Your home life was not only miserable; it influenced your life at school. How did you do in school? If you were like Emily, the super-achiever and responsible one, you did very well. You were there, doing whatever was asked of you. You got high grades and a lot of praise. You may even have been the kid who got to clean the black-board. And it was an escape for a while, from home and from your true feelings. Nobody thought you were a child with very serious problems. Teachers might have said to your parents, "I wish I had one at home like that."

If you fell into the other categories, your performance was spotty. Depending on how intelligent you were and how cleverly you had learned to manipulate, you could determine to some extent how well you did in school. You might do well one semester in one course and badly in another, until finally you gave up altogether. Or you slid through. Or, like Don, you tried to bully your way through.

Unfortunately, you took on many characteristics of your alcoholic parent. People behave as they have learned to behave, whether they like it or not—whether they want to or not. Alcoholics do not want to take responsibility for their behavior. Was that you? It certainly was Don.

Don is a seventeen-year-old high school senior living with a recovering alcoholic father. His father, during his drinking years, which were most of Don's life, was very argumentative and often violent. He invariably got his own way, because others were afraid of him.

Don came to see me because he was in danger of failing his health class. If he failed, it would mean that he would not graduate. The reason the health teacher gave for his imminent failure was that he had never attended health class.

His first response to the situation was identical to what he had heard his alcoholic father say when he was actively drinking. "He can't do this to me. He has no right to do that. Who does he think he is? I'll report him to the Board of Education. I'll have that bastard's job." And on and on.

I said nothing.

He then tried the tack his father used when he was no longer drinking but still muddled and still sick. "I know what I'll do. I'll go to his home. I'll throw myself on the ground at his feet. I'll beg. I'll plead. I'll kiss his ring."

With no response from me, he moved to a third phase—one that demonstrated he had worked long and hard on himself. "I guess what I will have to do is make an appointment with him and sit down and see if there is anything I can do to make up the work."

Don had learned to take responsibility for his behavior. It was a hard lesson because it did not automatically come out of his life experience. Responsibility had to be taught.

If he had remained belligerent, he would have failed and not understood why. He could consider himself a victim and blame others. The child who continues with this behavior becomes more and more antisocial and is likely to end up in a penal institution. Those around him judge his behavior harshly, and he will not understand because he did not learn the alternatives.

If he had gotten stuck at the second stage, he might have been able to *pull it off*. The con artist can generally get away with it for a while. This, too, is what he learned at home. The highly manipulative behavior of the alcoholic for a while reaps rewards in terms of achieving the ends that he thinks are desirable. But manipulation doesn't work forever; others stop being fooled and the alcoholic gets caught. This happens to the child of the alcoholic, too. He gets away with it—for a while. Having a distorted sense of his own power, he doesn't quite know what hit him when he is finally caught.

The third alternative is the desirable one, as it gave Don the greatest opportunity to resolve his problem in a satisfactory way. It is a way that allowed him to take some pride in himself, no matter what the results. If the teacher will work out a compromise, he will graduate with the class. If the teacher will not work out a compromise, he did what he could to better the situation. He can begin to respect himself.

This particular case has a happy ending. The teacher and Don worked out a program whereby he could make up the work. He was able to graduate with his class.

Another problem in school was the inability to concentrate. Quite often your thoughts were directed to the fantasies you constructed to make life okay, or to stop worrying. *What's going to happen to me? Will everything be all right? What will happen when I get home?* You might have gotten into trouble for staring out the window. The teacher said, "Suzy daydreams all the time. I wish she'd pay better attention."

Well, if you were Suzy, you probably wanted to pay better attention—but how could you? Especially if you had been up all night listening to your parents screaming and yelling at each other. How were you going to concentrate in school if you hadn't had a good night's sleep? And what difference did it make anyway? Things were so bad. Who really cared? Who really gave a damn if you did well or poorly? If you did well, it wasn't good enough. If you did poorly, you got yelled at. But it passed—nobody really noticed. If you needed help, you knew better than to ask for it. You might get a promise, but nobody had time to help you. So you felt sorry for yourself.

And if by chance there was someone sympathetic to you, a teacher who said, "Is something wrong, Johnny? You look like there is something bothering you," you automatically said, "No, everything is fine," and walked away, wanting desperately to cling to that teacher, wanting desperately to say, "Oh my God, it's so terrible at home. . . . I'm not really sure what is wrong, but I know something is wrong. Please, please help me." But you knew that you didn't talk outside the home about what was going on in the home. At the same time, you wished the teacher hadn't let you walk away. You wanted someone to understand without your having to tell them, but you didn't really believe anyone could.

You had learned to keep your feelings to yourself, perhaps not even acknowledging them to yourself. So school, which could have been a haven, became a kind of hell. After a while, you may have misbehaved or stopped going. Maybe, maybe, maybe someone would pay attention. If you got into trouble, you might be pressured into telling the truth.

If you withdrew, you knew you'd be left alone, because you were quiet and didn't cause anyone any trouble. And the more you did this, the more alone you would feel and the harder it would be to do anything else. Becoming the class clown, a welcome diversion to the students, if not the teacher, worked for a while. You got some attention that way—not the kind you wanted, but at least you weren't ignored.

But if you stopped going to school, if you got into big enough trouble, somebody would surely pay attention. You cried for help in the only way you knew how. And then you would be punished, but at least they would have noticed. So that was what school was like. It was an additional punishment, simply a place you had to be. If you were lucky, it offered you a little relief. But mostly it was something that you *had to go through.*

Friends

What about friends—other kids your own age? You might have played with them but somehow you didn't feel you were one of them. As involved as you looked in the game, you always felt a little different. You didn't completely belong, so you always felt like an outsider.

It was difficult to make friends for a couple of reasons. One, because it was hard to believe that people really liked you. After all, you had been told all your life that you were such a crummy kid. And if you hadn't been told in words, you knew it was true, because if it wasn't, your father wouldn't have to drink. And even if someone's good feelings toward you were real, it was a little scary to know that if they got to know you a little better and found out, they wouldn't be your friend.

You probably got to know some kids. But that caused problems, too. How many times could you go over to your friend's house without inviting him to your house? There was always a sense of that dreaded day when your friend would say, "Let's play at your house this afternoon." You could only go to your friend's so often without having to face the inevitable. Maybe it just wasn't worth it to have a friend.

So you might have withdrawn, or you might have behaved in such a way that the kids walked away from you. That way you didn't have to face them at all. But if you took the risk and made a friend, you knew the day of being found out would come.

When a sixteen-year-old girl met the older brother of a girl she had made friends with when she was younger, it brought back a lot of memories. And she wrote him this poem:

TO

I remember you from long ago,
When I was living in a hell
built especially for children.
The walls of your home
were my only salvation.
I'm sure you were never aware of this, though—
because I never really knew you.
This is why I've always known you,
but you never did me.
I was a lonely, horrified child—
with nowhere to go
and no one to turn to . . .
So many years later.
You don't remember knowing me,
but I do you.
I needed to be where you stood—
a place so unlike my own.

◆ ◆ ◆

That household meant a lot to this little girl. However, the dreaded day came—she had to invite her friend to her house. When she brought her friend home, her father was passed out on the living room floor. Her mother very quickly made up a face-saving lie and said, "Oh, he sleeps on the floor because he has a problem with his back and the doctor told him that would be good for his back." The little girl seemed to accept that but she never came back again. The risk was real. How hard it was to make friends!

And, as you grew up, it became harder and harder because you reached a point where you simply didn't know how to make friends. "What do I talk to them about? Why would they be interested in me? Why would they like me? I'm not a good person. Why would they want me for a friend?" With all those questions going through your head, how could you feel spontaneous or free? How could you relate well to other kids?

Even if you wanted to stay after school and play with the other kids, it may have been impossible. You may have had to rush home because of responsibilities like taking care of your little brothers and sisters. You may have been worried that your mother was drunk and you would have to take care of her. You may have worried all day and you had to rush right home to see what had happened. In this strange life, you wanted nothing more than to run away, and yet you had to go back as soon as possible.

But that wasn't your life, your reality. It doesn't make a whole lot of sense when you look at it now, but it was what you knew then. A child goes away for a camp experience. She went to a camp designed for children of alcoholic parents.

When the child returns home, she sits down and writes about what it felt like inside. Because, although she knew how to behave, she brought all of the confusion and all of the concern of being a child living with alcoholism with her. Nobody saw it, but she shared it with me in the following poem.

C.A.M.P.

I don't want to be here.
I want to go home.
I'm not going to have a good time.
I don't have any friends here
And nobody likes me.

Hey! I just had fun!
And I laughed and smiled,
And I feel pretty happy!
Maybe it won't be so bad after all,
Then, again, I want to go home.

I want to go boating again!
When is it time for lunch?
Can we go on a hike?
I want to go fishing some more!
A campfire!

I don't understand these "meetings"!
Everybody is saying all these horrible things
And I know exactly how they feel!
Do they understand how I feel, too?
Hey, let's have another one!
No—they put me to sleep.

I really like my counselors, too.
All of them are really nice.
We do whatever we want
And that's okay!

What! We're going home tomorrow?
We just got here, didn't we?
Go away! You make me mad!
You're ugly!
And your mother dresses you funny!
I hate you!

Wow, it's really time to go home.
I don't know how I feel about this.
I hope I can come back next year.
I don't want to go home,
I want to be here!

Well, I guess coming here really doesn't matter after all,
Because you still have to go home
To exactly what you left.

◆ ◆ ◆

What about your sense of yourself? Did you have high self-esteem? Did you value yourself? Or consider yourself worthy? Did you consider yourself at all?

In order to measure self-esteem, you need a sense of self. Did you have one? I'm not so sure. A child determines a sense of self by the input of significant people around him or her. As children get older, they make those decisions for themselves or, ideally, they should. But initially they find out who they are by what other people say to them, and they internalize these messages.

But you got a lot of double messages, things that seemed to contradict each other. You didn't know which part was true, so sometimes you picked one part and sometimes you picked the other part. You were never really sure. Paradoxically, these contradictory messages were probably both true. As a result, your sense of self became somewhat distorted. The messages were not clear. They didn't make a lot of sense. So who you were and whether or not you valued that person were very difficult to determine.

For example, you heard, "I love you, go away." What did that mean? Your mother would say to you, "I love you." You heard and felt those words. But you knew that you were in the way, that she didn't have time for you, that her concerns were not with you and that you were in her hair. "I love you, go away." How does that make sense? Which part did you believe? If you believed both, you were confused.

If you believed "I love you" and yet had to go away, what did that do? If you believed both parts, what was the implication as you grew up? People who told you they loved you and yet pushed you away could be extremely desirable.

How about the set of double messages, "You can't do anything right. . . . I need you!" The perfectionism of the alcoholic criticized whatever you did. You got the A, you needed the A+. No matter what happened, it wasn't good enough; there was always a way to find fault. You certainly couldn't believe you were able to do anything right, no matter how hard you tried.

But the other part of the message, "I need you. I can't get along without you," caused you to do a lot of chores around the house. You ended up being, to some degree, the emotional support. Why did they need you if you couldn't do anything right? It didn't make a lot of sense, but you knew it was true, because both of those messages were coming through loud and clear.

Next we come to the *greatest* paradox. "Always tell the truth," and, "I don't want to know." You were told to tell the truth always, because being honest was of value. Moreover, you were told that if something happens and you tell the truth, you will get into less trouble. Remember that one?

You could never be sure about that one, as sometimes it was true and sometimes it wasn't true. "I don't want to know" certainly complicated the issue. Why overburden them? Why overburden an already over-burdened parent? This is a wonderful rationalization for someone who doesn't want to take responsibility. What kid wants to own up to a bad deed, especially when he has a parent who models that behavior?

Why give them more to worry about? That is encouraged, at least covertly. Pretty soon you learned that "Always tell the truth" is something you should tell your kids. But the truth really had very little meaning in your household. You heard your parents lie all the time. You heard your nonalcoholic parent covering up for your alcoholic parent, and that was apparently okay. Also, your alcoholic parent was always making promises and never following through. But he didn't seem to be lying when he made the promise.

What was real and what was unreal got very distorted in your household. So there's not a whole lot in it for you to tell the truth. And what happened for a while is that you started lying automatically. And since you didn't feel that you were lying, because everybody's lying, you didn't feel too guilty about it. You may even have fooled yourself into believing you were protecting your family. *They'll feel a lot better thinking my ride home was late*, you thought, rather than saying, "They caught us smoking a joint on the street and brought us to the juvenile center."

"I'll be there for you" and "I give you my word, next time," are another set of double messages. Your parent was always making promises like, "Saturday we will do this. We'll get out of this some-how. Everything will be fine. Don't worry about it. I'll buy you the dress. I'll be home for dinner. I care, I'm interested, let's talk about it sometime." And then these things never happened. All lies!

In the other part of the message, "I give you my word, next time," "Well, it didn't work out this time, but it will work out next time," the desire to get points for intent and not for behavior became evident. And what did you do with that? Not now, later! The later never came. So there was a third message in there. "Forget it." You learned how not to want.

We then move into the paradox of, "Everything is fine, don't worry." The other part of the message your parent sent out is, "How can I deal with all of this?" A sense of hopelessness, but telling you not to worry. "Okay, okay, I won't worry." Somehow it didn't work that way.

One other confusing message is a judgment on the alcoholic because he or she is an alcoholic, and a dismissal of unacceptable behavior for the same reason. "John is a drunk," was said with contempt. But then you heard, "Yes, he broke his glass, but he couldn't help it, he was drunk." It made no sense. He could not help being drunk if he was an alcoholic, but it was not okay for him to break the glass.

The behavior of the alcoholic got explained away because of the disease. Nobody was allowed to be upset because he or she didn't mean it.

This double standard had to be confusing. The real message was, "If I am drunk, I can do whatever I want." Not only was alcoholism used as a cop-out for the alcoholic, but you probably learned how to use it as a cop-out for your own behavior. For example, "Tell your teacher you've got family problems and she'll let you get away with not having your work done. It works every time."

Ginger was referred to me because of her own drinking, but it was not long before she made sure that I knew how rotten life was because of her father's alcoholism.

"He's down on me all the time. He is always on my case."

"Tell me, Ginger, what are you talking about specifically?"

"If I get in after curfew he yells at me. (Ginger, at fifteen, had a curfew of 1:30 A.M.) If I don't say 'good morning,' he really lets me have it."

My response to her was, "Ginger, I don't drink a whole lot but in my house your curfew would be 11:00, and I would do more than yell if you got in late. You would also say 'good morning' to me, whether you wanted to or not."

It's easy to see that she was using the alcoholism as an excuse to run amok. Then, when her father's strong reactions proved how terrible he was, in effect, she had set him up. I was pretty rough on Ginger, telling her exactly what I saw her doing and what I thought of it. I also acknowledged the real difficulties in her life.

The following week when she returned I said, "I was pretty hard on you last week; I'm surprised you came back."

"When I left here last week, I felt terrible, so I knew something must be working," she replied.

Not really wanting to get away with her bad behavior, she felt relief at someone finally calling her on it. Her mother's fear of making a bad situation worse by taking a stand had left Ginger very confused. If the child of the alcoholic, not unlike the alcoholic, is ever to mature, there must be accountability. Part of having a strong sense of self is to be accountable for one's actions. No matter how much we explore motives or lack of motives, we are what we do. We take credit for the good and we must take credit for the bad. The key is to take responsibility for all of our behavior.

The double messages you received as a child caused you to lose sight of yourself. Where are you in the mix? Who's really concerned with you anyway? Your parents don't seem to be. Even if you don't seem to be, your self-image is confused.

The bottom line is that you know your parents love you. You can't prove it, but you just know it. This fact alone is the reason you can overcome the difficulties of your childhood. It is the critical component that not even alcoholism can destroy. The love may have been distorted, but it was real . . . your reality was distorted.

Therefore, your sense of self is distorted. Because of this, there are many aspects of life, many aspects of growing up and living life fully, that you haven't learned. You missed the discussions between parent and child of, "How do I handle this?" and, "What do I do if he says this?" "What do I do with this problem? How can I figure it out?" Your parents were so absorbed in the madness of alcoholism that they had neither the time nor the energy to discuss these problems with you.

So there are a lot of things you are unfamiliar with, things that you simply don't know. Moreover, there are many things that you don't even know you don't know, so you don't even know what questions to ask.

What you do know is that you never really feel that you fit in, and you can't figure out why. Everyone else fits in, and you don't even ask why.

Your childhood feelings, thoughts, experiences and assumptions are carried with you, in one form or another, throughout your life. Adults who don't work to change and develop remain tied to their parents and/or spouses, react in the workplace the same as they did in school, feel isolated despite the presence of other people, and are afraid to let others know them.

These adults also increase the likelihood that they will become alcoholics, marry alcoholics, or both, thereby perpetuating a vicious cycle.

2

What Is Happening to You Now?

The child grows into an adult. We all know what an adult is, until we are asked to define the word. When we begin to search for the answers, we wonder. I cannot define for you what an adult is. You have to define it for yourself. Maybe it's the point in your life when you are where the buck stops. Maybe that's when you become an adult—the time when you are in charge of your life.

For the purposes of this book, we're talking about someone who has grown up, who has reached his or her majority. Then you can wonder, even though you are all grown up, "How adult are you?" What role has your history played in your life? What things about your history have you been able to use to your advantage? What things about your history tend to get in your way? What is your perspective on yourself? How do you really, truly see yourself?

You have a lot of questions, many of which lead to new questions. Because your foundation has been ambiguous, you've always had a lot of questions. You may not even have known what all those questions were, but one thing was clear. You didn't have a lot of answers.

Let's take a look at who you are today. Simply take a look. Try not to make the assumption as you look over these characteristics that

39

they are further proof of how damaged you are. If I know you as well as I think I do, that's exactly what you will do.

This list is not the result of a scientific survey. It is a list of statements that a consensus of adult children of alcoholics say describe themselves. They agreed that these characteristics are part of who they are. They may not all be true for you, or only be true to some degree. This is not an attempt to label you, but if the following discussion does nothing else, it will give you a little understanding of why you react the way you do, of what some of the reasons are for some of the behaviors that you have not been able to understand. It's a way to show you that some of the things that have caused you to wonder about your emotional health are carryovers from your childhood.

They may simply be carryovers from being the child of an alcoholic. The form may have changed, but the substance remains the same. In this context, you can look at these characteristics, begin to explore them, and make an effort to change.

Now, let's just take a look at what these characteristics are, what they mean and what some of the implications are.

1. Adult children of alcoholics guess at what normal is.

The significance of this statement cannot be overestimated, as it is their most profound characteristic. Adult children of alcoholics simply have no experience with what is normal. Many of them join AA or Al-Anon. I am often amused at what happens when they reach the second step: "Came to believe that a power greater than ourselves could restore us to sanity." They absolutely believe that. It's certainly true. It's certainly significant and important and essential to recovery. However, they don't know what sanity is. They look at things that appear to be normal and try to copy them. Yet, what they are copying may or may not be normal, so they're behaving as if they are normal, without having a sound basis for making that decision.

It's very similar to the kinds of feelings homosexuals have before coming out of the closet. Having spent a whole lifetime covering up in order not to be found out, they are suffering from a great deal of confusion. They've spent much of their time guessing at what they would be feeling if they were straight, so that others don't have certain information about them.

I don't find this a lot different with the grown children of alcoholics. Throughout life, to keep others from finding out that they don't know what they're doing, they guess at what is appropriate. They get concerned and confused about things that they believe other people do not get concerned and confused about. They don't have the freedom to ask, so they never know for sure. Even more important, they don't want to look stupid. When people like me make statements such as, "The only stupid questions are the ones that are left unasked," they say nothing out loud. But to themselves, they say, "That's what she thinks! If she only knew . . ."

After all, when you take a look at your history, how could you have any understanding of normalcy? Your home life varied from slightly mad to extremely bizarre.

Since this was the only home life you knew, what others would consider "slightly mad" or "extremely bizarre" were usual to you. If there was a day in there that one could characterize as "normal," it certainly was not typical and therefore could not have had much meaning.

Beyond your chaotic day-to-day life, part of what you did was live in fantasy. You lived in a world all your own that you created, a world of what life would be like IF. . . . What your home would be like IF . . . The way your parents would relate to each other IF . . . The things that would be possible for you IF . . . And you structured a whole life based on something that was probably impossible. The unrealistic fantasies about what life would be like if your parent got sober probably helped you survive but added to your confusion.

You saw *The Brady Bunch* or *Father Knows Best* and assumed that people really lived like that. What did you know? The other homes you went into were different from yours, and your hosts probably put their best foot forward. Even if they didn't, you couldn't have a real sense of what life was really like in someone else's home, because you didn't live there.

Children from more typical homes know that these programs don't show life as it really is. They see them as fairy tales and either enjoy them or get annoyed by the sweetness and perfection, because they know nobody really lives like that and everything doesn't always work out well in the end.

It becomes very clear that you have no frame of reference for what it is like to be in a normal household. You also have no frame of reference for what is okay to say and to feel. In a more typical situation, one does not have to walk on eggshells all the time. One doesn't have to question or repress one's feelings all the time. Because you did, you also became confused. Many things from the past contributed to your having to guess at what normal is.

Not too long ago, a thirteen-year-old boy was referred to me for counseling. Both of his parents were recovering alcoholics and both were children of alcoholics. Because the boy was having difficulty in school, the vice principal said that he had serious emotional problems and should go for counseling. Knowing that this couple were children of alcoholics gave me some very important information: They did not know what it was like to be thirteen. I knew that as children of alcoholics, they had not been typical thirteen-year-olds.

Before I even saw their son, I described to them what it was like to be a thirteen-year-old growing up in a typical home. They were greatly relieved, because I had described their son. No normal thirteen-year-old is all that easy to live with. After seeing the boy a couple of times, I was pleasantly surprised to find nothing wrong with him. Yes, he was having difficulty in school. Yes, he was very competitive. Yes, he was having a personality conflict with the vice principal. Yet there was no reason for him to see a therapist. There was nothing wrong with this boy that getting over being thirteen wouldn't cure.

Disruption is not exclusive to the alcoholic family system. So-called "normal" families have their share of ups and downs as well. Children living in "normal" families can have behavior problems and be disrupted emotionally. Some of this is part of growing up, and some of it may mean more serious difficulties. The key is to know the difference, and in the family complicated by alcohol, it is harder to sift things out realistically.

Had the parents not been children of alcoholics, they might have recognized typical adolescent behavior. It is to their credit, certainly, that they cared enough to find out. Yet it was a little sad that they were unable to recognize the very fine job of parenting they were doing . . . how they were bringing up a very normal, healthy child who would have all of the usual and normal crises of growing up. Because of their own histories, they simply did not know what normal was.

That is one example of how being the child of an alcoholic, and having to guess at what normal is, can influence parenting.

The following shows how it can influence a marital relationship.

At the time Beth and James came to see me, James had been recovering in AA for sixteen years and Beth had spent the same amount of time in Al-Anon. They were a very devoted couple who had worked long and hard on themselves individually, on their family relationships and on their marriage. Beth, who was about to have a hysterectomy, saw this as a very significant milestone in her life. She had spent a lifetime taking care of her husband, six children and the house.

She wanted to be completely pampered for a while. She wanted her kids to take care of her and her husband to leave his work if he had to, even though he had just become president of a company. She demanded that he take care of the kids and support her emotionally and physically. That this was to be her time, she made clear, and she wanted everybody to like it.

James was supportive and was encouraging, but she wasn't quite sure he meant it. When they came in, they were at odds.

I knew that James, as well as being an alcoholic himself, was the adult child of an alcoholic parent. This meant that he had grown up in an environment where he wasn't sure how to feel. He wasn't sure what response to the situation was okay. He was in turmoil and I could see that the problem needed to be defined.

So I turned to James and said, "If I were you, I would be feeling a whole lot of things right now. I would want to be very supportive of my wife, because I care about her a whole lot. I would also be thinking that she was making a very big deal out of this hysterectomy, that women all over the world have hysterectomies, and although it is a major operation, it is rarely, if ever, fatal, and she is really making more of a fuss than necessary. Many of my friends' wives have gone through this operation, and it wasn't as big a deal as Beth is making out of it. If I were you, I would want to be there for her to the degree that I could, but I would be very concerned about canceling business trips and leaving the office early when I need to see that things are done there; and with the difficulties I am having at the office, to also have to worry about running the household and taking care of the kids, you know, I'd really consider it a burden on me. And I would be feeling like no one was considering me at all. And that I am supposed to forget about myself altogether, take over all of these roles and like it, too. I would be somewhat resentful, although I couldn't really admit it because what a crummy way for a man to feel about a woman he loves at a difficult time in her life when I am supposed to be supportive."

What I had described to him were typical reactions to this situation. Although his feelings were typical and predictable, he didn't know that they were. As a child, he had only been allowed to express the feelings that his mother found acceptable. Gradually, over the years, he had learned to keep his feelings to himself. This was far more satisfactory than risking his mother's disapproval. In this circumstance, since he judged his feelings as inappropriate and didn't want to risk the disapproval of his wife, he kept them to himself.

He stared at me with his mouth open. He certainly felt as if I had taken off all of his clothes and that he was sitting there naked. Beth then said, "Of course you have all of those feelings, James. Of course you do. That's precisely the way I felt when you were in the hospital the last time and I had to take care of you."

You could feel the relief in that room. He found out that all of the feelings he had were okay, that they were perfectly fine, natural and *normal*. He hadn't known that having all of those feelings didn't mean that he was a bastard and didn't care about his wife. He had to be told.

As soon as I had the information that he was an adult child of an alcoholic, it was not very difficult to focus on precisely what was giving this couple trouble.

As it happened, she recovered very quickly from the operation, he was able to be supportive and the marriage is fine. She is more mindful of the fact that he simply does not know some things and he understands that his reactions are not all that strange, especially the ones that he learned to suppress when he was a child.

2. Children of alcoholics have difficulty following a project through from beginning to end.

The topic one evening in an adult children of alcoholics meeting was procrastination. When I asked them to talk about what it meant to them, the opening response was, "I'm the world's biggest procrastinator," or "Somehow I just don't seem to be able to finish anything that I start." When I asked some grown children of alcoholics to be a little bit more specific, this is what I heard:

Bob said, "I know what you mean. I'm facing that right now. I've been running into a problem at work trying to organize information and write it down on a piece of paper. I have this incredible difficulty seeing what it is and putting it down simply on a piece of paper. I sit and flounder until somebody says, 'What the hell are you doing? Do this and this and this and I want this!' And all of a sudden it's obvious, and why the hell didn't I think about it? I'm scared. This is my job. It is essential to what I do now. I can't go on like this forever. I'm not going to be a six-month newly hired forever, and I'm alarmed."

Amy's statement went like this: "In organizing a long paper, I get stuck. I really wonder what the hell it is with me, I just can't plot it out. I've got all this stuff and I can't sift it out. It's so hard for me not to abandon it, even if I'm interested in it and I want to follow through with it. It's such a fucking struggle.

"When I was going to college, I had all these incompletes that turned to Fs. The courses I did were all As, but all the Fs really sickened me. I'm scared, too, because it's affecting my job as well."

These comments are fairly typical, and it's not too hard to understand why a difficulty exists. These people are not procrastinators in the usual sense.

In the typical alcoholic home, there are an awful lot of promises.

The great job was always around the corner. The big deal was always about to be made. The work that needed to be done around the house would be done in no time. The toy that would be built—the go-cart, the dollhouse—and so on.

"I'm going to do this. I'm going to do that." But this or that never really happens. Not only doesn't it happen, but the alcoholic wants credit even for having the idea, even for intending to do it. You grew up in this environment.

Remember the projects that got a little further than that? Painting the living room, for example. Remember when the alcoholic went out, bought the paint, came back, covered everything with the drop-cloth and it was years until the living room was finally painted? That is, unless your mother got disgusted somewhere along the way and painted it herself.

There were many projects like that. Lots of wonderful ideas, but never effected. If they were, so much time passed, you had forgotten about the original idea.

Who took the time to sit down with you when you had an idea for a project and said, "That's a good idea. How are you going to go about doing it? How long is it going to take you? What are the steps involved?" Probably no one. When was it that one of your parents said, "Gee. That idea is terrific! You sure you can do it? Can you break it down into smaller pieces? Can you make it manageable?" Probably never.

This is not to suggest that all parents who do not live with alcohol teach their children how to solve problems. But it is to suggest that in a functional family, the child has this behavior and attitude to model. The child observes the process, and the child may even ask questions along the way. The learning may be more indirect than direct, but it is present. Since your experience was so vastly different, it's no surprise to me that you have a problem following a project through from beginning to end. You haven't seen it happen, and you don't know how to make it happen. Lack of knowledge isn't the same as procrastination.

In chapter five of this part, we are going to talk about how you can change this alarming state of affairs.

3. Adult children of alcoholics lie when it would be just as easy to tell the truth.

Lying is basic to the family system affected by alcohol. It masquerades in part as overt denial of unpleasant realities, cover-ups, broken promises and inconsistencies. It takes many forms and has many implications. Although it is somewhat different from the kind of lying usually talked about, it certainly is a departure from the truth.

The first and most basic lie is the family's denial of the problem. So the pretense that everything at home is in order is a lie, and the family rarely discusses the truth openly, even with each other. Perhaps somewhere in one's private thoughts there is a recognition of the truth, but there's also the struggle to deny it.

The next lie, the cover-up, relates to the first one. The nonalcoholic family member covers up for the alcoholic member. As a child, you saw your nonalcoholic parent covering up for your alcoholic parent. You heard him or her on the phone, making excuses for your mother or father not fulfilling an obligation, not being on time. That's part of the lie that you lived.

You also heard a lot of promises from your alcoholic parent. These, too, turned out to be lies.

Lying as the norm in your house became part of what you knew and what could be useful to you. At times, it made life much more comfortable. If you lied about getting your work done, you could get away with being lazy for a while. If you lied about why you couldn't bring a friend home or why you were late coming home, you could avert unpleasantness. It seemed to make life simpler for everybody.

Although your family said that telling the truth was a virtue, you knew they didn't mean much of what they said. So the truth lost its meaning.

Lying has become a habit. That's why the statement, "Adult children of alcoholics lie when it would be just as easy to tell the truth," is relevant. But if lying is what you have heard comes naturally, perhaps it is not as easy to tell the truth.

In this context, "It would be just as easy to tell the truth" means that you derive no real benefit from lying.

The following are comments made by adult children of alcoholics who are concerned about their lying. You will probably recognize yourself, at least in part.

Joan, a twenty-six-year-old guidance counselor whose mother was alcoholic said,

> *I find myself lying and about halfway through the lie wanting to say, "Stop! That's a lie, that's not it. Let's start over again," but too embarrassed to do it. I don't know that I had to lie growing up. I just know that I did. I used to make up stories in order to be noticed, I think, and I think I feel bad that I didn't get caught, because if people had talked to me and listened to me and known me, they would have known that I was bullshitting and I was really good at it. I'd start out faking being sick sometimes and then get really sick. I was really an expert at it. It was so much easier to do that than to say that I just couldn't do what others could do. I felt like it would be terrible not to be able to cut it. I'd lose face. It was sad, though, and I didn't like doing it. There was always this panic about getting caught. I wouldn't have minded getting caught so I could stop the charade. It seemed to be because I didn't believe I could keep it up. I just didn't know how*

to do it, and then I would start making things up. It gets very complicated. There has been a need in the past to end friendships because I couldn't keep track of the lies anymore. I want to stop lying. I really want to stop it. When I find myself in the middle of one, I'm just scared to death. I just want to say, "Hold it," and back up and go to the truth. I really don't know what to do. When it's just an inconsequential, silly little dumb thing, I feel like an asshole.

◆ ◆ ◆

Jeff, a thirty-year-old engineer with two recovering alcoholic parents, said,

I can remember an occasion when I told a really big lie. I was on a hiking trip in the White Mountains with some friends of mine. We were hiking from one hut to another place a few miles away in the snow. The temperature dropped and it was really, really cold. I had skipped breakfast, we were in a real hurry to get packed, and I had just eaten some candy bars or something. I ran after the rest of them. On the way over, we started to get strung out. The wind was blowing very hard and there was snow all over the place. I began to fall behind the others, and I remember being in extreme resentment that they wouldn't slow up and wait for me, but at the same time I was annoyed at myself that I couldn't keep up with them. I had gotten this book on hypothermia. I knew how to do it and I faked them out. I slowed up behind them, and part of the symptoms were to get vague and hazy mentally, so I started to wander off the trail. By the time they got together and started wondering where I was, we had wasted a good hour. They came back and did all of the things that go along with trying to pull someone out of hypothermia. I really wanted that attention, and I guess I had just reached the point where I was willing to do just about anything to get it. They were leaving me. I was slipping behind and nobody had noticed. We were in the mountains and I could freeze to death, and with the statements I made to myself, it was easy to make the progression. All right, I am gonna freeze to death. We'll see how you respond when I come down with hypothermia.

In reality, I had spent two hundred dollars on the fancy equipment, and I could have laid in the snow for a month without freezing to death. So, I simply faked it. I was nervous about getting caught. I knew how to do it, but I wasn't physically able to do what the other guys were doing.

I knew that when I was growing up the truth was irrelevant. When my parents were three sheets to the wind, it didn't matter what you said or what you didn't say. When my mother was drunk, she was in her own world, and the conversation revolved around the age of the washing machine or the refrigerator, or something like that. I just didn't come into it. There was no "Your grades aren't good enough" or anything like that. I just wasn't there.

The same thing is pretty much true of my father. He was isolated also. So, there wasn't any truth or lying. You could say anything you liked. You could dance naked with a rose in your teeth; they simply wouldn't notice.

◆ ◆ ◆

Steve, a thirty-six-year-old alcoholism counselor with two alcoholic parents, said,

What about wanting to survive? When I was a kid, I became a very accomplished liar, mostly by selecting what I would say. Whenever my father asked me something, if I gave him a straight answer he would always criticize the answer. I stopped giving him a straight answer, and I realized that it worked very well. If he criticized the not-straight answer, I could discard the criticism as being of no practical value, because what I gave him wasn't true anyway. Over the years, I've kept that. Ninety-eight percent of the time I'm honest and I have a reputation for honesty, but I always keep that other two percent in reserve. I think I started keeping my lies down to a minimum with other people, because I got into a thing of not being able to remember what it was that I said.

I have to distinguish between lying about things and lying about feelings. When it comes to feelings, I have a tough time being honest about my feelings, being honest with myself and honest with others.

In my family, my mother had a reputation for being a pathological liar, and I suspected that in order to get any attention at all, I had to make things bigger than they really were. I mean, especially to get recognition from my parents. When my parents were drunk, one or both of them, it was easy to lie and get away with it. They weren't dealing with things very well either. If I came up with a story sometimes, I really got the feeling that they preferred that to the truth. They didn't want to know, as long as I wasn't arrested or causing them any embarrassment.

I soon learned that telling the truth was probably the worst possible thing I could do. Lying was okay, and I just needed to be smart enough to cover up. I rarely ever got into trouble, so my credibility was rarely questioned.

◆ ◆ ◆

Sandra, a twenty-three-year-old child of two alcoholic parents, said,

> *Lying is one thing I absolutely will not tolerate in other people. My ex-husband lied to me before we were married and it almost broke us up. I lie to myself constantly and don't know it. I'll fabricate an idea or concept and I'll say that's what I feel and I'll believe it with every inch of me. Somewhere down the road, just like a smack in the face, I'll say to myself, You don't believe that. I've been deluding myself the whole time, and I still can do that—lie to myself—but I do have a lot of trouble lying to other people. That is to say, I won't deliberately lie. But, if it gets to the point where I have to be too honest, then I've been known to end the friendship. I will walk away when it becomes work to be honest.*
>
> *There are very few people with whom I'm honest about my feelings. I can feel absolutely shattered inside and someone will ask me how I'm doing and I'll say, "Fine."*
>
> *In my job I'm honest, but I don't share, so what's there to be dishonest about? In AA, I share somewhat. I don't share all that much. The times I'm really honest, people look at me like I'm strange.*
>
> *I think of myself as being honest because I was the minister's daughter and thou shalt not lie. And now, thinking about this, I realized that my mother never believed me. She never believed me when I was a kid growing up.*
>
> *One time I ran home from school and some kids had been throwing rocks at me. I got home and told my mom and she said, "That didn't happen. You're lying." I was out of breath, I was exhausted, there were tears rolling down my face and she didn't believe me. It happened all the time.*
>
> *One time some kids dragged me down some brick steps and scraped my back up. She didn't believe it happened. She didn't believe*

kids would do that to her daughter. I felt as though I was hitting my head against a brick wall and nothing was getting through.

That's probably why I'm so careful about what I share today. I don't want to not be believed, if I'm telling the truth. I don't want to take that risk. So, I would prefer to share very little.

These people, in discussing what lying means to them in their lives, have a high level of self-awareness and a fearless honesty with which they share their difficulty in telling the truth. It is the first step of changing this aspect of their personalities. If you wish, you can change, too.

4. Adult children of alcoholics judge themselves without mercy.

When you were a child, there was no way that you were good enough. You were constantly criticized. You believed that your family would be better off without you because you were the cause of the trouble. You may have been criticized for things that made no sense. "If you weren't such a rotten kid, I wouldn't have to drink." It makes no sense, but if you hear something often enough, for a long enough period of time, you will end up believing it. As a result, you internalized these criticisms as negative self-feelings. They remain, even though no one is saying them to you anymore.

Since there is no way for you to meet the standards of perfection that you have internalized from childhood, you are always falling short of the mark you have set for yourself. As a child, whatever you did was not quite good enough. No matter how hard you tried, you should have tried harder. If you got an A, it should have been an A+.

You were never good enough. I have a client who told me that his mother was so demanding that when he was in basic training, he found the sergeants loose. So, this became a part of you, who you are, a part of the way you see yourself. The shoulds and should-nots can become paralyzing after a while.

One aspect of this is how some people are able to successfully maintain a negative self-image when there is evidence to the contrary. This is how it works. If anything goes wrong, it is your responsibility. Somehow, you should have done it differently and things would have been better. Anything that goes right has to do with something other than yourself. It was going to happen that way anyway. Or, if it is very clear that you are the one who is responsible for a positive outcome, you dismissed it with, "Oh that was easy. That was of little consequence."

This is really not a sense of humility but a distortion of reality. It feels safer to keep a negative self-image because you are used to it. Accepting praise for being competent means changing the way you see yourself and means that maybe you can judge yourself a little less harshly—and be a little more accepting and say, "I made that mistake; however, I am not a mistake."

An example of the kind of automatic judgment that I hear is very well exemplified in Ellen's statement. She talks about having an operation and coming home from the hospital. She calls her mother, who comes to take care of her.

Okay, I'm the one who has had the surgery, and my mother starts attacking each of my friends as they walk in the door to see me. She had a royal fight with one of my friends, just tore her head off, and my friend just tore her head off. By the end of the night, I was taking care of my mother. I was the one who was getting my mother some hot tea to calm her nerves, when what I needed was some tea and some loving and some sympathy. But I really know that the only reason I got mad at my mother was because she was not taking care of me my way. She wasn't doing it the way I wanted her to do it, and I was being very selfish.

♦ ♦ ♦

Ellen found herself to be at fault because she wanted things done her way. She judged herself for not feeling well and for wanting to be taken care of.

She said to me, "I always do that. That is one of the strongest parts of who I am. It's that I judge everything I do, and it's partly because everything is so black and white. It's either all bad or all good. There's no middle ground. Most of what I see myself doing is bad; even though intellectually I feel that it's good, emotionally I can't."

What Ellen said is fairly typical. I was working with another client of mine on "shoulds." She had reached the point where she was completely immobilized, and I asked her to make a list of all the "shoulds" she gave herself in a day. The list was enormous. When she was able to look at it objectively, she laughed and said, "I'm going to stop judging myself. I'm not going to judge myself, even if I'm entirely at fault."

Judging yourself negatively is one of the things that you do best, because it is ingrained in your personality. Sometimes there's even a sort of pleasure or a comfort in it.

The adult children of alcoholics I know who have joined AA and Al-Anon absolutely cannot wait to get to the fourth and fifth steps. The fourth step is, "Took a searching and fearless moral inventory of ourselves." And the fifth step is, "Admitted to God, to ourselves, and to another human being the exact nature of our wrongs."

When I see them doing these steps shortly after joining the program, I know what they will do. They see Steps Four and Five as a good opportunity to come down on themselves. They judge themselves on characteristics that they never even knew they had. All of these characteristics are negative. There's never a positive characteristic in it. It has never been used positively. They take to it like a duck to water. Then, the idea that they can flagellate themselves to somebody else is absolutely super.

If I suggest that maybe counseling is a form of moral inventory, that maybe it could be done formally a little later, it makes no difference. There is no way to slow them down. I issue a warning that they're going to do a giant number on themselves. They do it anyway, then come back, and I get to help pick up the pieces. We move on. At a little later stage, they do the fourth and fifth steps much more successfully. But initially, it's a great opportunity to come down on themselves.

Your judgment of others is not nearly as harsh as your judgment of yourself, although it is hard for you to see other people's behavior in terms of a continuum either. Black or white, good or bad, are typically the way you look at things. Either side is an awesome responsibility. You know what it feels like to be bad and how those feelings make you behave. And then, if you are good, there is always the risk that it won't last. So, either way, you set yourself up. Either way there is a great amount of pressure on you at all times. How difficult and stressful life is. How hard it is to just sit back and relax and say, "It's okay to be me."

5. Adult children of alcoholics have difficulty having fun.

6. Adult children of alcoholics take themselves very seriously.

These two characteristics are very closely linked. If you're having trouble having fun, you're probably taking yourself very seriously, and if you don't take yourself all that seriously, chances are you can have fun.

Once again, in order to understand this problem, you need to look back at your childhood. How much fun was your childhood? You don't have to answer that. Children of alcoholics simply don't have much fun. One child of an alcoholic described it as "chronic trauma." You didn't hear your parents laughing and joking and fooling around. Life was a very serious, angry business. You didn't really learn to play with the other kids. You could join in some of the games, but were you really able to let yourself go and have fun? Even if you could have, it was discouraged. The tone around the house put a damper on your fun. Eventually, you just went along with everybody else. Having fun just wasn't fun. There was no place for it in your house. You gave it up. It just wasn't a workable idea. The spontaneous child within was squashed.

Last summer, at a camp for children of alcoholic parents, the staff, who were mostly adult children of alcoholics, were playing for probably the first time in their lives. "The only other camp I ever went to was in Vietnam," said one of the counselors. Others reported that it was the very first time they had thrown a Frisbee. They were becoming very childlike in that they were having fun and it was a new experience.

So it's really no wonder that you don't have fun. You may even disapprove of others who act silly, thinking, "Oh look, she's making such a fool of herself." But in a little place inside of you, you really wish you could do that, too.

At Rutgers University Summer School for Alcohol Studies, some of us were throwing a ball around and others were watching. Some adult children of alcoholics told me later how badly they wanted to join in. "I wanted to get up and join in so badly, but I just couldn't get up and do it. I didn't want to make a fool of myself. I didn't want to look foolish."

The spontaneous child that got squashed so many years ago struggles to be released. The pressure to be adult helps to keep the child repressed. You are at war with yourself. But fear of the unknown wins out. After all, what would happen if that child gained freedom? What would it mean? So you rationalize.

Having fun, being silly, being childlike, is being foolish. It is no wonder that adult children of alcoholics have difficulty having fun. Life is too serious.

You also have trouble separating yourself from your work, so you take yourself very seriously at whatever job you have to do. You can take the work seriously, but not yourself. You are therefore a prime candidate for burnout.

One night on the subject of work, Abby turned to me with a very angry face and said, "You may make me laugh at myself, but I want you to know, I don't think it's funny."

7. Adult children of alcoholics have difficulty with intimate relationships.

Adult children want very much to have healthy intimate relationships, and it is extraordinarily difficult for a number of reasons.

The first and most obvious reason is that they have no frame of reference for a healthy intimate relationship, because they have never seen one. The only model they have is their parents, which you and I both know was not healthy.

They also carry with them the experience of come close, go away—the inconsistency of a loving parent-child relationship. They feel loved one day and rejected the next. The fear of being abandoned is a terrible fear they grow up with. If the fear isn't overwhelming, it certainly gets in the way. Not knowing what it is like to have a consistent, day-to-day, healthy intimate relationship with another person makes building one very painful and complicated.

The push-pull, approach-avoidance, the "I want you—go away," the colossal terror of being close, yet the desire and need for it, is beautifully shown in a poem by John Gould.

WHY DO YOU COME?

> *I don't want you.*
> *I don't need you.*
> *I don't want to see you.*
> *Yet you keep coming back.*
> *I can't figure you out.*
> *A pretty girl like you*
> *Should be able to find*
> *Someone else.*
> *I reject you and*
> *Yet you keep*
> *Returning.*
> *Everywhere I turn,*
> *You're there.*
> *You're just taking*
> *Up too much of*
> *My time.*

Why do you come?
Why don't you leave?
You are?
Good!
What did you want
With a guy like me?
Love.
Please come back.
She's gone.

The following demonstrates the same conflict. Sam was involved in one of his first relationships and describes what happened.

Last week Cindy brought me some fruit. I drink a lot of Hawaiian Punch. She had cut some labels from the cans, put them on the fruit, and brought them and gave them to me. I felt like crying. She thought my nutrition wasn't good enough or something, and she was going to bring me this fruit. She didn't just bring me the fruit. She went and stuck those stupid little labels on them!

♦ ♦ ♦

It meant so much to him that he wanted to cry but he had to find a way to diminish it. Push, pull. The internal struggle goes on and on.

Karen talks about it from another vantage point. She has the same confusion as an adult because of her past experiences.

It's so much easier to deal with deep negative emotions about myself, especially in terms of my relationships with men. I'm rejecting

who's willing to love me. I have this feeling that the only way I'm ever
going to fall in love with somebody is if they are absolutely perfect and
they walk in the door and it's an automatic, instantaneous, perfect
relationship. Otherwise, I don't want any part of it. I'll get interested
in somebody, start going after them and the second they're interested
in me, I don't want any part of it at all. It's just completely gone. It's
gotten to the point where most of the time I don't bother, because I
know what I'm going to do anyway, so why even bother trying? I'm
not sure if I'm afraid of loving or if I'm afraid of being loved. The
only thing that comes to mind is that I'm afraid of not ever knowing
that love is real or if the love is real, having it taken away, somehow.

◆ ◆ ◆

Thus, the fear of abandonment gets in the way of the development
of a relationship. The development of any healthy relationship
requires a lot of give-and-take and problem solving. There is always
some disagreement and anger which a couple resolve. A minor dis-
agreement gets very big, very quickly for adult children of alcoholics
because the issue of being abandoned takes precedence over the
original issue.

Karen is deeply affected by concerns over abandonment.

I take everything so seriously with relationships. If I don't feel like
I'm being treated in the right way, I react with anger and panic and
"Oh, my God!" I'll get really uptight and I'll say something and react
with anger, but I know that they're not going to want to stay with me.
Somehow I'm not worth it. I always see them as being all right. It's
always that even if I feel I'm worth it, they leave anyway and there's
nothing I can do to make them stay, and it's easy to make them leave
somehow. I feel as though I'm always having to do things to make

them stay. And it's not me doing things because it's me and I'm doing them. I'm doing things to make them stay or keep them from leaving. It's always like "Don't leave me."

◆ ◆ ◆

These same feelings are expressed by Nancy.

I have a real strong panic reaction to someone's anger with me. The panic that I experience is so extreme that I really don't know what to do with it, so that whenever there's a small argument, the fear is so great that it always escalates, and I guess I would love to know how people handle rejection because to me it becomes more of an issue of abandonment.

◆ ◆ ◆

As a result of the fear of abandonment, you don't feel confident about yourself. You don't feel good about yourself or believe that you are lovable. So you look to others for what it is that you cannot give yourself in order to feel okay. You feel okay if someone else tells you that you are okay. Needless to say, you give away a great deal of power. In a relationship, you give the other person the power to lift you up or knock you down. You feel wonderful if they treat you well and tell you that you are wonderful but when they don't, these feelings no longer belong to you.

Some clear examples of this came through in one of the groups of children of alcoholics that I ran:

Ed said,

I fear rejection. I'm very dependent. All the time that I'm involved with the group, I'm looking for praises from Jan. I know that that's dumb. It would be nice but I would like to not have that need. I would like to wean myself off that need to constantly seek approval for everything that I do. It's a pain in the ass and it occupies a lot of my time. I'm constantly fighting for the audience.

Ray agreed with him.

I've wondered about that in myself, too. I wonder about struggling in front of audiences who approve of people who are trying to come together to work on themselves because I am sure that that generates approval. The thought has occurred to me that maybe sometimes what I'm doing in becoming a part of the group is just a very sophisticated mechanism for getting approval.

♦ ♦ ♦

These overwhelming fears of being abandoned or rejected prevent any ease in the process of developing a relationship. Coupled with a sense of urgency, "This is the only time I have; if I don't do it now, it will never happen," they tend to put pressure on the relationship. It makes it much more difficult to evolve slowly, to let two people get to know each other better, and to explore each other's feelings and attitudes in a variety of ways.

This sense of urgency makes the other person feel smothered, even though it is not the intent. I know a couple who have tremendous problems because whenever they argue, she panics and worries that he is now going to leave her. She needs constant reassurance in the middle of the argument that he's not going to leave her and that he still loves her. When he is in conflict, which is difficult for him as well, he tends to want to withdraw and be by himself. Needless to say, this makes the issue at hand more difficult to resolve than if it were only the issue itself needing to be confronted.

The feelings of being insecure, of having difficulty in trusting, and questions about whether or not you're going to get hurt are not exclusive to adult children of alcoholics. These are problems most people have. Few people enter a relationship fully confident that things are going to work out the way they hope they will. They enter a relationship hopeful, but with a variety of fears.

So, all of the things that cause you concern are not unique to you. It's simply a matter of degree: Your being the child of an alcoholic caused the ordinary difficulties to become more severe.

Adult children of alcoholics do not appear to have any more or any fewer sexual problems than the general population.

In talking with many adult children of alcoholics about their sexuality, I found that their conversations, their attitudes and their feelings were no different from any other group. The hang-ups that some of them had related more to the church and the culture than what went on at home. This is not to say that some pretty bizarre things did not go on at home. This is to say that what went on in the alcoholic home was no more or less bizarre than things I've heard of or seen going on in other kinds of homes.

Professionals in the alcohol field are now taking a look at the problem of incest. We are trying very hard to understand it in order to help to effect healthy changes in our clients. I doubt that alcoholics are any more guilty of incest than anybody else. It may be that incest occurs more often when the adult is drunk than when the adult is sober, but we're talking about alcoholics here, not about someone who is disinhibited from alcohol.

With respect to sex in general, the children of alcoholics have not been able to sit down with their parents and discuss it. However, I don't believe this is exclusive to them. Talking about sexuality is difficult for people, regardless of whether or not they are living with alcoholism. Somehow, it's easier to excuse within the alcoholic family system. If you're in too much of a squirrel cage to discuss anything, sex is just like anything else.

We know that the sexual relationship of the parents breaks down as does every other form of communication. We know that offering and withdrawing of sex becomes a weapon, and we know that the experience becomes unhealthy between the two partners as other things become unhealthy. I know that sex is used as a weapon in households that are not affected by alcoholism.

I am not suggesting that the adult child of the alcoholic is necessarily healthy in terms of sexual attitudes. I am just not suggesting that they are not. It has been my experience that adult children of alcoholics have no more and no fewer problems with their sexuality than anybody else.

8. Adult children of alcoholics overreact to changes over which they have no control.

This is very simple to understand. The young child of the alcoholic was not in control. The alcoholic's life was inflicted on him, as was his environment.

In order to survive when growing up, he needed to turn that around. He needed to begin taking charge of his environment. This became very important and remains so. The child of the alcoholic learns to trust himself more than anyone else when it's impossible to rely on somebody else's judgment.

As a result, you are very often accused of being controlling, rigid and lacking in spontaneity. This is probably true. It doesn't come from wanting to do everything your own way. It isn't because you are spoiled or unwilling to listen to other ideas. It comes from the fear that if you are not in charge, if a change is made, abruptly, quickly, without your being able to participate in it, you will lose control of your life.

There is no question that this is overreaction. And when there is an overreaction, it generally means that it is caused by something in one's past experience. At the moment, the thing you overreacted to may seem foolish to others. But it is an automatic response. "You can't do that to me. No, I will not go to the movies when we decided we were going roller skating." It's almost an involuntary reflex.

When you look back on your reactions and your behavior later, you feel somewhat foolish, but at the time you were simply unable to shift gears.

9. Adult children of alcoholics constantly seek approval and affirmation.

> *Searching eyes,*
> *Questioning all corners of the room*
> *in split seconds—*
> *Brows which aspire*
> *to the heights of the forehead;*
> *darting, cool and somewhat unsure fingers*
> *examining the air around her—*
> *reassuring her doubtful mind*
> *of the truth of her existence;*
> *Seeing herself in the mirrors of others' minds,*
> *She rarely believes her own—*
> *accepting her existence as a reflection*
> *the haze rarely clears,*

the mirror is a glass
and her soul is bare.
Does she know that she is her own—
For real.

—Marya DePinto

We talk about an external and internal locus of control. When a child is born, the environment pretty much dictates how that child is going to feel about himself or herself. The school, the church and other people all have an influence, but the most important influence is what we call "significant others." In the child's world, this means parents. So children begin to believe who they are by the messages received from parents. And as children grow older, these messages become internalized and contribute significantly to self-image. The movement is toward the internal locus of control.

The message you got as a child was very confused. It was not unconditional love. It was not, "I think *you're* terrific, but I'm not too happy about what you just did." The definitions were not clear and the messages were mixed. "Yes, no, I love you, go away." So you grew up with some confusion about yourself. The affirmations you didn't get on a day-to-day basis as a child, you interpret as negative.

Now, when affirmation is offered, it's very difficult to accept. Accepting the affirmation would be the beginning of changing your self-image.

Lou had this very problem but was beginning to change.

In the last four months at work, a lot of people have come up to me and said, "You're a really nice person. I'm glad you're here." People have said this more than once, and I have a tough time accepting that. I wonder what's going to come after that. "Lou, you're a nice person, but. . . ." *That's what I heard in my childhood. "But" was always devastating. What I'm doing with that now is I'm saying, "Thank you." I'm still wondering about the but, but I'm beginning to believe that I'm the one who's putting it there and they're not.*

◆ ◆ ◆

Another member in the group talked about a relationship he backed away from because the affirmation would cause him to change. He said, "After last week, it occurred to me that perhaps the reason why the relationship didn't get anywhere is because Cindy did like me, and since she did like me—I judged her as being worthless."

Anyone who could care about him could not be worth very much. This self-defeating reasoning resulted in his losing the affirmation and approval that he wanted so desperately.

10. Adult children of alcoholics feel that they are different from other people.

Children of alcoholics feel different from other people because to some degree they actually are. Yet, there are more of them than they are aware of.

They also assume that in any group of people, everyone else feels comfortable and they are the only ones who feel awkward. This is not peculiar to them. Never, of course, does anyone check it out and find out that each person has his or her own way of trying not to look awkward. Is that true of you, too?

Interestingly enough, you even feel different in a group of adult children of alcoholics. Feeling different is something you have had with you since childhood, and even if the circumstance does not warrant it, the feeling prevails. Other children had an opportunity to be children. You didn't. You were very much concerned with what was going on at home. You could never be completely comfortable playing with other children. You could not be fully there. Your concerns about your home problems clouded everything else in your life.

What happened to you is what happened to the rest of your family. You became isolated. As a result, socializing, being a part of any group, became increasingly difficult. You simply did not develop the social skills necessary to feel comfortable or a part of the group.

You guessed at what would work. Dana tried bribes. "I used to have this thing about Barbie Dolls. I had such an incredible collection of them, and I used to give my prized ones away to people so I would have a friend. Usually they thought I was a jerkoff for giving it away and thought less of me."

Dave said, "I lent my books. My books were my most prized possessions."

Another child of an alcoholic said, "I tend to give people whatever they need at that moment, so that's a hook into them to like me and maybe I try to get the hook in first. As a child, I watched how my father manipulated people this way, and I saw how well it worked for him, so I guess I thought it would work for me the same way."

On the subject of picking a role model, Dana reports: "I kind of pick people with this unrealistic image in terms of being the bright ones, the smart ones, the loving ones, the Peace Corps types. I'd pick role models that were just sweet, kind, loving and that kind of stuff. I don't pick people who are appropriate, but who seem perfect. I never picked anyone who was a bully or a tyrant to model myself after. I would look at that and think that that is not the way it should be, but I do know that the people I picked were not appropriate."

Dave agreed. "When I was a kid, I used to pick inappropriate role models also. But I went to the other extreme. All the people I hung out with were worse than I was. I picked out all the teenage alcoholics, the guys who drank codeine cough syrup, women who could not have close sexual relationships with men. I was very frustrated as an adolescent. I picked out the fat ones. I would not dare to date a good-looking woman. I still have very few friends."

It is hard for children of alcoholics to believe that they can be accepted because of who they are and that the acceptance does not have to be earned.

Feeling different and somewhat isolated is part of your makeup.

11. Adult children of alcoholics are either superresponsible or super-irresponsible.

You take it all on or you give it all up. There is no middle ground. You tried to please your parents, doing more and more and more, or you reached the point where you recognized it didn't matter, so you did nothing. You also did not see a family that cooperated with each other. You didn't have a family that decided on Sunday, "Let's all work in the yard. I will work on this and you work on that, and then we'll come together."

Not having a sense of doing a part of a project, of how to cooperate with other people and let all the parts come together and become a whole, you either do all of it or you do none of it. You also don't have a good sense of your own limitations. Saying no is extraordinarily difficult for you so you do more and more and more. You do it, not because you really have a bloated sense of yourself but rather (1) because you don't have a realistic sense of your capacity, or (2) because if you say "no," you are afraid that they will find you out. They will find out that you are incompetent. The quality of the job you do does not seem to influence your feelings about yourself. So you take on more and more and more and more. Until you finally burn out.

The constant fear of being found out takes much of your energy. It even takes some of the energy that you could be using to do a better job. Not better in terms of what the employer asks for because you're probably giving the employer more than he asks for, but better in being more efficient.

Dana talked about her feelings about herself on the job.

Nobody has said anything. Nobody has complained about my work. If anything, they've praised it. They've all been good to me. They've been very understanding when I've been sick, and I am still there looking for the pink slip. And the thing is, I know I'm doing a good job. It's just that I'm so insecure, and that insecurity overrides any good thing that I'm doing. I continue to wait to be fired.

♦ ♦ ♦

Because of her insecurity, this is the way she behaves.

I've been getting myself crazy in terms of organization, scheduling my time and energy in such a small place that the pressure I put on myself is incredible. It sent me to my office in such a state today that when one more piece of "I want you" was handed me, I started to cry. I seem to have this responsibility thing where I feel I have to take it all on, whether it's responsible for me to do it or not. I want to be able to do it and I think I should be able to do it.

♦ ♦ ♦

She finally worked herself up to this point.

I'm not going in to work tomorrow. There's no way in hell that I'm going in to work tomorrow. I don't think I have any time left and I know that I'm going to be docked, but I just can't go in there anymore. Not this week. I can't go in and look at those people and work. I can't work. I can't do anything. I'm just blocked. It's frustrating as hell. I had a lot of work today, and I was sick to my stomach. I got home and I was hysterical. Walking around, pacing around, and I tried calling everybody and nobody was home. The whole world's out to lunch. I'm sorry. It's gotten to the point where I don't think I can manage anything.

◆ ◆ ◆

In talking to a group of adult children of alcoholics, I said somewhat sarcastically, "You book your days so full that there is no time even to go to the bathroom." One young man responded to me by saying, "That's not true. We do plan time to go to the bathroom. It's just that we bring a book along."

12. Adult children of alcoholics are extremely loyal, even in the face of evidence that the loyalty is undeserved.

The alcoholic home appears to be a very loyal place. Family members hang in long after reasons dictate that they should leave. The so-called "loyalty" is more the result of fear and insecurity than anything else; nevertheless, the behavior that is modeled is one where no one walks away just because the going gets rough. This sense enables the adult child to remain in involvements that are better dissolved.

Since making a friend or developing a relationship is so difficult and so complicated, once the effort has been made it is permanent. If someone cares enough about you to be your friend, your lover or your spouse, then you have the obligation to stay with them forever. If you have let them know who you are, if they have discovered who you are and not rejected you, that fact, in and of itself, is enough to make you sustain the relationship. The fact that they may treat you poorly does not matter. You can rationalize that. Somehow, no matter what they do or say, you can figure out a way to excuse their behavior and find yourself at fault. This reinforces your negative self-image and enables you to stay in the relationship. Your loyalty is unparalleled.

There is also a lot of safety in an established relationship. It is known, and the known is always more secure than the unknown. Change being extremely difficult, you would much prefer to stay with what is.

You also don't know much about what a good relationship is all about. So you stay with what you have, not knowing that there could be anything better or anything different. You just muddle your way through.

On this subject, Dana said:

It was like once I made a commitment, I was going to stick to it. It was because I was so scared of being myself. I didn't know that there were other types of marriages—other than the type my parents had or the type that his parents had. I wanted my marriage to work so that we would be able to buy a house, have babies, and do all the things right, and be happy and contented, and like each other and love each other. It didn't work out that way, but I couldn't let go.

◆ ◆ ◆

13. Adult children of alcoholics are impulsive. They tend to lock themselves into a course of action without giving serious consideration to alternative behaviors or possible consequences. This impulsivity leads to confusion, self-loathing and loss of control over their environment. In addition, they spend an excessive amount of energy cleaning up the mess.

This can be best characterized as "alcoholic." It may be modeled behavior without any conscious awareness. For example: The alcoholic gets an idea. "I'm going to stop off and have a (one) drink on the way home." Simple idea—any thoughts that would get in the way of carrying out this idea are rationalized away. "I promised to be home on time," or "One drink will not make me late," or "I promised I'd stop drinking—one drink is not drinking."

It is true that one drink will not make him late nor is it "drinking" within his framework, if he simply has one drink. So he stops for "the" drink.

From the time that the idea entered the alcoholic's head to have the drink, he was compelled. No other options were available. The idea extended only to the first drink.

The rest of the scenario is clear. After the first drink, the compulsion takes over and the alcoholic has lost control. He rationalizes for a while, and then is so far into it that he loses sight of what he had in his mind to begin with.

The idea that triggers the impulsive behavior has no timeframe. It is the "here and now." No serious consideration is paid to what happened the last time, nor what the consequences will be this time.

Since the idea is limited to the moment, "I'm going to have a (one) drink," thoughts of "I'll get drunk and be late and this will cause trouble" simply are not relevant. The fact that there will be loss of control and that the behavior will get out of hand is simply ignored. "I can control what I drink" is heard over and over, and evidence to the contrary is similarly dismissed, once the compulsion takes over and the uncontrolled behavior begins.

Impulsivity is a very childlike quality. Ordinarily, children are impulsive. But when you were a child you were more of a parent than a child, so your present impulsive behavior is something you missed during your childhood. If you miss out on one stage, quite often you make it up at another time in your life. When a child has a parent who functions as a parent and the child acts out impulsively, they say, "You cannot do that. Because you did that, there is a consequence."

As a child, you could not predict the outcome of any given behavior, so you don't know how to do it now. Also, there was no consistency at home. As a result, you haven't the following framework of "When I behaved impulsively in the past, this happened and that happened, and this person reacted in that way." Sometimes it would go okay, and sometimes it wouldn't. Essentially, it may not really have mattered. Nor did anyone say to you, "These are the possible consequences of that behavior. Let's talk about other things that you might do."

The situation is further complicated by a terrible sense of urgency. If you don't do it immediately, you will not get a second chance. And you are used to being on the edge of a precipice, living from crisis to crisis. If things go smoothly, it's even more unsettling than when you're in a crisis. So it's not surprising that you may even create a crisis.

This impulsive behavior is not deliberate or calculated. It is behavior over which you have lost control. This is the characteristic that is most unsettling to you, that frightens you the most and that you really want to change.

Rose expresses it this way:

It's not that I don't empathize with other people, because when I see the effect my behavior has, when it happens I can't believe I've done that. I care about that person, how could I have? I'm absolutely flipped out that it's me. I do care about the impact but somewhere between the impact and doing something about it, I have some kind of tunnel vision.

Dana:

I don't ever set out to intentionally hurt somebody else or to upset anybody else; it's just that that's the path I take and I just plunge right into it.

Mike:

It's like a plow. I mean, it's not something you do casually. I go full steam ahead.

Dana:

I'm walking forward with a wall on either side and I just go.

Cindy:

My capacity to think, to hear words in my head, disappears. I'm not aware of finding any words to fit together in a sentence. It just becomes a mass of energy. I seem to bolt out.

Mike:

It gives me bad judgment and that bothers me.

Cindy:

I only see in the moment.

Dana:

Sometimes it's like that's the only path I can take. It's not really a path, but it's the only action. There have been times when I knew this was the wrong thing to do and I've paid the consequences four or five months down the road. I knew before I even went into it that it was the wrong thing to do.

Cindy:

Once the feelings take over, I have to go with it. It has a propulsion that I'm powerless against. I wish a crane would come down and pick me up out of it.

Dana:

Once I take the first step, that's all that's needed. It's like going down a hill. You take that first step, and it's all of a sudden rolling.

Cindy:

It seems like a commitment to go with whatever decision I make.

Sam:

It's very rigid with me. It's not that I start out to hurt somebody, but that the other person usually gets hurt in the process. Almost always somebody gets hurt. Even after I recognize it, I keep on going anyway. Whatever my agenda is, I adhere to it rigidly. There's a great deal of momentum behind it. There's a lot of energy and it just keeps right on barreling through. There's this concept of blinders. I may have been told facts that would slow another person down or to check something out, but once I'm on this thing, rarely do I check things out. And if I do, I rarely listen.

Cindy:

It becomes compulsive, and I seem to lose the ability to project myself into the future to see what it really would be like, to see if that's really what I want to do. In the moment, if I'm feeling something negative with some-body, I seem to have a complete inability to feel and touch and taste the parts that are good, even though I know they are there. I can't feel them, so they are of no worth to me somehow.

Dana:

The emotion that I feel in the present is usually the only one that counts. I only feel the emotion I'm in at the time. It's so hard for me to remember that I can feel anything else but what I'm feeling at the moment. Or, that tomorrow I'll look at this and feel differently.

As a result of this behavior, more often than not, the light at the end of the tunnel is the headlamp of an oncoming train. You have not been able to see the reaction or the implications of what you do. As a result, you create many outrageous situations for yourself.

A client decided one afternoon to buy a horse. She brought the horse home and put it in the garage. It was very difficult for her to understand why her husband was very upset, because it seemed like a good idea at the time.

Once she had the idea, that was the end of it. She had to follow through. She could not stop herself.

You find that you will quit a job without realizing that you have no other means of support. You'll marry without really getting to know the other person. Buying horses is very unusual. I have only encountered that once, but the second two happen very, very often. You end up very concerned about your behavior, but before you can begin to look at it and change it, you have to spend a great deal of time and energy extricating yourself from a mess. So it is self-defeating on several levels.

Part of the difficulty is that adult children of alcoholics tend to look for immediate, as opposed to deferred, gratification.

The word I use most with my clients who are adult children of alcoholics is "patience." Whatever it is that comes up, whatever it is that you need to accomplish—be it emotionally or behaviorally—you want to accomplish it yesterday. You have some difficulty in being patient with others. The person you are most impatient with, however, is yourself. You want it all immediately.

This gets you into a lot of trouble because your lack of patience feeds into everything else that gives you difficulty. Especially, it feeds into your impulsivity, your judgment of yourself.

It's not very hard to understand why it is that you want everything immediately. Putting things off gives you so much trouble because when you were growing up, if you did not get what you asked for in that very moment, that was the end of it. If you said, "I want this now," and your parents said, "You can't do it now but you can do it by the end of the week," or, "We can talk about it later," you knew that was the end of it. You knew that promises for the future were broken. That was one consistent thing in your life.

That was the reality of your life. If you didn't do it immediately, it simply would not happen. This makes it very difficult for you to plan for the future. For you to say, "This is what I'm going to do two years from now and this is the manner in which I am going to do it" is very much of a struggle. You want what you want when you want it because a little part of you knows even though it is probably no longer true, that if you don't get it now, if you didn't go after it now, if you don't grab on now and grab on tight, it will never happen.

The sense of "This is my last chance" is with you all the time. You even become impatient with yourself when you decide to work on patience and don't become patient immediately. Patience, therefore, is something that you must work very hard to acquire.

3

Breaking the Cycle

1. Adult children of alcoholics guess at what normal is.

It is important for you to recognize that there is no such thing as normal. This is the foundation of the issues that will be discussed. It is critical, because something built on a false premise can develop logically but won't work. Like a house of cards, if the base is not secure, a small breeze will blow down the whole structure.

Normal is a myth like Santa Claus and *The Brady Bunch*. It is not realistic to talk in terms of normal, since it is something you have been fooled into believing exists. Other concepts like functional or dysfunctional are more useful. What is functional for you? What works well for you? What is in your best interest? And in the best interest of your family? This approach is realistic and varies from person to person, from family to family.

The task, then, is not to find out what normal is but to discover what is most comfortable for you and for those who are close to you. You bought the myth of normalcy and, in so doing, developed fantasies about your ideal self, ideal others and an ideal family. This has made your life extremely difficult. The ideal self you think about is the perfect child, the perfect spouse, the perfect friend, the perfect parent. Since the fantasy cannot exist, you spend a lot of time judging yourself because life doesn't work the way you decide it should.

In discovering what feels okay, what doesn't and why, you also need to take a look at this in terms of the way your family functions. It is now time for your family to learn how to solve problems and how to resolve conflicts. There are many ways to accomplish these things.

The first one is rather simple. Pick up a book on child development so that you can learn what is expected at different stages. Because you did not develop like most children, you may be unnecessarily concerned about your children. Such a book will teach you what to expect at various ages. This is not an attempt to mold your children according to stages but to gain a sense of whether or not they are somewhat predictable. This knowledge will give you a sense of security.

You might also take a course in parent-effectiveness to learn the skills and techniques for comfortably relating to children. Remember, you are not expected to know all the answers. You are there with a lot of other people who care about their children and want to develop better ways of communicating with them.

Barry and Aviva Mascari, who work with chemically dependent families, have developed an adaptation of the Adlerian family meeting. On a weekly basis, the family sits down and discusses the issues important to them, such as how much allowances should be, where to take the family vacation, and who is responsible for doing the laundry and taking out the garbage. This doesn't mean that your children take over the running of the family. It just means that all members of the family participate in the decision making, so that there are no giant secrets. Everyone is considered and no one is invalidated.

Much of your experience in growing up was that of being invalidated. You had the feeling that life would be better if you were out of the picture. It was a feeling that what you thought and said were not important. A first step in turning these feelings around, the family meeting will also make your children feel that their input is valuable. As a result, they will not have the feelings of invalidation that you had.

Something else you can do to discover what will work is to find a person you can talk to about anything. Have at least one person in your life with whom you do not have to worry about how stupid you might sound, to whom you can admit not knowing, to whom you can feel free not to even know the right questions to ask. A person like this is a treasure. I recommend that this person not be the adult child of an alcoholic because there is a possibility that he or she is struggling with the same things that you are.

It is important to be able to risk admitting that you don't know. Owning up to not knowing something in a group of people always elicits the response: "I'm really glad you said that. I didn't know that either." But there is always one person in every group of people who says, "You don't know *that?*" You can learn to laugh at that remark or to discount it completely. Instead, use the support of those who are willing to learn and explore and not worry about having all of the answers all of the time.

I encourage you to trust your own instincts, which much of the time tell you the most appropriate way to behave. You tend to pull yourself back too quickly and decide that your instincts are not valid. By starting to trust them, you will soon learn that your instincts are a very valuable tool in developing the kind of healthy relationships you want.

A client of mine told me how several people had gone to a lot of trouble to give her a special surprise party for her fortieth birthday. Her twenty-year-old daughter was completely obnoxious. My client said, "You know, I really wanted to let her have it in front of all those people, but I held back." I said, "How come? That's what I think she deserved." My client said, "Well, I will next time. First I wanted to check it out with you."

This incident illustrates how to deal with a difficult situation. When something makes you uncomfortable, identify it. Talk about it and then make the decision about what to do. Situational issues often can be solved rather simply and easily. But those relating to the past are much more complicated.

Sandra is struggling hard with giving up the idea that she has to be the perfect parent, and her children test her constantly. Her youngest child started a paper route. When the woman who gave him the route, who happens to be a fabulous Italian cook, said to him, "Can I pay you for this?" he said, "How about a hot meal?"

Sandra feeds her children, yet she became very upset and distraught because her neighbor might think she did not feed them. She had no sense of humor about the incident, nor did she know how to handle it. Her son was also having a breakfast of pancakes at another home, in addition to a full breakfast and dinner at home. Sandra needed to take a look at what caused her extreme discomfort. It had to do with her perfectionism, with the way she wanted to be seen in the neighborhood.

Another part of it was that she felt her son was taking advantage of her neighbors. That was the part that she could deal with, and so she called up the neighbor with the paper route. The neighbor thought it was quite funny and said, "That's quite a little boy you got there. I love to watch people eat. Feeding people is one of the greatest joys of my life. I know that he comes to my house directly from your house, but if you don't mind, I enjoy doing this for him."

Sandra felt relieved, and they continued to talk. She admitted to this neighbor, who was also a friend, that her biggest concern was that she would think she did not feed her children properly. Her neighbor started to laugh because even as the conversation took place, her neighbor was in bed running a high fever and feeling very guilty that she was absent from her graduate classes. She was not being the perfect student and Sandra was not being the perfect mother, and both of them were feeling guilty. Discussing their problems made them feel better because they became a little more realistic. This was important because being perfect is not realistic and attempting to be perfect causes a great deal of anxiety. One can strive toward certain goals, but the goal of perfection does not have rewards in it that are beneficial.

A fully functioning person knows how to handle conflict in a responsible manner. This includes how to confront, how to deal with and how to resolve conflict. When you were growing up, you did not learn how to resolve problems. Problems were avoided, not resolved. As an adult, you still behave in ways that are not useful in this area.

Take this simple little test. Imagine that you are walking down a hall. There is a door in the hallway. You are about halfway down the hall and coming out of that door is someone you are very angry with or someone you know to be angry with you.

What do you do? Do you stand your ground and confront that person and say, "It's good to see you. There are things we need to discuss." Or do you turn around and walk away? Do you make some frivolous remark that has nothing to do with what you two need to work out? Do you walk on and pretend he is not there?

What is it that you do when a potential conflict arises? How do you handle yourself? What is your initial reaction? To resolve conflict, you need to understand what you do and what goes on inside of you. This is a place to begin. Once you know that, you can make decisions about how you are going to deal with the problem and learn how to confront reality. Not really wanting to confront reality is the biggest issue in an alcoholic home. It is time to confront reality and realize there is no such thing as normal. There is only reality, which you determine for yourself with the help and input of people who are interested and willing and anxious to participate in your development—thereby participating also in enhancing their own.

2. Adult children of alcoholics have trouble following a project through from beginning to end.

It is time for you to find out whether you are the procrastinator you think you are or whether you simply lack information about how to complete a task. How does one follow a project through from beginning to end? How does that happen? It can, it does and it will. It has to be done very systematically. People who carry projects through to completion don't do it casually. They have what we call a "game plan." They may have developed it to the degree that it looks automatic but it is not. There is a process involved.

In the beginning, you need to be very aware of what the process is so that you can follow it and so that you do not get stuck along the way and begin to judge yourself. The first thing you need to do when you conceive the project is to take a look at the idea. Is it manageable? Is it possible to accomplish what it is you would like to accomplish?

You then need to develop a step-by-step plan in order to accomplish it. You need to set a time limit for each step. How long is it going to take you to do each part of your project? You don't need to know exactly how long it's going to take, but you need to have a sense of what all of the parts are and how much time you need to give to each part.

Once you have made that decision, the next step is to plan how you are going to meet the time limit. Is it realistic for you to do this project within this time limit, if all of these parts take this much time?

In developing the way you are going to meet the time require-
ments, you need to take a look at your own working style. The best
way to do this is to reflect back on your learning style. When you
were in school, how did you learn best? Were you the student who
did best by doing a little each day or by cramming the night before?
Did you cram the night before because you learned best that way or
because there was no alternative? What ways were you most satisfied
with what you were able to do? Study your own learning style.

If those steps don't fall into place and the goal isn't manageable,
rethink the idea. Perhaps your idea was not realistic. If not, be willing to revise it. Perhaps you have taken on something more than you
can do at this time. Or perhaps you need to approach the same idea
somewhat differently. Be willing to revise the idea or the time limit.
It may be that the idea is just fine, but you have not set aside enough
time to accomplish it. Be willing at each stage to rethink and
reassess. See if there are changes that might occur along the way that
will make a difference. You need not get stuck along the way because
you have not figured out how it is going to be accomplished.

An example of this process should make it clearer to you. Paul is
forty-eight years old and a very successful businessman. To a large
extent, his business involves high-pressure situations such as twenty-
four-hour time limits on preparing major reports. He goes from crisis
to crisis and does it extremely well. Crisis is something that he, as an
adult child of an alcoholic, understands extremely well. He has used
this aspect of his history to his advantage.

Paul decided that he wanted to get a Ph.D. After being accepted
into a doctoral program, he came to me in a state of panic. "I cannot do this," he said. "It is not possible for me to do this dissertation." I smiled. He was overwhelmed at the project taking over a
year to complete. Because he had no frame of reference for that kind
of thing, he was scared. He is also intelligent enough to recognize

that he was getting in his own way and needed help to overcome the problem.

The first thing we decided was that he had to limit whom he talked to about it, because he was getting too much input, too many different approaches. This, plus not developing his own approach, increased his anxiety. I simply said to him, "If I am going to help you, I am the only one to increase your anxiety at this time."

He also had the idea that his would be the most definitive dissertation of all time. He had to give up his grandiose notion and decide to research a subject that was manageable. He also had to name a committee of people whose input was pertinent and who wanted his project to be a success.

As soon as he did this, his panic started to subside.

The next step was to determine how long it would take to write the dissertation. He was in a panic as if it had to be done yesterday. The paper was going to take a year. It was going to take time to accumulate, assemble and assess the material. It also was going to take time to interpret the results and write the paper in a way that would be acceptable to the members of his committee. It could not be done yesterday, and it could not be done tomorrow. A year was the only realistic assessment of how long the project would take.

Once that was understood, we could take a look at his learning style. How did he learn best? Could he do this the way he had done other things in life? It became clear that he could not do this the way he did other things, in a cramming, last-minute way. In addition, he did not want to take a month or two off work to work exclusively on the dissertation. It was decided that he would work two hours a day.

We also needed to look at what this meant. Did it mean that he had to write two hours a day? Or sit at his desk for two hours a day? Could he think during this time? The conclusion was to do something related to the dissertation during those two hours. The time spent thinking would later translate to time spent in writing. He need not be rigid with himself. We also determined that the place he worked best was at home at a little desk he had in the back room, where he could have some privacy. The most productive hours of the day were the first two hours in the morning. He would thus use the time before the rest of his family arose and before the phone started to ring.

These decisions were very basic and simple. But they made the difference between accomplishing and not accomplishing the task. And they were arrived at by very careful consideration.

Paul had never had the experience of planning out anything before. This was the first time someone had sat down with him and said, "How are you going to accomplish this? How are you going to get this done? What is your game plan? How long is it going to take? Is it feasible?"

After working on the dissertation for two weeks, he said he could not work two hours a day, but he could work one hour. This was by far more manageable for him, and he felt he could accomplish what he needed to in less time. This was fine. He developed a game plan and was able to revise it, once there was a structure which made the task more manageable. He was no longer in a state of panic that drained his energy and got in his way. He will now have less difficulty following a project through from beginning to end.

The steps outlined here apply to anything that needs to be accomplished. That wonderful idea that you have may or may not be possible. It does not come about through luck. It results through careful planning. As you have more experience with planning, you begin to do it automatically. The difficulty you have now may not be because you are procrastinating but because you simply have not known about the process involved.

Your young children do not have to wait until they are adults to resolve this particular problem. If their teachers have been saying to you that they have not been living up to their potential, that they don't finish what they start, you can say, "My child needs to learn how to do it. My child may not be completing what he or she starts—not because she's not interested, not because she's not involved—but because we need to teach her how to do it." Sit down with the teacher, if he or she is sympathetic, and talk about how your child is going to develop the kinds of study habits that will make it possible to finish a project. Your children may not be doing as well as they would like to in school because they don't have the experience of seeing something begun and finished. This is no time to judge yourself and decide that you are a terrible parent. That will take energy away from helping your child and structuring the environment—a necessity for accomplishment. You can develop and organize a structure with or without the help of a teacher.

Guidelines need to be established. You don't need to be dictatorial; you can work them out with your children so that they become part of their life's design. They don't have to like it. It is time for them to begin to do things systematically. For example, homework should be done daily at a regular time and place for an agreed amount of time. This is the way to begin.

It is important to let them know they are not stupid, which they begin to believe very early on.

The difficulties result from lack of experience, but this is going to change. The family is going to enter into a partnership where they learn how to complete what they start. It is a process that everybody will be involved in, so they have more control of their lives. It also will improve your relationship with your children and break the cycle in the next generation.

3. Adult children of alcoholics lie when it would be just as easy to tell the truth.

Lying is a very difficult habit to break because when you were a child there was a payoff for not telling the truth. As an adult, you find that there is no longer a payoff, but the habit persists. I have seen the habit broken mainly when the penalties are so great that life becomes unmanageable. The idea here is to stop lying before that happens. First, one must differentiate between the measured lie and the automatic lie. There may be a small payoff for you in a measured lie. It is not for me to judge; it is to give you a choice: to lie or not to lie. The cycle we are trying to break is the one in which the lying is automatic and you have no control over it.

The initial step in overcoming any bad habit is becoming aware of it. If you have been lying automatically, you are not necessarily aware of what you have been doing. Promise yourself that you will not lie for one whole day. Then see what happens. You may or may not be able to do it.

If you can do it, fine. Was it easy or difficult for you? If you can't, write down what happened—what you lied about and what was going through your mind right before you lied.

Assess what happened at the end of the day without judging yourself. You did what you did. You accomplished whatever you could accomplish. It was easy or it was difficult. You were able to do it for part of the day but not for all of the day. You were able to do it in certain kinds of situations and not in others. Maybe you were able when you were relaxed and unable when you were stressed.

Just sit down and take a look at it. Rather than judging yourself, get to know yourself a little better by becoming a little more aware of how you behave.

Start the next day with the same resolve. Repeat the process. Do this for three or four days. At the end of that time, see what progress you have made. If you are still lying automatically, it's a good idea to make a commitment to yourself that the next time you find your-self lying, you will own up to it and correct any misstatement you have made.

This is a powerful commitment. It means saying to yourself, "Even though the habit is strong, it is important to me that I change it." If you cannot do this, at least be realistic in accepting the fact that you are not ready to change, for whatever reason.

If increasing your awareness and accepting your commitment does not lead to the disappearance of automatic lying, it is probably more than just a bad habit. It may be something you need to work on at a deeper level. It may be a survival tactic, one whose time has passed. Because of your history and the childhood fears you developed, you may have to seek help to change your behavior.

Some things are resolved simply and easily. Others require a lot more work and assistance in their resolution. This is not to say that there is anything wrong with you. It may simply be more difficult for you than you anticipated.

When I work with someone who has a problem with lying, I say, "I believe that you believe what you just said." Then we can take a look at it, see what it means and find out where the truth lies.

Many adult children of alcoholics go to the other extreme. Because there is so much lying, they resolve never to tell a lie. This is a more unusual way of dealing with that problem of growing up. It's a denial of the family pattern.

If you have been involved in the AA, Al-Anon or Alateen pro-grams, you can use their tools of recovery for breaking this habit. You can do what one does with alcohol. You commit yourself to stop drinking and, one day at a time, you stop. One day at a time, you believe in yourself. One day at a time, you can work to change any bad habit you have.

4. Adult children of alcoholics judge themselves without mercy.

Tim, a child of two alcoholics, wrote to me about himself and his feelings. He expressed his most significant discovery very simply: "Although I may make mistakes, I am not a mistake." These words show that he had achieved a certain amount of freedom. He had begun to look at himself honestly without judging himself. When one can separate the behavior from the person, one is free to change, develop and grow.

Although you have been told since childhood all of the ways you did not measure up, it is important for you to recognize that every statement has a positive and negative side. For example, if you are intelligent, that is wonderful because you can understand things that less intelligent people cannot. Yet, these things are often disconcerting. If you feel deeply, the joy is greater than the pain. Who is to say what is good? Who is to say what is not so good? The idea is just to explore it, become fascinated by it and see what it means.

You may have decided that your life is a Greek tragedy. I have a client who has done this, although there is very little evidence that anything other than her attitude is causing her problems. Life does not have to be perceived in various degrees of misery. If you perceive it this way, you might want to figure out what the payoff is. What do you gain by judging yourself? Why do you never judge on the good side? Why do you never pick out those things that make you special and wonderful? What is your need to come down on yourself? The answer is probably simple. Misery is familiar and you have learned how to deal with distress. Life going really well is unfamiliar to you, so you don't know how to manage it. It is not unusual for clients to find a kind of comfort in their poor self-image.

When things start turning around, when they start looking and feeling better, then life becomes unmanageable. It is not unusual for the progress to be sabotaged. Even with a warning, the need for the familiar often takes precedence. After all, your earliest influences are the most powerful ones.

An exercise that I do with my students shows that judgments, good or bad, are a function of the person who holds them. The group sits around in a circle. A decision is made to build a monster in the center of the circle. It is our opportunity to purge ourselves of any qualities, wholly or partially, that we no longer want to possess. If the qualities being discarded are ones that someone else desires, he can pick them up. We go back and forth in this fascinating game. A man decides that he wants to give up 90 percent of his procrastination, and it is hardly out in the center of the circle before someone says, "I will take 75 percent of that because I am much too compulsive."

Someone else says, "I want to give up all of my guilt," and somebody replies, "I need to take a little of that on. I don't want to look at my responsibilities in terms of the impact they have on others." People look surprised as we go on. When one person says, "I am tired of being so sensitive. I am going to give up 60 percent of my sensitivity," another says, "I have been insensitive long enough. I think I need some of yours."

This exercise clearly shows that our traits need to be looked at and explored. To what degree are they useful to us? To what degree do they get in our way? Certainly, judging them and judging ourselves is not useful. Who is to say what is good and what is bad? Somehow, if you step back and decide that you are you and that is okay, you have a lot more choices in life.

The monster ends up being a mixture—a confused mixture. And

just about the only things that all people agree that they want to throw into the center are extra weight and oppressive mothers-in-law.

Another aspect of judging yourself that needs work is your acceptance of compliments. How well do you accept them? Do you automatically throw compliments away? It has been my experience that if something goes wrong, you will take on all the responsibility for it. But when something goes right, you dismiss it with "It just happened" or "It was easy." You may call this humility, but it perpetuates your negative self-image. It does not allow you to give yourself credit for the things that you do well, so that you can begin to feel better about yourself.

You may choose to sound humble to others but be very sure that you accept what is due you. Because something is easy for you does not mean it is unimportant. Yet, if you make a careless mistake, that does not make that mistake any less important.

Try to be aware of the things that you do well. Do not dismiss them. Use them to build on, to become a whole person. You needn't judge them, as they are just part of the complete human being that is you.

5. Adult children of alcoholics have difficulty having fun.

It is the child in us that has fun—that knows how to play. Because the child in you has been repressed for a very long time, it needs to be discovered and developed. You need to be the child you never were.

A friend once presented, somewhat frivolously, a rent-a-kid plan. He said that there are certain things that adults like to do that are much more fun if you have a kid along. Fishing is one of them, and he wanted to adopt a little redheaded, freckle-faced kid to take along. At the amusement park, he also wanted to have a kid with him so that he wouldn't look foolish riding on the Ferris wheel.

This man also likes to swing at the playground. You know what people say when they see an adult on the swings or in the sandbox. But if you just happen to bring a kid along, you get a lot of credit, for being either a good parent or an interested adult. Children know how to have fun.

So if you want to learn, spend some time with a child who knows how to have a good time. Do some of those childlike things that you never tried. What fantasy did you have in childhood? What game did you want to play that you never played? Now is the time to begin to play.

The more confident you are, the less afraid you will be of looking stupid. You may need to learn how to relax and do nothing. Simply take time for yourself without deciding that each moment has to be spent productively. Ironically, you may have to plan it. Book it into your day so that you don't spend that time thinking about all the silly things you wanted to do that you never got around to. I can have a very good time, but I'm not good at initiating it. Because I can't think of things to do that will be fun, I spend time with people who can. Not surprisingly, they are not adult children of alcoholic parents.

However, I must admit that part of the fun is to bring some of you guys along. When you let go and are flabbergasted by the good time you are having, it increases the enjoyment for the rest of us. The "Aha!" of the first experience is something very precious to share with another person.

6. Adult children of alcoholics take themselves very seriously.

One of the reasons you have so much difficulty having fun, in addition to lack of experience, is that you take yourself too seriously. In order to overcome this difficulty, you need to separate yourself from what you do. You need to separate yourself from your responsibilities, such as your job. You do not have to be what you do. The key is to take your work seriously because it is relevant and important but not to take yourself seriously. Your work is not all of you.

A good way to begin separating yourself from your activities is to make a schedule. If your job is supposed to last from 9 to 5, leave at 5:00. Hanging around until 7:30 does not make you more productive; in the long run, it will impair your efficiency. It also may be a cop-out on life.

A client who did hospital volunteer work was very involved with the terminally ill. She was also a lay minister who gave the Eucharist to bedridden people. She spent a lot of time in service and being very supportive to people around her. When she came to see me, she was pretty much on the road to being burned out.

She didn't want to give up her work because she thought it was important and productive. She also felt that it was a part of who she was. I tended to agree with her, so we needed to find a way for her to make it manageable so that there would be time left over for herself.

She already knew what to do with the time she had for herself. She was an accomplished musician, enjoyed the theater, was very athletic and had many friends. She had worked out how to spend her leisure time, but somehow it was only talk.

What we did was set up a very flexible schedule. She decided that she was going to do this two days a week, spending her morning working and afternoon playing. This was a way that she could take her work seriously but still have time for herself. She now could do all of the things she wanted to do.

You need to plan conscientiously in order to begin to separate yourself from your activities. It will not happen on its own. It does not seem to work when you say, "I'm going to cut down on the hours that I work. I'm going to be different." One needs to be more specific.

You need to have other things to think about and other things to do in order to have a whole life. Otherwise, you will become narrow and limited, making it a lot harder to play. It also will make you a less interesting person. What are you doing for yourself? Or, more specifically, what did you do for yourself today?

7. Adult children of alcoholics have difficulty with intimate relationships.

This has many aspects to it. The first is that adult children of alcoholics simply do not know how to have healthy, intimate relationships. Your fear of intimacy, of letting anybody in, gets in the way. Part of that fear is of the unknown. What is it? What does it consist of? Intimacy implies closeness. How do you get close? What are the ingredients in a healthy relationship?

Keep in mind that healthy relationships do not develop overnight. There are many elements involved in a healthy relationship and all of them must be shared. When entering into a relationship with another person, it is important to offer your partner that which you would want your partner to offer you.

The degree of intimacy is determined by the degree of sharing— by how much each member of the partnership is willing to give. It is, in effect, a contract which is best served when understood and declared. Many contracts are implied, but you need to find a way to check it out.

Several ingredients are essential to a healthy relationship. They apply whether the other person is a lover, parent, child, friend, spouse or even an employer or coworker.

The form or degree, however, may change according to the nature of the relationship. There is no attempt in this list to specify order or significance. What is important is that all of these ingredients should be present, and there should be mutuality. If any of them is missing, one cannot sustain a healthy relationship with that person.

Once again, bear in mind that intimacy is determined by the degree to which partners are willing to work at each one of these criteria. In certain types of relationships, this is more important and more appropriate than in others.

As you read the list, you might want to explore each aspect with respect to your relationships with people. Are they all present? This will show why some of your relationships are working well and others not quite so well. If any of these ingredients is missing, there seems to be a hole in the relationship.

- VULNERABILITY—To what degree am I willing to let down my barriers? To what degree am I willing to allow the other person to affect my feelings?
- UNDERSTANDING—Do I understand the other person? Do I understand what she means by what she says or does?
- EMPATHY—To what degree am I able to allow myself to feel what he feels?
- COMPASSION—Do I have a genuine concern for the issues that cause the other person concern?
- RESPECT—Do I treat the other person as if she is of value?
- TRUST—To what degree and on what levels am I willing to let the other person gain access to the things about me that I don't want everybody to know?
- ACCEPTANCE—Am I okay the way I am? Is my partner?
- HONESTY—Is this relationship built on truth, or are there games involved?
- COMMUNICATION—Are we able to talk freely about issues that are important in the relationship? Do we know how to do it

so we are understood and the relationship goes forward because
of the sharing?

- COMPATIBILITY—To what degree do we like and dislike the
same things? To what degree does it matter if we differ in certain
attitudes and beliefs?
- PERSONAL INTEGRITY—To what degree am I able to maintain myself as well as offer to the other person?
- CONSIDERATION—Am I mindful of the other person's needs
as well as my own?

These are the ingredients that people have shared with me as
essential to a healthy relationship. These are the parts of which it is
made.

The bottom line in a healthy relationship and the one premise
upon which everything else is based is, "Am I seen and do I see the
other person realistically? Am I able to see him for who he is? Is he
able to see me for who I am?"

If you are not realistic, the attributes do not matter. They are neither relevant nor valid. The ability to be seen and to see the partner
realistically, regardless of the nature of the relationship, is critical to
its health. It is perhaps more critical than if you had a different history because you will react in ways that are inconsistent with developing a good relationship.

If you are realistic, you and your partner can talk about and learn
from problems which can bring you closer together. If the relationship is based on fantasy, it may not be sustainable.

For example, adult children of alcoholics are afraid of being abandoned. When a problem arises, they panic, so the problem hardly
ever gets discussed. If you are with someone who needs space and you
panic, it will be extremely destructive. Try saying to your partner, "I
have a problem in that I panic when we have a conflict. It's hard for

me even to look at the problem. I know that you react differently, but promise me that even if you're angry at my behavior, you will reassure me that you love me. That way, we may be able to get back to the problem."

In a healthy relationship, these reactions are discussed. They should be discussed ahead of time so that when they come up, they are seen for what they are. The discussion itself will take away some of the fear of abandonment. Then you can say, "Now what was the problem that we had before I panicked?"

In any relationship, many of the problems that come up have to do with one's relationship with oneself. They are often disguised as problems in the relationship and can also cause problems in, and even destroy, the relationship. Let me give you some examples.

Cheryl is the adult child of two alcoholics. She is ending a ten-year bad marriage and has a very loving relationship with a young man named Ivan. It is the healthiest relationship she has ever known. One of the problems that she has is that he wants to touch her. He wants to hold her and be physically demonstrative, and she finds that she backs away from this. She is almost averse to the touching, except periodically. It seemed that her reaction was an overreaction, since he didn't seem to be an oppressive person. He was willing to give her whatever space she needed, along with time by herself.

Ivan was not oppressive in his demand, but he needed to touch and be touched as an expression of feeling for her. He had been brought up in a physically demonstrative family. Her negative reaction was causing great problems in the relationship.

Since it was clear that she was overreacting, we needed to look at her history to find out why.

It happened quite unexpectedly, when her mother came for a visit. She came around noon, started to drink and continued to drink all

afternoon. As she became drunker and drunker, she made more and
more demands on her daughter. "Please touch me. Please hold me. I
need you just to hold me." Cheryl said, "I did as my mother had
asked, but it turned my stomach. She had been doing that to me
since I was a little child."

When she told me about this, it was pretty clear where her aversion
came from. It was no longer a big, dark secret, and now we could begin
to overcome it. She reported to Ivan what was going on. She needed
to let him know that her reaction had nothing to do with him; it was
a result of her being a child of an alcoholic. That eased the situation
somewhat, and we can now begin to work on changing her reaction to
Ivan. If they hadn't been able to talk about it and had lacked the ingredients of a healthy relationship, especially the ability to see each other
realistically, this problem might have ended the relationship.

Kelly, too, is working on a new relationship that she is determined
will be healthy and good for both her and her partner. Kelly, a nurse,
came into therapy with this as her primary agenda. The child of two
alcoholics, she had never seen nor had a healthy relationship. And
she felt that, if left to her own devices, she never would. Her friend,
a doctor, seems to be a considerate and thoughtful person who is willing to work on building a good relationship and who wants to share
his life with her.

One night she said, "This is it. It is done. It is over. I am finished
with him. I never want to see him again. I thought maybe we could
make it, but now I know that it is simply no good."

"What happened?" I asked.

"Last Wednesday night," she replied, "we talked about going out
to dinner, and I decided that I really could not do that because I
really had to clean the house. Once I get an idea in my head, that's
the end of it. I knew that if I went out to dinner, my mind would be
on cleaning the house and I wouldn't have a good time. So I said, 'I

will see you tomorrow but I am going to stay home and I am going to clean the house.' Then, an hour later, he stopped by with a bottle of Lestoil and some Chinese food. His statement to me was, 'I knew you had to eat anyway and I thought I would help you clean the house.' Can you imagine such a thing?" she said. "I went right off the wall. I don't think I have been quite so angry in my life."

I said to her, "It sounds to me like he was being thoughtful. Sounds to me like he was looking to spend time with you, and didn't want to miss out on it."

She answered, "That's what he said. He said, 'I knew you had to eat anyway and I wanted to help you clean if you had to clean. I don't care what I do, as long as I spend time with you.'"

I told her I thought that was a wonderful thing for him to do. So we began to explore what made it difficult for her to accept his kindness. No one had ever said, "Let me help you out. Let me do this for you, just because I care about you." It was an experience that was foreign to her. As a young child, she went out begging on the streets because it was the only way to keep her and her brother out of a children's shelter and the authorities from finding out that they were being neglected. Her friend's kindness did not fit her frame of reference, so instead of accepting it, she became angry.

After we talked about it, she was able to understand his point of view a little bit better. It is still very hard for her to accept his kindness, but she was able to explain her reaction, even though it didn't make much sense to him. It wouldn't be understandable to anyone who didn't know what it was like to be the adult child of an alcoholic.

A lovely young couple came to see me because of a problem they couldn't resolve. Once again, the fact that the wife was an adult child of an alcoholic was relevant. The man had a problem with high blood pressure. His high blood pressure was related to the stress from his job, which he planned to change, and was a condition that ran in his family. The medication that his doctor put him on had a lot of side effects, and he preferred not to take it. In order for him to get off the medication, it was important that he not repress feelings such as anger, so he started letting it out in ways which were not harmful. He closed the car windows and screamed at his boss or at the other drivers on the road. He had a tantrum when a window wouldn't open. His yelling was harmless to others and healthy for him in maintaining his blood pressure at the necessary level.

His wife, however, reacted very badly. She said, "I wish he wouldn't do that. He's yelling in the car all the time. He's screaming around the house all the time. I know he's not going to hurt anybody, but even so, I just can't take it. I just can't live with it."

He decided that rather than do anything to upset or hurt her, he would stop his yelling. He was also reluctant to tell her that it was healthy for him to yell. She kept saying, "Don't be afraid to tell me what you feel." But there was very clearly a double message. Don't be afraid to tell me what you feel, as long as what you feel is what I want you to feel.

We took a look at it. What did it mean? She said, "I'm not afraid of him. I know he will not harm me. There is no question of that. I don't understand what it is." And all of a sudden she flashed back to a time when her alcoholic mother behaved the way her husband behaved. She was losing control, yelling and screaming and banging on doors for no apparent reason. This was very frightening to a little girl because her mother was her source of security.

When this woman heard her husband act out, she overreacted, because of her experience as a child. Now that they know what it stems from, they have a better chance of coming to grips with it. They can talk about it, and resolve the issue.

One of the things that happens when couples care about developing healthy, intimate relationships is that once the process is started, it has its own momentum. They really begin to enjoy exploring themselves and each other, and they have a commitment not only to the relationship but to the self, which becomes more and more special as time goes on. Couples that begin to work on these skills, even if they start out ready to call it a day, are able to develop worthwhile relationships. They begin to enjoy communicating with one another, recognizing that they simply had not known how to do it. This knowledge gives them what they need in order to grow together, offer more to each other and develop more fully as individuals.

If you have sexual concerns about yourself, they result largely from lack of information. The remedy is not complicated. There are several very good books on the subject. *Our Bodies, Our Selves* gives you a lot of very good information—very clearly and very frankly expressed. There are a lot of technical "how-to" books. Why don't you read them so you can become familiar with different techniques of lovemaking?

The physical relationship that you have with another person is based not only on the technical know-how you can easily acquire but is an aspect of a larger relationship. The physical relationship is one form of communication. All of the characteristics attributed to an adult child of an alcoholic can affect the sexual relationship. How well a couple relates sexually is symptomatic of everything else that is going on in the relationship.

As you grow as a person and are able to relate better on a variety of different levels, you also will be able to communicate sexually in ways that are more satisfying to you. The sexual relationship is just one part of the total picture. It fits into place as everything else fits into place.

Your confusions about sex roles, masculinity and femininity, and appropriateness of behavior toward the opposite sex are issues that concern everybody. They are not exclusive to adult children of alcoholics.

We are going through a time when the norms are very unclear. Traditional forms are gaining power and the not-so-traditional is losing power. Even with that trend, just about everything goes. All of these norms are operating at the same time. So if you are confused, you are in very good company.

There was a time when the male role was very clearly defined and the female role was clearly defined. This was true in the workplace, in the home and in the bedroom. This is no longer true, and the definitions are changing.

The only way to know for sure who you are is to find out what works for you. That is essentially the whole message of this book. Find out who you are, feel good about who you are and be willing to act upon it. That way you will be whole. You will be healthy in all aspects of your life. And you will be free.

8. Adult children of alcoholics overreact to changes over which they have no control.

On the surface, adult children of alcoholics appear to be very rigid people. They seem to want things their way and no other way. This may be true, in part, but there is more to it than meets the eye. The issues that seem very simple to adjust to for others are a big deal for the adult child of an alcoholic.

I remember Martha falling apart because plans to go to the city fell through at the last minute when her friends chose to do something else. It was a very big deal. Joan burst into tears because someone was late. He was not very late, but just the idea of being late set her off. At one point, another adult child of an alcoholic had her phone disconnected unintentionally. She decided that she was being punished, which was devastating to her.

These things on the surface do not seem big. Yet, if you are reading this and you are the adult child of an alcoholic, you know how big they are.

Yet, they are all overreactions, which generally are related to one's past history. Something like this has happened many times before, usually in childhood. A seemingly inconsequential incident is like the straw that broke the camel's back. It brings back all the plans that were never carried out, the promises that were never kept and the punishment that you could not relate to your crime.

This is what happens when plans to go to the city are disrupted, when someone is late, when the phone company inadvertently disconnects your phone. The pain you experienced as a child is experienced in the moment and *nobody, nobody* is ever going to do that to you again.

Coming to grips with this issue requires a great degree of self-awareness. The first thing that you have to do is recognize it when you overreact. You may be able to do that for yourself. Is your reaction inappropriate to the circumstance? Is somebody whose opinion you respect saying to you that you are overreacting? Have you become irrational? Is the situation worth reacting to as strongly as you are reacting? What is your response when someone says to you, "Why is it such a big deal?"

If you become defensive with that question, then you have overreacted. If you are not reacting in an appropriate way, you need to ask yourself, "What was the circumstance in and of itself that made it so big?" Why did it really matter to you that the change occurred without your helping to effect it? And what did that mean to you? When did it happen before?

Lack of awareness created the feeling that an injustice has been done deliberately against you. The extension of this kind of thinking is a paranoic attitude toward life. "They're out to get me, because they changed the plans at the last minute, or they were late, or they unintentionally disconnected the phone. They did it deliberately." This extreme attitude can develop if you don't understand that your overreaction results from your history.

The first and perhaps most significant way to overcome this is to increase your awareness of overreactions and what has happened in your past that causes them. Another way to change is to deliberately change your normal routine. Take a look at the day. Are you rigidly locked into everything you do? Can you go home a new way? Is it possible to shop on Thursday this week instead of Wednesday? Can you shift things around without causing yourself a lot of turmoil?

You may find that it is harder than you think to break your routine. But it is a place to start being somewhat flexible. Flexibility in one area will generalize to other areas. You probably will be surprised at the degree to which you have settled into a routine and how carefully structured your days are. You might, from time to time, throw it all up in the air and run in another direction, almost as if you are rebelling against yourself. But, in terms of the overall design, you probably are very routinized. Easing that up will help to ease you up, which will help you develop some freedom to affect the things you can and to accept the things that you can't. This doesn't mean that you have to like everything that happens. You don't have to be the adult child of an alcoholic to be disappointed when a change occurs that you did not anticipate or you did not want, but you do not have to be devastated by it and that may be the difference. It does not have to affect your whole being.

9. Adult children of alcoholics constantly seek approval and affirmation.

The issue here is one of self-confidence. There are a variety of ways to become more confident in one's own abilities.

The first way is concerned with the support and encouragement of other people. Adult children of alcoholics are constantly seeking that encouragement, but they don't seem to be able to use it. It is very hard to trust when you have been taught trusting will only offer you pain. It is very hard to trust when the messages you received as a child were very inconsistent. You were programmed not to trust, but to believe what is said is not necessarily what is meant. Adults did not say what they meant, nor did they mean what they said. This makes trusting extremely difficult. So when someone gives you support and encouragement, it is very hard for you to feel it, accept it and use it.

So you continue to look for it because it is so difficult for you to internalize. Only if you become bombarded with encouragement to such a degree that you can no longer deny it will you begin to believe it.

So the first step is to decide that you are going to take the risk and allow some of the support and encouragement to be felt. Begin by identifying a few people whom you can trust. There are certain criteria that you might set up. How well does this person know you? Is it someone with whom you have a lot of contact? To what degree does this person accept you as you are? To what degree do they trust you? How much do you accept the other person? (This might make it easier for you to trust the other person's judgment.) Is this person an expert in the area in which they are offering you support and encouragement? These are the questions that people ask themselves when they are trying to decide whether or not they can use and trust someone's support and encouragement.

One young person who is not the child of an alcoholic said to me, "I do something very different. Support and encouragement are good energy. I take that energy and use it in order to be able to accomplish even more. I take those good feelings and use them in order to feel a little more. I like that." She didn't have to judge. For whatever reason, when she was told, "Try it. It's a good idea," she decided, "Why not?"

While you are working on being more receptive to support and encouragement from others, you also need to work on building self-confidence. Here are some ways that you can begin.

Ask yourself what you did today that you feel good about. The answer to that will not come quickly or easily. Then ask yourself what happened today. Is there something, no matter how little or how simple, you can count as a little success? Go through the day. You didn't wake up as a grouch. That may be an achievement for you. You got to work on time. That may be something you don't do often. Whatever it is, don't throw it away. Don't throw away the credit for any little successes just because anybody can do it. You did it. It therefore is your success.

You need to continue to strive, giving yourself credit for whatever you accomplish. You will gain self-confidence if you accomplish the tasks that you set for yourself. They may be very simple tasks, or they may be big tasks, but commit yourself to accomplishing the task, once you recognize that it is realistic.

If you have a difficult task, practice rather than project disaster. If you are going for a job interview, don't waste your time in a state of panic. Practice by yourself. Practice with a friend, so that it will not be completely new to you when you go for the interview. Don't spend time projecting disaster or success. Spend your time in the present moment.

Not everything will work out. If it does, that's terrific. But it didn't just happen. You were responsible for the success. If it doesn't work out, then you will go out and try something new. It doesn't have to devastate you. You are not responsible for everything that doesn't work out and everything that does work out is not a matter of coincidence.

Again and again, people will come into my office and say, "Things really went well," and they are astonished. I look at them and say, "It was no accident that it went well. You have been working on that for several weeks. You have been working very hard on having things go well. When they go well it is a result of your hard work. Step by step. Little by little. It's not an accident that it went well."

These are some of the ways to build up self-confidence—by little successes and by acknowledging the little successes. Little things that come easily for you are not without value. Build on the things that you can do well. Take it one step at a time, one day at a time. Begin to trust yourself and others. You never again will be in a position where you have no option but to trust those who cannot trust themselves. You now have a choice. You know better now who to trust. You know better now where you can trust yourself and where you can't trust yourself. You know where the help is. All you have to do is use it.

10. Adult children of alcoholics usually feel different from other people.

The feelings of isolation you had as a child make connection with other people extremely difficult. You longed for connection but could not effect it. As an adult you find that these same feelings persist.

It is difficult, if not impossible, to wholly overcome these feelings but there are ways of reducing the feelings of isolation. They may require some risk and some hard but necessary effort. First, you need to take the risk of sharing with others. This will help you to realize that although you are unique as a person, you are not all that different from others.

Find out all you can about what children of alcoholics feel like. This will help you to understand that you are not different.

Intellectual understanding will not really change your feelings much, but it will make it a little easier for you to push yourself.

Joining a group will be helpful. It can be an adult children of alcoholics group or any group of people who share their thoughts and feelings. Since not all of your feelings are related to your history, it may be helpful to learn which ones are and which ones are not. You will not find any group that does not have some adult children of alcoholics in it. You will never be the only one, yet this fact is not often shared.

When I talk about risk, I mean putting yourself out. The risk involves letting people know who you are and getting to know yourself better. The payoffs are getting to know others better and starting to feel a little bit connected. Feeling alone in a crowd will begin to diminish.

The only way to get the things you really want is to give them away. If you need to be loved, offer love to others. I know if I need to be understood, the way to ensure it is to offer understanding. The same is true if I want to feel close. The only way I know for sure that I can be close to another person is if I can allow that person to be close to me. I can say (not necessarily aloud), "You can come in close. I'm not afraid of your coming in close. I will offer you myself, my friendship, my caring. I will offer you the things I need for myself, and this will help reduce the isolation for both of us."

I'm not sure one ever completely loses the sense of isolation. I'm not sure anyone with this kind of history ever feels wholly connected. But it is not only adult children of alcoholics who feel somewhat different from other people and who do not feel a part of the group.

For example, if you are a professional or a boss, you will be isolated from those who work for you. They will be friendly to you but you will not be one of them. Because you may be in a more prominent position, you will feel separated from the group. If you are in a helping profession, your clients will not connect with you as a person. They will see you as separate and apart, which they do for their own well-being.

If you are becoming self-actualized, if you are discovering who you are and living your life on your own terms, you will also feel somewhat alienated. The only way to avoid this feeling is to make, from time to time, the decision to do it their way and accept the norms of the group you happen to be with. If you have decided to accept the norms of AA, you probably will feel a sense of connectedness at an AA meeting. This also will happen in a church group. You will not feel connected all the time, but you will feel connected when you have not made decisions for yourself that are different from those of the rest of the group.

It is important to select just a few special people in your life and offer them what you want and they, in turn, can offer you what they want. Not taking the risk leaves you isolated. But taking the risk gives you the opportunity to change. Trying it once is not enough. Promise yourself that every day, in a very small way, you will reach out to another person, either by getting to know them better for who they are or by letting them know you a little better for who you are. You will initiate the interaction and will try to accept that which is offered you.

11. Adult children of alcoholics are superresponsible or super-irresponsible.

The issue here is the need to be perfect. "If I am not perfect, I am nothing. If I am not perfect, I will be rejected. I will be abandoned. I know that I am not perfect but if I try hard enough, no one else will know. Therefore, I will be the perfect employee, the perfect spouse, the perfect parent, the perfect friend, the perfect child. I will always look perfect. I will always say the right thing. If I am perfect, my boss will love me, my parents will love me, my friends will love me. All I have to do is whatever I am asked and more. All I have to do is everything. But please don't let them look under the rug!"

Can you feel the pressure from just reading that? It's enormous. The task to change is also enormous. If you are not the superachiever but are the super-irresponsible one, the task to change for you, too, is enormous, but it's much more easily expressed. The other side of the scenario goes, "If all that is true, why bother?"

They may or may not love you. People resent perfect people because they can't compete, but others love you if they love the image that you have projected. Of what use to you is the love? You have to continue to be stressed in order to hang on to it. If they love you and know the real you, chances are they won't run off into the night if you run downstairs with your hair in curlers.

Therein lies the risk. Many superresponsible people, in order to stop, have to get sick. It is the only way out, and it is very predictable. They give and give, and take more upon themselves until they no longer have anything left, and they get sick. In effect, they burn out. They cannot find an acceptable way to stop short of this.

Eric is a perfect example. He is still in the process of recovering from a terrible automobile accident that happened two years ago. He's in a new marriage, with a new set of children and new problems. He is beginning a new career and looking for a job.

Along with all this, he has invited his recently widowed and very depressed mother into his home. He has decided to be responsible for the emotional care of a brother who is just getting out of a relationship and for another brother who is trying to kick his chemical dependency, besides making sure that every whim of his mother-in-law is carried out. The statements I made in terms of relieving the pressure were countered with, "If I don't do it, who will?"

Eric reached the point where he simply could not do it anymore. His body refused to get out of bed. To all the people in his life, he looked sick. He was sick, and it gave them an opportunity to be responsible. They took charge of their own lives, which gave him an opportunity to stop being such a superperson. Yet, he had to get sick to do it.

The same is true with Paula, a divorced woman with an alcoholic mother who is still drinking. She has one child of her own and has been involved with a father of five. Paula has a full-time job. She also has taken over the responsibility for her boyfriend's home and his children. This means that before she goes to work and takes her own son to school in the morning, she stops by another household and makes all of the lunches, does all of the laundry and gets the five children off to school.

Paula had only been seeing me for a few weeks when she broke her foot. I told her it was no accident. The only way she could slow down, the only way that she could stop proving herself was for something to happen that incapacitated her. Not surprisingly, her lover is quite angry that she hurt herself, and she is now looking at the relationship a lot more closely. Her mother now has a reason not to drink for a while, so she can play mother. And Paula can begin to find ways to become somewhat less responsible.

In order to help these two people start living realistic lives, it was necessary to give them very specific guidelines. In Paula's case, it was easy. Her son broke out with a very serious rash. She promised me that she would not consider going back into the relationship with her boyfriend until her son's skin cleared up. This contract allowed her to begin to change.

In Eric's case, his family became very concerned about his health and promised they would help him and find the strength that they had within themselves all along to become adults and confront their own problems. He had become just too convenient for everyone. That has now changed.

In both cases, somebody took over and was supportive. It may not always happen this way, but unless you give others a chance, there is no chance that it will.

You do not have to wait until you are in such an extreme position to begin to work on the problem. A part of your difficulty may lie in not realistically assessing your own capabilities. You may not have assessed what is fair for someone else to ask of you. Perhaps you may not have learned how to delegate responsibility.

Looking first at your work, you need to set up some specific guidelines for yourself. How late am I willing to work? When is it time to quit and go home? Check it out with others. What do they do? What is your job description? What is expected of you in this position? What can be asked of you? What is reasonable? What is fair? How much responsibility is yours and how much responsibility for the work belongs to somebody else? What is workable and what isn't workable? These things really need to be looked at very carefully. You also may need to discuss them with another person.

One of the most outrageous circumstances that I've encountered involved a woman who had gone home from work because someone very close to her was dying. While she was sitting in the hospital's intensive care unit, her boss called and told her to return because of a deadline. Since she was the child of two alcoholics, she didn't know what was appropriate and came back. Needless to say, I was flabbergasted. She simply did not know the answer to the question, "Do I really have to do that?"

When someone asks you to do something, ask yourself, "Do I really have to do it? Do I really want to do it?" The answer may not always be "no," but "no" is an option that is always available to you.

When I was in Israel one summer, I was touring with a group. It was 115 degrees, and they started climbing up a mound to see Jericho, which is just a pile of ruins. I started to climb with them, then stopped and said, "Hey! I don't have to do that!" They looked at me in great surprise, and another woman on the tour said, "You know, you're right. I don't have to do that either!" They never forgot that. Later on in the tour when we were in a cable car climbing up Masada, she turned to me because she had a fear of heights and said, "Do I have to do it?" Since we were halfway up the side of the mountain, there was no choice.

"Do I have to do it?" is a question you need to ask yourself. If you're not sure, discuss it with someone you can trust, not someone who has a vested interest in your completing the task.

The next step is for you to learn to say no if that is your decision. This is very hard to do. It involves practice and it involves taking a risk. People may not like it when you say no and accept saying no as part of who you are. Look at the possible consequences and be ready to handle them. Is it worth it and what is your motive in saying no?

It may be that you don't want to jump right into saying "no." You may not want to do this as compulsively as you have done other things. Instead, you might decide to buy time with, "I can't make a decision right now. Let me get back to you." If they want an immediate decision, then you can say, "I need time to think about it."

Giving yourself time to think should make it easier to say "no" if that's how you feel. It will also give you an opportunity to figure out an alternative. Buying time can enable you to make a responsible decision, and everybody will be satisfied.

If you think about it, and part of your message to yourself (since you are such a superachiever) is, "Maybe I can fit it in," the next question to ask yourself is, "Do I want to?" That may be the key. "Do I want to? Or is there something I would rather do with my time?" Maybe you would rather do nothing. That can be as important for you as anything else, if you choose it because you want to do nothing, not because you've reached the point where you no longer have the energy.

Being super-irresponsible can result from one of two things. The first is that you chose never to get started, and the second may be because you burned out. Although the results of these two look similar, they are very different and they need to be looked at differently. If you have burned out, you need time to rest and recover. You may need to opt out for a while. There's nothing so terribly wrong with that. You need time to regroup, to heal, before you can go forth again. However, the next time you get up the energy, you may need to live in a more measured way.

In recovering, you need to begin giving to yourself. You probably need to learn how to do this. Think about the things that make you feel good. You might go to a burnout clinic and find out the specific ways people use to recover. You need to begin to learn how to take in energy, not only to give but to get.

Take a look at the people in your life, at the nature of your relationships. Are you getting to the degree that you are giving? Have you surrounded yourself with people with strength to offer you as well as your offering to them? It may be that if you look around carefully, you will discover that you are involved with a population that is drawing from you but giving nothing. You may need to change this by developing relationships with people who have as much to offer you as you have to offer them. It also may be that you have not allowed the people around you to offer to you. You have been playing superstrong, and now is the time to let others help you so that you can regain your strength.

This time you need to do it more realistically, not being all things to all people all of the time. You now see that the payoff is not worth it. Martyrs rarely are appreciated in their lifetime.

Superresponsible people tend to be exploited. Somehow they almost demand it. So this time, when you look at what you plan to do for your life's work, make sure that you do not get exploited. Find out if you are being paid what the job is worth. Find out all you can.

Jen did this, and once she found she could not work in such conditions, she confronted her boss. She had decided she would prefer to lose the job rather than allow herself to be exploited. It worked out well for her. Her employer gave her what she considered reasonable. It does not always work out so well, but your self-respect may be worth it.

If you are super-irresponsible and it does not result from being burned out but from never having gotten started, the problem is somewhat different. Your decision to read this book probably means you are ready to change. This is a difficult problem. You may need to find out what it is you want to do. You may have to begin in a direction and start by having little successes. You may want to do some testing and find out what vocational areas are of interest to you. You may think about going to school. It probably will be a good idea to do this with some professional direction—to work out a plan with someone who understands what is happening to you psychologically and how difficult it is for you to become more responsible and to become less afraid of success and all that it implies. This may be something you cannot do alone. You can certainly begin. But if you find yourself becoming paralyzed at the moment things begin to work for you, you may find what one of my clients found—he could go so far and no further. He found he could get up to the college campus but not go to the registrar's office. He could fill out the application forms but he couldn't make it for the interview.

Check out how far you can go alone, but this may be something you will need help with. It doesn't mean that you are sick. It just means that this is a hurdle that you need professional help in order to overcome. The decision to do so is probably the hardest part.

12. Adult children of alcoholics are extremely loyal, even in face of evidence that the loyalty is undeserved.

Loyalty is a very admirable quality. Yet any quality that is extreme may not be beneficial to you. You are indiscriminately loyal to all those who come within your circle and touch your life. Your loyalty extends to lovers, to friends, to family and to employers. To have you in any of these relationships is extremely valuable. And your fears of being abandoned make it almost impossible for you to abandon others.

If you are involved with people who are not treating you as you need to be treated, it is important to rethink your loyalty. It may not be appropriate. You do not automatically owe loyalty. The relationships I'm talking about are the ones where you say to yourself day after day, "Why do I bother? Why do I stay with it? Is it worth it? Why am I such a fool? Why can't I let go?"

To overcome a tie that you no longer desire, there are a number of steps you can take. The first is to specify the reality of the situation. Ask yourself, *What is the nature of this relationship? What is going on at the moment?* Then you will hear yourself begin to say, *But, but . . .* When the "buts" start, you are no longer in the moment. You are no longer in the reality but into a fantasy of the past or a fantasy of the future. *Why can't it be like it was?*

It can't be like it was because it is no longer like it was. You need to understand what the difference is. In the initial stages of reality of a relationship, people often treat each other differently from the way they do after it becomes a part of the routine. You may not do this but others might. And you find yourself assuming that if he or she is no longer treating you as in the beginning, then there is something wrong with you. *If I could only do or say the right thing, life would be as it was.* That is not realistic.

As a relationship develops and the people get to know each other better, the relationship has to change. It can become more meaningful or less meaningful. People can become more considerate or less considerate. Many things happen. Nothing stands still, so what existed in the beginning no longer exists.

The notion that if you can just get through a difficult time, things will be wonderful, may not be realistic.

Living in the future is not a good idea because the future cannot be predicted. When couples in healthy relationships go through difficult times, they share their feelings with each other. If they take out their aggressions, they talk about it and how to prevent its happening again.

How much energy you put into a relationship is an important consideration. When you start to back off, to want more equality in the relationship, very interesting things start to happen. If you look back realistically at what happened in the initial stages of a relationship, you may find that you put an awful lot of energy into it. This is your way and you enjoy doing it.

The other person responded. And then somewhere along the line, you may have felt a need yourself. You may have withdrawn a little bit of energy, and the other person didn't like it. This may be the time when she stopped treating you the way you wanted to be treated. This may be the point at which you started to become unhappy—when you withdrew a little bit, and he was no longer riding on your energy.

I know a man in a situation like this. When the woman, who was an adult child of an alcoholic, withdrew some energy, people started to see him as shorter. She had given so much to him that when she slowed down, he literally looked shrunken.

The first step in deciding whether or not your loyalty is appropriate is to be realistic about what the relationship consists of. Do not allow yourself to live in the past or future projection. The present is what is real. Ask yourself, *What is best for me now? Is my loyalty to the person I know in the moment?*

A certain amount of loyalty is appropriate if the relationship is with a child who is going through a terrible stage or if the relationship is with someone who is very ill and cannot offer what they offered at one time. You might want to remain loyal but need to make this a conscious decision. You may need to say, *I care about Janine. I'm going to stay with her. I will be loyal to her, even though she is not good for me right now. I will be careful. I will protect myself in the hope that this will be resolved.*

The next thing that you need to do if you want to make decisions about loyalty and not have it be automatic is to begin to say to yourself, *What is in this for me? What is the payoff? Why do I maintain this relationship? Who is this other person to me?* The answers to these questions are often quite surprising. You may find that a person represents someone else in your life. Your lover may be very much like your alcoholic parent was when you were growing up. You may be repeating a pattern because it is familiar. You may not have broken early ties and may be setting yourself up again.

How is that person like you? Have you been drawn to someone who is very much like yourself? Who is that person? What does that person represent to you?

After you have the answers, you need to begin separating yourself from the other person. Begin to acknowledge where the other person ends and where you begin. Differentiate between what has to do with that person and what has to do with you. When this is clear, the other person's hold on your feelings will decrease.

The people who are undeserving of our loyalty quite often are very critical of us. They spend a lot of time telling us what is wrong with us. Be careful when you hear this. If you decide to listen, be sure who the other person is really talking about. Do those statements really have to do with you, or is that person merely projecting herself on you? Be mindful of where the other person ends and you begin. Another's pain, sorrow or anger belongs to that person. You may be compassionate and empathetic, but it is not yours. The loyalty where you lose yourself and become submerged into another person is not in your best interest.

You may get hooked through guilt into a relationship that is not good for you. If you are easily manipulated by guilt, you think you owe the person something. When I ask my clients what they owe, I hear, "Well, he was nice to me. Well, she cared about me."

You become guilty and feel that you owe for the wrong reasons. If someone cares about you, it is because you are worth being cared about. Your friendship is a gift. You are under no obligation to people just because they befriended you. You are of value. If you owe them because they befriended you, you are saying, "I am not of value." When you begin to back away, the other person will try to make you feel guilty. He will talk about how much he wants you and needs you, and you will find it very difficult to break away.

This may be a time when the relationship can change. You can say, "I don't want to end this but I can't continue in a relationship that isn't good for me. If we can talk about it and if it can change so that it can be good for both of us, maybe I will think about it some more."

To stay in a relationship out of guilt is something you have to look at carefully. Your friendship is a gift. It is to be cherished. It is not something that you owe because somebody accepted it from you. Take a good, hard look at what you have offered and what has been offered to you. Do you still feel that you need to be indebted? Have you looked at it fairly and realistically? Swallow that "but, but, but. . . ."

You also may continue in relationships that are not good for you because you are afraid of being alone. You have a fear of loneliness and isolation. This is probably not your last opportunity to have a friend or a lover, or the only person in the world who will ever care about you. You may have made this somewhat bigger than it is. Remember, you have yourself. Isn't that glorious? It can be, if you get to know yourself. Being alone with yourself can be turned from something fearful into a desirable experience.

You may also be staying in a relationship because it makes you feel superior. If your partner does not offer you all that you can offer, you can feel more important and feel that she should be indebted and loyal to you. In effect, you are saying, "The only way I can feel good is to be involved with someone who is less than I am. This way I can build my ego. If you are lower than me, I can elevate myself."

This may be the payoff. "Although you don't treat me as I need to be treated, I feel superior, and that is a way I falsely build my self-esteem." This is something you may need to look at very carefully. Even though you complain, is there something about it which gives you pleasure?

You may sincerely think that you are in love with someone, and I would never argue about that. If I were to define it, I would define love as enhancement. If you and I are in a loving relationship, we enhance each other. We are more than we would be if we were not involved. That is probably where your loyalty is inappropriate—even if you call it love.

What you did call it may not be very important. The important question is, "Is it good for me?" It's very much like discussing whether you're an alcoholic. I won't enter into that discussion either. I don't know if you're alcoholic, but why don't you just not drink? I don't know if you love this person, but why don't you just decide that nobody has the right to treat you less than well because you love yourself and because you are important to yourself?

If you decide that you need to change a relationship and that your loyalty is best offered elsewhere, it may be hard for you to break away completely because of your fears. Why limit yourself? Why not develop other friendships? Why not put your energy into those and try to be more realistic with them? As those relationships develop, you can begin to make the one that is not good for you less important. It does not have to be all or nothing. You may not have to eliminate this person completely but simply lessen the impact of the relationship. There are many choices and many directions. Being realistic about who and what you want is the place to begin.

13. Adult children of alcoholics tend to lock themselves into a course of action without giving serious consideration to alternative behaviors or possible consequences. This impulsivity leads to confusion, self-loathing and loss of control of their environment. As a result, they spend tremendous amounts of time cleaning up the mess.

The impulsive behavior we are discussing is not unlike a two-year-old who has a temper tantrum because he wants what he wants when he wants it. The toy he has his eye on is the only thing that is important in his world. It is not unlike the two-year-old who decides to run across the street in the middle of heavy traffic.

A two-year-old also will hold his breath until he turns blue. Because he wants attention so badly, he will punish himself by hurting himself. Your behaviors are not much different. The main difference is that you are the one who is held responsible for these behaviors. The two-year-old has someone else to hold responsible. It is quite possible that in a different environment, you might have developed differently, and your desires would now affect you differently.

But that's not the issue here. It is what you are going to do so that you don't behave like a two-year-old. You know that it can't work for you, which may be the only thing that separates you from the child.

The key here is to head you off at the pass, get in the way of your impulses until you have examined what the consequences and the alternatives are. It is important to slow you down, so that once locked in a course of action, you do not throw reason away.

If you are working with a counselor or if you have a sponsor whom you speak to on a regular basis, you may be able to buy a little time. The following examples show how the problem was resolved for my clients.

One female client had many disastrous relationships with men. We began to look at just exactly what was happening. What was she contributing? Who was she selecting? We were beginning to look at all the issues involved and decided that she could not be considered a victim.

She called me one afternoon right before I was leaving on a business trip and said, "I have discovered the answer. You and I have been looking in the wrong place. It is not that I have problems with relationships. I have problems with men. I think the truth is that I would have a much easier time if I were involved with a woman, and I think that is what I am going to do. I met this woman and that is a new direction for my life."

The thought that went through my head was, *What can I do to slow this down?* The sex of the person involved is not the point. If you can't relate to a male, you can't relate to a female. And it certainly would have made her life a lot more complicated to enter into a homosexual relationship.

My answer was, "Could you wait until I get back from my trip?" She agreed, which was reasonable. If this was, in fact, the direction for her life to take, waiting a week or two would make no difference. It turned out that was all the time she needed. By the time I returned, it was no longer even something she wanted to discuss. It was over. The impulse of the moment had passed.

A similar thing happened with Harold. He called to tell me that he hated his boss and his job and that he was in the wrong field. He had written a letter of resignation which he planned to give his boss in the morning.

I suggested that he wait until we looked over the letter together. He agreed to do that. It wasn't all that urgent. It had to be done very shortly, but it certainly didn't have to be done the following morning. He agreed. By the time that he came in three days later, his position had changed. He was no longer quite so angry, and his sense of urgency was gone.

These are two circumstances where the people were aware enough to know that maybe they were on the wrong track. There was a chance that the behavior they thought very rational and reasonable in the moment might cause them stress later on. It's more usual for me to hear what someone did last night than what they are going to do tonight.

If you are not receiving professional help, there are ways that you can begin to overcome impulsivity yourself. You will recognize that impulsivity because there is a lot of energy involved. You will recognize it because you will feel driven, impelled, and you can think of nothing else.

When you get that feeling, say to yourself, *Who else is going to be affected by this behavior?* I'm not suggesting to you that you say, "This is good" or "This is bad" or "This is poor" or "I shouldn't do this" or "I should do this" because, in the moment, this is the only way that you see it, and it really doesn't matter whether you like or dislike it. It's the only way.

What you need to do then is to look at the other people involved in this behavior. *Who else is going to be affected by what I do? How are they going to be affected by what I do?* You may not care how you are going to be affected at a time when the action seems to take over. Your sense of yourself seems to be lost, although you think that you are experiencing yourself fully.

Asking yourself those two questions should be enough to delay the action. Delaying the action will give you time to look at the consequences and the alternatives.

A decision made impulsively might not always be bad for you. Quitting a job could be the best thing that you can do for yourself. It might be that homosexuality is preferable for you. But these decisions should be made after consideration of the alternatives and consequences. They should be made with a clear mind, so that you will be certain you are comfortable with what you are doing. Then you won't have to say to yourself, "I wish I hadn't acted so rashly."

Perhaps what is good for you is not good for the other people around you. Considering them may be important, too. Quitting your job because you hate your job may be good for you. Yet, if you are the sole support of dependent minors, it's not an appropriate move. If you believe that many of your problems are caused by trying to be straight and you are married, acting out in the moment could be damaging to your spouse.

I am not telling you what decision to make. I am suggesting that you find a way to buy time, so that you consider the implications of your actions. Here, as in every other aspect of your life, choice is important. If you make a conscious active choice and are willing to be held accountable for your behavior, you will feel much better about yourself, regardless of the choice you make.

Your life experience has been such that if what was promised didn't happen immediately, it simply didn't happen. Now that you are not living in the same environment, however, the rules can change. Look back at the things you did so quickly and at the gratification that you had to have in the moment. What was in it for you to do it that quickly? Was it to your advantage in the short run? Was it to your advantage in the long run?

For example, many of you quit school. What did you gain? What do you regret most about the things that you did too quickly? The things you regret may have been the things you thought you wanted in the moment. You need to begin taking a broader look at your life.

One of the ways to do it is to fantasize. Where would you like to be in five years? Do you want to be doing what you're doing now? Do you want to take a different direction in your life?

Think out the necessary steps to get there. When you look at those steps, you will see all of the gratification is not at the end. For example, in studying for a degree, you don't get all of the gratification the day you get the diploma.

There are many little gratifications along the way. Think about that. Build in those gratifications. Build in your own reward system. When the elementary school teacher gave out gold stars to the children who handed in good papers, it served a purpose. It said, "You did this well." No situation is an all-or-nothing proposition.

When you do things too quickly, you sometimes ask the wrong questions or make the wrong decisions. "I want a divorce" may mean "I don't want to live like this." These are very different statements. The decision "I don't want to live like this" can change into "I'm not going to live like this." It does not necessarily mean divorce.

It may mean a change of lifestyle. It may mean going into counseling or many other things. It also may mean divorce, but not necessarily. If you defer the gratification, you will have an opportunity to find out what it really does mean. You might be feeling stifled.

That doesn't necessarily mean divorce. It probably means making some new decisions with respect to your life.

I'm not going to pretend that the gratification you wait for is always more wonderful than what you decided in the moment you wanted.

That would be foolish and unrealistic. Sometimes deferred gratification is more wonderful and the experience is richer, but it does lack the excitement of doing what you want when you want to do it.

The problem with immediate gratification is not how it feels in the moment. It feels great in the moment. Walking out of school and knowing you never had to face your geometry teacher again felt super. That gooey, gooey dessert you ate last night tasted delicious. That person you went to bed with in a moment of extreme passion was a real turn-on.

All of this is true. However, there is the other part of it, which doesn't reflect on the joy of the moment but is greatly affected by it. Walking out of school and not having to face a teacher again also meant you would not graduate with your class and do the kinds of things you fancied afterward. Eating that gooey dessert meant you couldn't wear the outfit you were hoping to get into. Going to bed with someone in the height of passion meant an unwanted pregnancy or some other disaster. It's not as simple as experiencing something in the moment. What you need to recognize is that you're conning yourself. Whenever you decide something has to be done right now, this very minute, see it as a con and ask yourself what the consequences would be if you get caught. The used car you absolutely had to buy today with your family's vacation money might not work out to be as satisfying in the long run as in the short run.

Try to realize that you're conning yourself, you're fooling yourself and you're playing games with yourself. At the very least, you're rationalizing.

Ask yourself at the moment you must have a dessert, *Am I going to get caught?* It's an interesting question, isn't it? From the moment you decide, you begin to rationalize. *It's really a small portion. I'll only eat the crust. I'll start dieting tomorrow. I was good yesterday. I only had a light lunch.* I don't have to tell you all of the things you say to yourself.

If you ask yourself if you're going to get caught, your response might be different. Yes, you're going to get caught. You're not going to lose the weight that you want to lose. Or, at the very least, you're not going to lose it quickly. Yes, you are always going to get caught.

Can you get caught quitting school? You need to think about it. Think of alternatives which are more desirable to you than going to school. Consider also the advantages to you in not quitting. If they outweigh the former, you can get caught.

The implications of having intercourse without preparation don't need much elaboration. Yes, you can get caught. And the same is true for the car versus the family vacation.

After realizing you can get caught, the next question to ask yourself is, *Is it worth it?* If the answer is yes, enjoy the experience. If the answer is no and you decide either to delay or give up an experience that is only offered in the moment, you also will feel good about yourself. You will feel a sense of satisfaction because you had a choice.

Having a choice is critical. It allows you the freedom to act or not to act, which is the greatest gift we can give ourselves. It frees you from the necessity of acting out your impulses and puts you in charge of your life. What a very special place to be.

4

What About *Your* Children?

Children of alcoholics and children of children of alcoholics are no more or no less harmed emotionally than children living in any other kind of stressful situation. Alcoholism cannot claim exclusive rights to distressed children. The guilt that you carry because of your inability to provide an ideal home environment regardless of the circumstances will not do you a bit of good. It will not do your children a bit of good either. All it will do is take energy away from the things you could be doing to change the situation.

Much of the pain suffered by your children is reversible. Not only that, but with your help, your children can be stronger and have greater self-esteem because of their experiences. Yes, I mean that. Negatives can be turned into positives. It is all in knowing how. It has been my experience in counseling your children that improvement is immediate and dramatic. More often than not, enlisting your help is of great benefit in turning your child around. You are a significant person in your child's life and can be a strong force for well-being. There are many things that you can do that will enhance a sense of self-worth in your children.

What About My Kids?

The following are some guidelines that will be useful to you in helping to break the cycle of problems caused by alcoholism in the next generation. There are ten very simple points.

Since many of you developed alcoholism yourselves and many of you have married alcoholics, there is a good chance that your children are living in an active situation. The guidelines are developed with this in mind. If you are fortunate enough not to have become alcoholic yourself and are not living with alcoholism again, the guidelines will still be helpful. They can be adapted to any situation.

1. Work on yourself and your own personal growth.

Children learn through imitation. Be the kind of person you want your children to imitate. You are a role model—like it or not. You set the example. If you are upset and confused, your children will be upset and confused. If you are irritable, your children will be irritable. Your children became fearful and guilty and obsessed with alcohol, just as you did. Just as you can set a negative tone in the house, you can set a positive one. If you have a smile on your face, your children will smile. One can feel tension in the air. Not a word has to be spoken, but everybody feels it. If you can work on relaxing, the mood in your home will be more relaxed. It is a place to begin.

2. Listen to your children.

Sit down with them and hear what they have to say—regardless of what it is. Let them know that you are interested and that they have your attention. Because you listen does not mean you agree. It just means that you are willing to listen. Work on accepting their right to be who they are and to think what they think, just as you want them to accept your right to be who you are and to think what you think. That is an easy thing to say but it is a lot harder to do. Some of what you hear will be outrageous, but you had outrageous thoughts when you were that age, too. Or even today. Because you listen without preaching does not mean you agree. It is simply a beginning of opening up the lines of communication. It is a beginning of talking to and not at.

3. Tell the truth. Be honest with them.

Your children's sense of what is reality is badly distorted. They have difficulty in knowing the truth. The active alcoholic lies mostly in terms of broken promises. He means it when he says he will be home in time for dinner, even though this may not happen. This confuses children. The alcoholic is not lying but does not get home in time for dinner. The child hears the nonalcoholic covering up and follows that example. The child also doesn't want to face the truth. No one does. But confronting reality is what will bring you back to health. Not having to hide feelings will ease the burden on your children.

Feelings are not *right* or *wrong*. They just are. "You shouldn't feel that way" is not a helpful thing to hear or say, because we feel however we feel. Maybe there are certain ways we should not behave, but feelings have no right or wrong value. If we feel that what we are feeling is wrong, then we will feel guilty and it will make matters worse. Your child might say, "I hate my father!" For you to say, "You shouldn't hate your father, he is sick," is to lay guilt on the child. What a terrible person he must be to hate someone who is sick. It is better to explore the feelings with the child. "I know what you mean. Sometimes I think I hate him, too, but it is really the disease that I hate. What I really hate is the way the disease makes him behave." Help to clarify. In so doing, you will help to clarify your own thinking.

The anger you feel is real. It is not helpful to decide that you are wrong to feel angry and should feel compassionate instead. You can feel both those things. Talk about it. Be open about it. Decide what you are going to do about it. Why not ride your bike if you're angry, or hit a punching bag, or find a place where you can scream to your heart's content? Yes, being angry is okay. Behaving destructively because of the anger you feel is not okay.

I am more concerned with the child who remains passive in a situation that I know he resents. I know that the anger the child turns inward will result in stomach problems, depression and all sorts of other symptoms. If your children yell at you, as difficult as it is to take, it is healthier for them to get it out. Once it is out, you can sit down and talk about it. Children also worry a lot. They worry and they feel powerless. They are not comfortable confiding in their teachers and counselors. They don't want "outsiders" to know. So much of what concerns them is held inside. You can provide a haven. Worries, when talked about openly, seem more manageable.

4. Educate them.

Tell them everything you know about the disease of alcoholism. Give them literature and sit down with them and answer whatever questions they may ask. There may be some things they want to know that you cannot answer. "Yes, I understand that once Daddy starts to drink he can't stop, but why does he start?" And when you answer with, "He's so sick. The compulsion is a part of the disease." And the child says, "Yes, but . . ." At this point, there is nothing wrong with saying, "I don't fully understand it myself. The only answer I know for sure is that not letting it get us down is really hard work. I need your help to remember, just as you need my help to remember."

5. Encourage your children to attend Alateen.

Alateen will help to reinforce the idea that alcoholism is a disease and must be looked at as such. Once your children can accept the disease concept, they can start to build their self-esteem. As children, we see ourselves as others see us. Those terrible things that the alcoholic says to the children affect the way they see themselves. Many times I have had children sobbing in my arms, "If I wasn't such a rotten kid, my parent wouldn't drink. Everybody would be better off if I were dead."

One cannot cause alcoholism, nor can one cure it. The child must understand that alcohol cannot be allowed to determine his value as a human being. This, again, is much easier said than done. You can help by constant reminding and by your own behavior toward your child.

Alateen is wonderful in reinforcing these ideas. If your child will attend Alateen, she will feel understood and have a sense of belonging. It is a place where she will be able to talk out her problems and begin to feel better about herself.

6. Give up denial.

Denial is the greatest ally that alcoholism has and the biggest enemy that you who combat it have. Reality, however, is easier to deal with than the unknown. This is true even with a disease as insidious as alcoholism. Say to your children: "Your daddy has an allergy to alcohol. It causes him to behave in ways that he does not want to and we do not want him to, but we must not forget that when he acts those ways, it is the disease talking and not your daddy. That will be hard to remember, because he still looks like Daddy. When you forget, come and talk to me about it, and when I forget, I will come and talk to you. This is a family disease, and we will feel better as a family."

7. Do not protect your children from knowing the ravages of alcoholism.

If the alcoholic in your home destroys things, it is best for the alcoholic to see the evidence of the destruction. Unfortunately, the children may have to see it, too. Say, "I feel bad that you have to see this, but Mommy must know what happened or she will not remember." To protect your children is to make them weak and confused. They know something went on, so why leave it to their imagination? The imagination will make it far worse, no matter how bad it was. Reality cannot be denied. To spend energy denying what is real is to take that energy away from other things that can be more beneficial—like getting well.

8. Don't be afraid to show affection to your children.

There is no way that you can offer a child too much love. Giving in to his every whim to overcompensate for the difficulties of his life is not loving. To tell a child that you love him, to hold him, to kiss him, to let him know how lucky you feel that he is your kid is loving. He needs to hear it. For you to say that he knows you love him is not enough, just as it is not enough for you. The child needs to hear it, as you need to hear it. This does not mean that everything he does and says is lovable. It just means that as a human being he is lovable. "I love who you are. I do not have to love all your behavior, and if I do not, I do not love you less." This message needs to be clear. You can love the alcoholic and hate the disease. One thing does not have anything to do with the other. Some behaviors are acceptable and some are not.

9. It is important for children to have clearly defined limits.

Let them know that dinner is served at a particular time, that going to bed and doing homework are scheduled. Give them parameters around which to order their lives. Their home life needs to be consistent, for inconsistency so disorients children that they lose a sense of who they are. A child cannot feel good about herself if she doesn't know what is going on from day to day. It will throw her off balance. Offer her an ordered life with rules that are reasonable and demand that these rules be followed. Children test limits, just to know if you really mean it. If the rule is fair, it does not matter whether or not the child likes it. Few do. But that does not mean that he will not be grateful for it and feel more secure because of it. A child must feel secure if she is to improve her sense of self. You can help with this feeling.

10. Children need to take responsibility for their behavior.

If your child breaks a window, it is his problem to figure out a way to replace it. His failures are his and his successes are his. If he is late for dinner, it is his problem—not yours. Learning to manage difficulties is a part of building self-esteem. It means that he has some control over his environment. When your child has a problem, help him think through alternatives but don't always supply him with the answer. Children of alcoholics feel helpless. Their lives are inflicted on them. They need help taking charge. Encourage them to try out new things. Succeeding is not as important as trying. Although a child cannot fail if he does not try, a child cannot succeed either. Any little success should be supported.

Think about the things that make you feel more worthy. Offer these same things to your children. Self-esteem does not change as one grows older without hard work. Work at it as a family. You suffered as a family—divided by alcoholism. Now recover as a family—united because of alcoholism.

Ironically enough, the terrible illness that has hit your family can be used against itself. Because of alcoholism, you became aware of yourself and your need to be a fully functioning family. Take advantage of it. The power of self-growth—enhanced self-worth—renders alcoholism harmless. Your children will be stronger because they have dealt with reality. They will be less vulnerable because they have experienced the pain and faced it. We grow from the challenges in our lives. We grow from the hard times, not the easy ones. As a family, you can become more fulfilled than if you were never forced to face yourselves. Helping your children build their self-esteem will help you build yours. And building your self-esteem will help your children. This time, the spiral goes upward. Slowly, but surely, the pattern reverses itself and you are in the driver's seat—because YOU ARE WORTH IT!

CONCLUSION

There are three statements in the alcoholism field with which there appears to be agreement:

1. Alcoholism runs in families. Rarely do we see a case in isolation. Someone, somewhere else in the family usually has been or is currently suffering from the disease.
2. Children of alcoholics run a higher risk of developing alcoholism than children in the mainstream of the population. There may have been some discussion of environment or genetics or a combination of both, but the truth of the statement is without question.
3. Children of alcoholics tend to marry alcoholics. They rarely go into the marriage with that knowledge, but we see this phenomenon occur over and over again.

These statements demonstrate the undeniable links between and probably among all aspects of the family disease we call alcoholism. The characteristics of the alcoholic and the family responses, as I point out in *Marriage on the Rocks*, clearly influence the variables that relate to adult children of alcoholics, as discussed in this book.

In *Marriage on the Rocks*, I talk about qualities that are prevalent among alcoholics, such as (a) excessive dependency, (b) inability to express emotions, (c) low frustration tolerance, (d) emotional immaturity, (e) high level of anxiety in interpersonal relationships, (f) low self-esteem, (g) grandiosity, (h) feelings of isolation, (i) perfectionism, (j) ambivalence toward authority, and (k) guilt.

The family responds with (a) denial; (b) protectiveness, pity—concern about the drinker; (c) embarrassment, avoiding drinking occasions; (d) shift in relationship—domination, takeover, self-absorptive activities; (e) guilt; (f) obsession, continual worry; (g) fear;

(h) lying; (i) false hope, disappointment, euphoria; (j) confusion; (k) sex problems; (l) anger; (m) lethargy, hopelessness, self-pity, remorse, despair.

In taking one last look at the characteristics that predominate with adult children of alcoholics, it is not hard to make linkages between these characteristics and what they experienced as children from both alcoholic and near-alcoholic parents. The qualities discussed as emanating from the alcoholic and the near-alcoholic contribute in part to each characteristic. You may want to add to or modify my list. Perceptions may vary, but regardless of the differences, the connections become obvious.

KEY

Alcoholic (A)

a. excessive dependency
b. inability to express emotions
c. low frustration tolerance
d. emotional immaturity
e. high level of anxiety in interpersonal relationships
f. low self-esteem
g. grandiosity
h. feelings of isolation
i. perfectionism
j. ambivalence toward authority
k. guilt

Near-Alcoholic (NA)

aa. denial
bb. protectiveness, pity—concern about the drinker
cc. embarrassment, avoiding drinking situations
dd. shift in relationship—domination, takeover, self-absorptive activities

ee. guilt

ff. obsession, continual worry

gg. fear

hh. lying

ii. false hope, disappointment, euphoria

jj. confusion

kk. sex problems

ll. anger

mm. lethargy, hopelessness, self-pity, remorse, despair

Characteristics

1. Adult children of alcoholics guess at what normal is.
    A—b, g, j; NA—aa, dd, hh, ii, jj

2. Adult children of alcoholics have difficulty following a project through from beginning to end.
    A—c, f, i; NA—ff, jj, mm

3. Adult children of alcoholics lie when it would be just as easy to tell the truth.
    A—g, i, j; NA—aa, ee, hh, ii, jj

4. Adult children of alcoholics judge themselves without mercy.
    A—i, j, k; NA—ee

5. Adult children of alcoholics have difficulty having fun.
    A—all; NA—all

6. Adult children of alcoholics take themselves very seriously.
    A—e, f, j, k; NA—all

7. Adult children of alcoholics have difficulty with intimate relationships.
    A—a, b, c, d, e, k; NA—aa, dd, jj, kk, ll

8. Adult children of alcoholics overreact to changes over which they have no control.
   A—cc, i; NA—dd

9. Adult children of alcoholics constantly seek approval and affirmation.
   A—a, d, f, i, j; NA—ff, gg

10. Adult children of alcoholics usually feel different from other people.
    A—e, f, h; NA—cc, jj

11. Adult children of alcoholics are superresponsible or super-irresponsible.
    A—all; NA—all

12. Adult children of alcoholics are extremely loyal, even in the face of evidence that the loyalty is undeserved.
    A—a; NA—aa, bb, gg, ii

13. Adult children of alcoholics tend to lock themselves into a course of action without giving serious consideration to alternative behaviors or possible consequences. This impulsivity leads to confusion, self-loathing and loss of control of their environment. As a result, more energy is spent cleaning up the mess than would have been spent had the alternatives and consequences been examined in the first place.
    A—c, d, g, j; NA—ii, jj, ll

This demonstrates very clearly how adult children of alcoholic parents are the products of their environment. It is most fortunate that we know about the alcoholic home environment because it offers answers to questions that might otherwise not be understood.

If knowledge is freeing, and I believe it is, knowing what happened and what can develop as a result is a very significant tool in understanding who you are and why. The guesswork goes out, the self-indictment loses its power and you are free to work on what you choose. You are no longer a victim. You are in the center of your own universe. What a special place to be.

When you start to feel pulled or driven, explore those feelings, don't judge them, and then let go of them in order to maintain your serenity and stay in the flow of your life.

The process of life is an adventure. Twisting, turning, going where it needs to go and you with it right in the center but letting it take its course. This is a peaceful and serene attitude, like that of Alcoholics Anonymous and the gifts of "Easy Does It," "One Day at a Time" and "Let Go and Let God."

Life is an ongoing process. If you are centered, if you are in control of your feelings, thoughts and desires, you journey through life taking many little roads along the way and experience each phase fully and completely. If you are in the center of your life and not being pulled and swayed by your own impulses and by the desires of others, you will have a sense of serenity, a sense of real comfort within yourself.

That's what this book is all about. It offers the knowledge of where you were and where you are. It puts today and tomorrow firmly in your hands. The choices are yours, whatever they may be. You are in charge of you, and that's all that really matters.

5

Recovery Hints

It is important to be clear what recovery means for adult children. Alcoholism is a disease. People recovering from alcoholism are recovering from a disease. The medical model is accepted by all responsible folks working in alcoholism treatment.

Being the child of an alcoholic is not a disease. It is a fact of your history. Because of the nature of this illness and the family response to it, certain things occur that influence your self-feelings, attitudes and behaviors in ways that cause you pain and concern. The object of ACOA recovery is to overcome those aspects of your history that cause you difficulty today and to learn a better way.

To the degree that none of us have ideal childhoods and to the degree that even an ideal childhood may be a cause for some concern, we are all recovering to some extent or other, in some way or other. Because there are so many alcoholic families and because we have been fortunate in being able to study them, it is possible to describe in general terms what happens to children who grow up in that environment.

To the degree that other families have similar dynamics, individuals who have grown up in other "dysfunctional" systems identify with and recover in very much the same way.

RECOVERY HINTS FOR
ADULT CHILDREN

Reading the book *Adult Children of Alcoholics* is the first step toward recovery. This section addresses the questions "What now?" and "How can I protect the quality of my recovery?"

For those recovering from addiction to alcohol and/or drugs.

If you have been in recovery for a year or more, you are ready to proceed to the next step. Many folks who are doing well staying sober experience the nagging feeling that there is a piece missing. Addressing the ways in which your past impacts on your present and filling in those empty spaces will enrich the quality of your sobriety.

If you have been in recovery for less than a year, give yourself the rest of the year to concentrate on staying sober or clean. That has to be your first priority. There will be plenty of time to go on from there, but it has to be first things first, and sobriety comes first.

If you keep relapsing or can't put ninety days together . . .

Many times folks find themselves unable to maintain sobriety because they are using the substance in order not to feel the pain of their secret. "You are as sick as your secrets" is an expression that makes a lot of sense. Keeping the secret keeps you stuck. The alcoholic family system is a place of lots of secrets. You may need, if this is your situation, to work first with a professional who understands substance abuse and understands what it means to be an ACOA. The purpose of this is to expose your secret—if only to you and your therapist—and drain some of the pus out. (Some folks are able to use the fifth step of AA to do this, but it doesn't work for everyone.)

Most of the secrets in my experience relate to shame. Many men and women have been sexually molested or were unable to stop the abuse of siblings. Others are gay or lesbian and, because of parental, religious or societal attitudes, believe that is not an okay way to be.

Once the secret, whatever it is, is exposed and the weight of keeping that buried is no longer present, your next chore is to get clean or sober and maintain that for a year. Then it will be time to go on to the next step.

For those recovering from addictions that are not alcohol or drug related, such as gambling, food or sex, it is possible to combine that Twelve-Step recovery and ACOA recovery.

Any recovery program should work well alongside ACOA recovery. If it doesn't, you need to discover what is going on. Read the pamphlet "Guidelines for Self-Help Groups."

For folks not in recovery from addiction.

Go first to Al-Anon and learn the principles of a Twelve-Step program and how to work the steps. Not all ACOA support groups follow the steps, but since so many of their members belong to other Twelve-Step programs, the principles are followed and the language is used.

For everyone.

All folks in ACOA recovery need to learn the Al-Anon principle of detachment regardless of whether or not they are recovering from addiction or are living with an addict. Until you do this, you can go no further. Detachment is the key. Because of the inconsistent nature of the nurture a child receives in an alcoholic family system and the child's hunger for nurture, many of you are still joined to your parents at the emotional hip. Even if you are no longer with them, you continue to seek their approval and are strongly influenced by their attitudes and behaviors. You will need to learn to separate yourself from them in a way that will not add to your stress. This is one of the primary goals of the Al-Anon program.

Once you have learned how to detach (it will take six months to a year), you may now be ready to join an ACOA support group. Keep in mind that the goal of a support group is to share experience, strength and hope. Many groups do this very well, and by identification and example, members learn how to make healthy choices.

If the group you attend does this—wonderful, but if the group you attend spends its time sharing horror stories and blaming parents, be warned: You may not be in the best place for you. Living in the past and blaming parents are ways to avoid living in the present and taking responsibility for your own behavior. They are ways to stay stuck. It doesn't mean that your life wasn't a horror show and that your parents didn't do terrible things. What it does mean is that you are now an adult: You create your own horror show and you must be accountable for your behavior. You are also the only one who can make you feel better about yourself.

Talking about the past is appropriate in a beginners meeting or with a professional but not in the meeting itself. Folks in recovery from addiction need to keep their memory green but folks recovering from the behaviors of others do not share the same benefit. People recovering from the behaviors of others need to change their response to other behaviors, and that can best be done by focusing on the present.

What you learn about yourself as you are growing up becomes a part of who you are and how you feel about yourself. No one can change that but you. Your parents, even if they recover and treat you differently, cannot fix what makes you feel bad about yourself. You may start a new and healthy relationship with them in the present but no amount of amends on their part will fix the past. That is why dwelling on their part in your ongoing pain will not get you through it or past it. Your present difficulties are your problem. To put the focus outside yourself is to delay your recovery.

Emotions that have been held down for years and years will come to surface. That is why it is suggested that if you are recovering from an addiction, you need to focus on that first so that you will not be tempted to relieve those feelings in destructive ways. You will go through a number of powerful emotions in your recovery. It is part of the process.

Not everyone goes through the stages of the process in the same sequence, and many of you may block some of those feelings. There is no "right" way. I just tell you about the process because those feelings may surface without your conscious direction and frighten you. And they will resurface many times with each new discovery. The recovery process is different for different folks. Only you can determine the way that will work best for you.

Your immediate response to reading this book may be:

1. **Relief.** The realizations that you are not alone and that you are not crazy will be freeing. It may be a life-changing event.
2. **Pain.** The awareness of the amount of your suffering and your powerlessness may overwhelm you along with the knowledge that you have been living a lie. It will be similar to the extraordinary pain you experienced as a child before you learned how to numb out.
3. **Anger.** It is not unusual for all the anger that you've been sitting on for all these years to begin to bubble up to the surface, and you may become fearful of your own rage.

4. **Grief.** The losses that you have experienced have to be grieved for, and you may feel this level of pain as well. You may believe that if you begin to cry you will never stop.

5. **Joy.** Going through the process eventually will allow you to experience a freedom that you have never felt before. When you are an adult you can be the child you were unable to be when you were a child.

For some of you, reading books and attending support groups may be enough. I will give a suggested reading list at the end of this book. Others will need additional tools to manage these feelings and begin a new life.

Some of you may find counseling useful. A counselor is like a coach who helps you find a better way to live in the here and now. You may have a difficult decision that needs to be made and be having trouble filtering out the various possibilities. Someone without a vested interest in the outcome, who is trained to help others to do this, can be most useful.

Some of you may have suffered early trauma that is getting in your way. You can use the help of a therapist to look at your life with attention to understanding, reframing and desensitizing the past, making use of the light of the present.

Some of you may enter a therapy group. Self-help support groups assist in individual growth but do not focus on interaction. A therapy counseling group will help you understand and modify both your behavior and your reactions to others in an interactive context. That is, others will share their responses to you and you to them in useful ways. In one-to-one therapy or counseling, the professional only knows what you report and sees you through that lens. The one-to-one relationship does not show how you appear to others. You may come across to others in ways that are inconsistent with how you feel inside. Learning those differences and making those changes may greatly enhance your recovery.

SELECTING A THERAPIST

If you choose to see a therapist, there are some things to keep in mind.

1. The therapist needs to have an understanding of addictions.
2. The therapist needs to have an understanding of self-help programs.
3. The therapist needs to understand what it means to be an ACOA or come from a dysfunctional family but does *not* have to be from one.
4. The therapist needs to have at least a master's degree in counseling, social work or psychology.
5. The therapist must be willing to answer your questions.
6. The therapist need *not* self-disclose—sponsors self-disclose.
7. The therapist may be friendly but is not a friend.

You can interview therapists. You don't have to continue seeing the first one you check out. You are obligated to pay for the time but if you don't have a good feeling about the person, check out someone else. If you interview several potential therapists and no one satisfies you and if the people fulfill the above criteria, you may be not as ready as you think.

At some point in your recovery process it will be important to reconcile yourself with your spiritual side. There are some empty places and some painful places that can only be filled with a spiritual relationship. It will happen in your own way in your own time.

Recoverer beware.

1. The process of recovery for adult children is very disruptive. It means changing the way you have perceived yourself and your world up until now. This is a tall order. In comparison, "Don't drink and go to meetings" is a piece of cake—and you know how rough that can be. The volcano, once erupted, cannot be put back neatly in the cone. It has to be addressed. Don't be surprised if you feel like you no longer belong in your skin. It is to be expected.

2. Remember that your need to save everyone else from their ignorance is saying to them not only "There is a better way," but also "Turn your whole life upside down and inside out." That's quite a lot to ask of another person. So, if you choose to do so, ask yourself:
   - Am I prepared to be there for this person through this process?
   - Am I willing to accept this person's right to make the choice not to change?

   If you're not, you may be better off waiting for others to come to you.

3. If you're not in an intimate relationship, try to hold off until you get some of your issues sorted out. You will only repeat old mistakes and overcomplicate things. You will not be the same a year into the process as you were when you started, so your choices will be different.

4. If you are currently in a relationship, keep the other person apprised of what is going on with you. Have that person read this book and *Struggle for Intimacy*. Encourage working on this process together. If you have been enmeshed and now back away to be your own person, be aware of the fact that it is a

change not only for you but also for others in your life. They may or may not react well. But remember, if you change the rules and you are in a relationship, two people should be involved in the rules change or the relationship will become dysfunctional regardless of whether or not you know it is "the best thing for both of you."

5. If you have been neglectful as a parent and are now aware how you may be perpetuating the cycle, your becoming hypervigilant all of a sudden will not be well received.

6. Reading material and talk shows will add to your store of knowledge and may give you insight. Although they may have some therapeutic value, books and media are not therapy. The good feeling from the power of the identification does not effect a lasting change.

ACOAs are creatures of extremes. "Nothing worth doing is worth doing in moderation." What I am suggesting is: Recovery is a slow process. It has to be or it is not recovery. You may make rapid strides but it takes a while for the growth to belong to you.

Recovery is discovery.

Remember that recovery is a process you have not failed if something you thought you had resolved pops up in another form. It may now be on a deeper level. You have not failed if you go through a stressful time and find yourself reverting to old behaviors.

I found my "child within" today;
for many years so locked away.
Loving, embracing—needing so much,
if only I could reach in and touch.
I did not know this child of mine—
we were never acquainted at three or nine.
But today I felt the crying inside.
I'm here, I shouted, come reside.
We hugged each other ever so tight
as feelings emerged of hurt and fright.
It's okay, I sobbed, I love you so!
You are precious to me, I want you to know.
My child, my child, you are safe today.
You will not be abandoned—I'm here to stay.
We laughed, we cried, it was a discovery—
this warm, loving child is my recovery.

—KATHLEEN ALGOE, 1989

Recovery is, as they say, one day at a time.

PART TWO

In Love:
Struggle for Intimacy

A Message from
DR. JANET WOITITZ

Preface

Several months have passed since I first made the commitment to write this book. It has been a great struggle to begin putting these thoughts on paper. If I considered myself a writer, I could call it "writer's block."

Since I consider myself a clinician, I know that there is something more to it.

For me, writing has been a compulsive act; when, for some reason, I find the words won't come, I need to look further. Writing *Marriage on the Rocks* happened so quickly and so easily that I wondered if I was really the one writing it. It was a cleansing act for me, and for others like me, and it served a purpose. When I wrote *Adult Children of Alcoholics*, I wrote that, too, with relative ease. I wrote it for my children—the hundreds of my children who have been part of my life and part of my counseling practice.

I felt confident when I wrote both of these books that I was answering some questions, providing some "how-to's" that I knew would work.

To write about the struggle for intimacy is quite another matter. It is a much more complex issue, key to the happiness of every man and woman. It is quite clear to me that I am not as detached as I was when I wrote the other books. My own feelings are affected by the magnitude of this problem.

Maybe the reason I have had such a struggle in writing about intimacy is that I'm not sure this time that I can make things better for you. I think this book may help to clarify, but I am not so sure that it will heal you. What I do know is that the issues in this book need to be discussed in this context.

What I hope is that you are reading this book with the intent of airing some issues, so that wounds will be lanced and disinfected, knowing that they will then have the opportunity to heal. I am fearful that you will be disappointed if you expect to find *the one answer* in this book.

The struggle for intimacy goes on for all of us as long as we live. But it is especially difficult for those who have grown up with alcoholism. To be intimate, to be close, to be vulnerable, contradicts all the survival skills learned by children of alcoholics (ACOAs) when they were very young. Acquiring intimacy skills requires a complete relearning process and is, to say the least, a monumental task. Let us begin.

Introduction

Even though divorce statistics and the number of unhappy people we all know confirm that not only adult children of alcoholics (ACOAs) struggle with relationships, those of you who fall into the ACOA category have some very special problems and very special needs.

Although the struggle for intimacy is not yours alone, the ways needed to fix the problems may be unique.

First, you were set up for the situation in which you now find your-self. You never had a chance to "do it right" because you've never experienced what "doing it right" looked like, or felt like. It hasn't been your fault if you have always felt that other people knew some secrets about successful relationships that you didn't know.

You may feel overwhelmingly guilty because you have been so inef-fectual in your intimate relationships. Even if you learn nothing else from reading this book, please accept, right now, that you are not to blame for the pain you have suffered—and inflicted—to this point.

You didn't have an effective role model for loving relationships. You have had to make it all up. What you *did* know is that you didn't want to be like your parents, but you didn't know how to filter the destructive actions from the good actions. So you created a fantasy about how ideal relationships work from a fanciful blend of what you imagined, saw at a distance or observed on TV.

All of us learned to relate to others by watching how our parents interacted with each other, and with their children. Take a minute before you read further to create a visual picture for yourself of the interactions you observed between your parents. Think how you related to your mother, to your father. Do not judge. Just look objec-tively at your childhood experiences as you remember them. Your relationship behavior as an adult, no matter how different it may look, is, in large measure, a reaction to those experiences.

You will learn better ways to interact with others as you read this book. You will have new options and choices. And you will have a new responsibility to choose the better ways.

I want you to picture the model for your adult relationships which you learned while you were growing up in an alcoholic family. The following pages, originally published as an article in *Focus* magazine, will give you a broad overview. Think about your own childhood and your own family as you read it.

Chemical Dependency: The Insidious Invader

Where did it go wrong? What happened? Who is responsible? Where is the sense? What does it mean? Where will it all end? Circles and circles of circles and circles—all filled with confusion. Where did we go off the track? Is it possible to understand?

For each couple, the beginning is different. Even so, the process that occurs in the chemically dependent marital relationship is essentially the same. For the starting point, let's take a look at the marriage vows. Most wedding services include the following statements: for better or worse—for richer or poorer—in sickness and in health—until death do us part. Maybe that's where the trouble began. Did you mean what you said when you said it? If you knew at that time that you were going to have not the better but the worse, not the health but the sickness, not the richer but the poorer, and the potential suicide, would the love that you felt have made it worth it? You may say so, but I wonder. If you were more realistic than romantic, you may have interpreted the vows to mean: through the bad as well as the good, assuming that the bad times would be transitory, and the good ones permanent. The contract is entered into in good faith. There is no benefit of hindsight.

The idealizing that takes place at this time is not realistic. This is true not only for those who will live with chemical dependence, but for everyone. The difference is that the reality continues to be distorted in the chemically dependent relationship, and little by little the couple loses touch with what a happy marital relationship is all about. If the statistics are accurate, and they probably are understated, then a very large percentage of you grew up in chemically dependent households. This is important to be aware of, because you probably had no idea how to develop a healthy marital relationship to begin with. Your early attempts to "do it right" were built on models that you had not seen or experienced, but rather made up in your own head. Thus, the fancifulness of the vows would play right into this notion of "It will be different for us."

By the time help is sought, the expectations have changed a great deal. The sense of self is gone for the chemically free partner. "How can I help him/her?" The sense of what one can expect in a relationship has shifted. It is no longer Camelot. It is no longer even person-to-person. The distortion is bizarre. I will stay because "He doesn't beat me." "She doesn't run around." "He hasn't lost his job." Imagine getting credit for the behaviors we ordinary mortals do as a matter of course. Even if the worst is true—even if he does beat you; even if she does run around; even if he is no longer working—even with all this, you will then say, "But I love him/her!" When I respond, "Tell me, what is so lovable?" there is no response. The answer doesn't come, but the power of being emotionally stuck is far greater than the power of reason. I know it, but I plant the seed regardless.

Somewhere between the vows of everlasting wonderfulness and the acceptance of life as a horror story lies the reality. Somewhere hidden in the muck is the truth. It didn't get distorted overnight. It started out on one end of the pendulum and landed on the other. Somehow the process was so gradual that no one saw it happening, and the middle ground went unnoticed.

If I ask, "What *was* lovable when you decided to marry?" the response comes quickly. It is not unusual to hear answers like, "There was a strong physical attraction, and we could talk about anything and everything. He/she was my lover and my best friend."

These sentiments are sincere and important. It is important to recognize that people who start out as friends and lovers have something special. It is important, therefore, to recognize that chemical dependency affects everything. It turns lovers and friends into adversaries. Friendship is based on a number of things. It is based on mutual trust and honesty. It is based on the ability to communicate openly. It is based on a sense of understanding and being understood. The chemical eats away at this slowly, but surely.

The erosion probably begins in the denial phase. At this stage, the drinking is causing problems, but no one wants to face up to it. So the lies begin. First the lies to the self, and then the lies to each other. The dependent person will lie mostly in terms of broken promises. The chemically free person will lie to cover up. The trust begins to break down. True feelings are held back until they become explosive. The honest communication begins to dissolve.

The physical relationship is a good indicator of what is happening in the total relationship. The attraction may well continue through the denial phase. It will continue to be a way of sharing, even as the words become more difficult. Not only that, but no one has yet to come up with a better way of making up after a drunken episode.

Gradually, the interest in physical intimacy will decline on the part of the chemically free partner. The need to be less vulnerable will start to take over. At this point, the sexual experience may still be technically satisfying, but the emotion is held in check.

As in all other aspects, the deterioration continues, and what was a warm, loving experience now becomes a power play and a means of ventilating anger.

"Go to bed with your bottle—not me!" "I can't stand the smell!" "You have to make a choice!" "Who needs you? It won't be hard to find someone better than you!"

The gap continues to get greater. No part of the relationship remains unaffected.

The climate becomes confused and the open communication that existed before gives way to suspicion and anger. The underlying concerns are not addressed and the couple, even though they still care about each other, live a distorted lifestyle. Both partners are being directed by the chemical—one directly, the other indirectly. One is addicted to the chemical; the other is addicted to the chemically dependent partner.

The relationship breaks down even further. . . . If the chemical dependency was only destructive to this point, the damage to the relationship is repairable. It is possible to argue it out and, at the very least, clear the air. Feelings can be expressed and the lines of communication can remain open. But this is not simple.

This insidious illness does not stop here. It separates the couple still further. The chemically dependent partner stops developing emotionally. The chemically dependent partner no longer wants to deal with or confront problems. A large part of any marital relationship involves making decisions and resolving shared problems. Where will we go on our vacation? Johnny is failing algebra again. Can we redo the kitchen?

And so on, with the stuff that life is made of. These issues are no longer shared. The chemically free partner takes over more and more responsibility. The resentment grows deeper. The gap becomes even greater.

A saving grace during difficult times is the support of caring family and friends. This is true here, too, at least for a while, but if they have not experienced what you are experiencing, the support will only increase the pain. If only they could understand. The isolation of the chemically dependent couple becomes greater. They become isolated from other people, and they grow further and further away from each other.

And the sickness continues. The feelings shared are similar. The pain and the desperation are felt by both, but they blame each other. The guilt is felt by both, but the responsibility is placed differently. Once close, you are now strangers most of the time.

Occasionally, you will find yourselves in the eye of the storm, and you will be so grateful. The idea is that now the drinking will stop and all will be as it was. It is a shared belief. It is a shared deception. The reality is that the disease will progress. It will get worse . . . and so will whatever is left of your relationship.

The communication deteriorates into forms of anger. The inner feelings evolve into worry, fear, despair. The feelings are shared, but in isolation. The chemically dependent partner numbs the feelings, and the nonabuser is doubled over in pain—relieved only by anger and occasional fantasies.

The fantasy is that the drinking will stop, and everything will be as it was in the beginning. The miracle of abstinence. The fantasy is shared. Alcohol will lose its hold, and you will live happily ever after.

Somehow that is the greatest lie of all, and yet one of the most universally believed. The drinking stops. What does that mean in terms of the relationship? It only means that the focus is lost. It only means that the chemical is no longer the focal point. A huge vacuum now exists. Nothing else happens automatically. The trust that was lost does not come back just because the abuse stops. Just as a history of unfulfilled promises damaged the trust, a new history has to come into play, in order to rebuild it. The lies may stop, but sharing makes one too vulnerable to be open at this point. The anger does not auto- matically go away because the drinking stops. The feelings that were repressed by the chemical may want to come cascading out. How ter- ribly insecure—how terribly frightening. How hard to share these feelings and expect to be understood. The lines of communication have been cut off. You are two blind people without a road map.

Abstinence is not enough. A whole new relationship has to be built. The new starting point has to be different from the original starting point. The starting point this time is best served in learning how to solve mutual problems. It is best served in developing guide- lines of how to talk *to* and not *at* each other. How can each be heard and understood? If the relationship is going to be healthy, it is going to require a lot of hard work. The foundation will require careful and long attention. The attraction that enhances the beginning of a relationship is no longer present. The basis now has to be firmly grounded in reality. If both parties are committed to working, it can be more than it would have been, had the chemical not entered into the picture. If both people are looking for the same things, there is a great opportunity for mutual, as well as individual, growth. If not, the fantasy is over. The relationship is done. Abstinence is not nirvana.

Chemical dependency destroys slowly, but thoroughly. Chemical independence can lead the way to build a healthy marital relationship. It's the only winning game in town.

6

Who Do You Pick
for Your Lover?

Why Do You Pick the Lovers That You Do?

E verything is going wrong with my relationship. I know that it's all my fault. I try everything I know to fix it, but it doesn't work. I'm not even sure if I love him (her). Maybe I don't know what love is. I'm so confused."

Sound familiar? It should. It is almost verbatim the story I hear when an adult child of an alcoholic enters therapy because an intimate relationship is souring. And the story is the same whether the ACOA is twenty years old and in a first serious relationship, or forty years old and the veteran of one or more failed marriages.

"It just has to be my fault. Relationships always go this way. I thought it would be different this time, but it wasn't. Maybe I'm better off alone."

Have you felt that way? We all have—and we've all said similar self-deprecating things while in the midst of a troubled or troublesome relationship. Is it a "normal" way to feel? It depends upon whether you are feeling that way because of the current circumstances or whether these are deep-seated messages which have become a permanent part of your self-image because they were hammered at you

169

time and time again while you were growing up. In both cases, the feelings are equally painful, but they are more difficult to erase in the second case.

Read those opening statements again: "Everything is going wrong. I know that it is all my fault. I try to do everything that I know, but it just doesn't work."

Today you are saying those phrases about your relationship. The context may be new for you, but the phrases and the feelings are not. Once again, you are experiencing the helplessness of your childhood and reacting to an "old tape." Nonetheless, the feelings are real, and, oh, so powerful.

Other familiar feelings also well up, including confusion, the sense of being stuck, of being unable to change your destiny.

This is all part of being in an intimate relationship. It will drag out all things, old and new, that you have experienced and felt before. You will play it all out again. With work, the process and outcomes will be different, but the struggle cannot be avoided. Even those who have not been affected by living in an alcoholic family find one must work to have a good and healthy relationship. You have plenty of company in the struggle!

To probe a little deeper into the nature of the struggle you are facing, it is important that you recall some of the early inconsistent messages you were given by your parents. Like it or not, want to believe it or not, these messages are still influencing you on an unconscious level throughout all aspects of your life. *To change your life, you must change the message.*

And, awareness is the first step toward changing the message. The knowledge of how your current patterns were formed will begin to release you from the self-critical indictment which is such a basic part of your nature. Let's take a look at these double-bind messages and how they affect you today:

"I love you. Go away."

Sometimes your alcoholic parent was warm and loving, sometimes rejecting and hostile. Although your nonalcoholic parent told you that you were loved, he or she was often so absorbed with worry and so irritable that you rarely felt loved. There was no consistency.

This is love as you understood it as a child, and are still experiencing it. Ever wonder why you are attracted to that person who is warm and loving one day, and rejecting the next? Ever wonder why the person who says he or she will call and doesn't seems more desirable than the one who is consistent?

If, by chance, you do become involved with a lover who is consistent, you find that sort of person very unsettling, because you have no frame of reference for this kind of behavior. I am talking about the type of individual with order in her life, the person who can predict with a reasonable amount of certainty what tomorrow will bring. This also is someone who will behave, feel and think tomorrow much as he behaved, felt and thought today. The challenge to win the love of the erratic and sometimes rejecting person repeats the challenge of your childhood. You are grateful when the inconsistent person throws you a crumb, but get bored quickly with the one who is available all the time.

You are playing out your childhood all over again, because the only consistency you knew was inconsistency. The only predictability you had was the lack of predictability. You lived your childhood on an emotional roller coaster. And that is what you understand. Think a minute: How many times have you created a crisis in your relationship to get the energy flowing again, and bring the relationship back to more familiar ground?

Even though this may be obvious to you on an intellectual level, bear in mind that it may take longer for you to truly feel this truth because you were conditioned at such an early age.

"You can't do anything right. I need you."

Here is another set of conflicting messages which you play over and over again. When you were a child, you could never meet your alcoholic parent's perfectionistic standards, no matter how hard you tried. You were never good enough. And you truly believed that everything that went wrong was your fault. If you would have been good enough, things would have been better for your family.

Yet you knew you were needed, and that they couldn't get along without you. That was perfectly clear also. Since it was impossible for them to get along without you, even though you were so worthless, you would struggle until you could find a way to "fix" things.

As an adult, do you find yourself drawn to partners who are both extremely dependent and highly critical? Are you drawn to those who repeatedly put you down, although you know they can't get along without you? You continue to strive for their approval, because on a deep level you believe that there would not be so much trouble in the relationship if you were only good enough. And you know you can't keep letting down someone who needs you so desperately. Sound familiar? Another setup.

"Yes, it's true that your mother/father did/said those terrible things. But you must understand that he/she was drunk."

The implications of this double-bind message are especially destructive to you when you are in an intimate relationship. Your unconscious tells you that if you can find an explanation for inexcusable behavior, you must believe that the behavior is excusable.

In the family system affected by alcoholism, the alcoholic is rarely held accountable for his or her behavior. More likely, the child hears from the other parent, "What did you expect from a drunk?" Or, in early family recovery, "You have to understand that your father/mother has a disease." The child hears the message that the parent can do whatever he or she wishes by simply using the excuse of drunkenness or alcoholism.

Now that you are an adult, you have become the most understanding person in the world when it comes to your loving relationships. Right? In almost every situation, you will find a way to make everything okay—certainly if *someone* must be at fault, you will take that fault upon yourself. You have learned how to understand, and you have learned how to take full responsibility upon yourself.

Therefore, when you are treated in a lousy way, you analyze the situation and don't allow yourself to experience any angry feelings. Understanding a behavior does not make it automatically acceptable. But you learned to do that very well when you were a child, and denied yourself the pain for maltreatment because you believed that "My father/mother wouldn't have done that to me if he/she were sober."

This also has elements of control and elements of guilt. Here is the kind of thought pattern that runs through the mind of the child in the alcoholic family system: *If I feel guilty, then I am responsible. And if I am responsible, then I can do something to fix it, to change it, to make it different.* Giving up your guilt also means giving up your sense that you have control over the situation. And, of course, loss of control is a disaster. You have grown up to be the perfect doormat for an inconsiderate person. Often you end up in a perfect give-and-take relationship . . . you give, they take.

"I'll be there for you—next time. I give you my word."

The underlying message here is—forget it! So you learn how not to want so that you don't get disappointed.

Sometimes you unwittingly become the doormat for a partner who truly doesn't want to treat you that way. Often you become tired and resentful. You complain about having to do everything in the relationship—yet it is almost impossible for you to ask for anything for yourself. You want your partner to be a mind reader.

Your fear of asking for something and then not getting it is as unsettling as your fear of asking for something *and* getting it! The first outcome reinforces your belief that you are too unworthy to deserve what you want, and the second possibility is so unfamiliar that you actually don't know how to react. Even a simple compliment may cause you great discomfort.

You deal with the whole situation by abdicating responsibility for your happiness. You decide that your partner should know what you want and act on it without ever having been told. For example, "If I have to tell him I want to go to the theater for my birthday, it proves that he doesn't really want to please me." Your lover is now set up so that you can decide he doesn't love you if he doesn't pick up whatever vague hints you may have sent his way. You'll only be happy with a mind reader, a fantasy hero who will automatically know how to please you.

"Everything is fine, so don't worry. But how in the world can I deal with all this?"

Both of these messages come through. "Don't concern yourself—everything is going to be okay." Yet the underlying sense you get from your parents is that everything is *not* okay. The result is you develop into a superperson by the time you become an adult. You can (and will) take care of everything. You are in charge. Nobody else around you has to be concerned about anything. You can manage. How often do you say the following things: "Don't worry, we'll take my car—I've got enough money—I'll pick up the food—I'll make the arrangements—Don't worry—It's no problem for me!"

7

What Is a Healthy Relationship Anyway?

What does a healthy relationship look like? What does it feel like? How do I get one? How will I know if I have one?"

These are very important and real questions that need to be addressed. Wanting to be involved in a healthy, intimate relationship is a universal condition. And defining just exactly what "healthy" is, is a universal question.

You know you are in a healthy, intimate relationship when you have created an environment where:

1. I can be me.   4. I can grow.
2. You can be you.   5. You can grow.
3. We can be us.   6. We can grow together.

Essentially, that's what it's all about. It's paradoxical that a healthy relationship frees me to be myself—and yet I don't know who I am because acquiring self-knowledge is a lifelong process. Although you may not have a strong sense of who you are, you recognize clearly when you are not being allowed the freedom to be you. It is clear when you are feeling judged. It is clear when you feel that you are walking on eggshells. It is clear when you worry about making a mistake. In effect, the freedom to be you means that your partner will not inter-fere with nor judge your process of being and becoming.

You offer your partner the same freedom that you are asking for yourself. And you accept your partner as she is, and do not try to use the power of your love to turn her into a swan. You do not get caught up in your fantasy of who you want her to be, and then concentrate on making that happen. You focus on who that person really is.

"I accept you unconditionally, and you accept me unconditionally." That's the bottom line. It does not mean that changes in personality or actions are undesirable or impossible—it merely means that you begin by accepting your partner as he is.

"We are free to be us." Each couple defines their own relationship built on shared values and interests. First, they must decide what they each value as individuals and then they can build a oneness out of their separateness. Some of their differences are unimportant, and can either be ignored or worked out. For example, issues such as "You always leave the cap off the toothpaste," or, "I hate church socials," can easily be worked out.

Other differences are significant and need to be worked out, if the relationship is to remain healthy and survive. Examples of more crit-ical issues are, "I don't want any children," or, "I'll never have any-thing to do with your mother again."

Many experiences are enhanced because the two of you are a couple. Enjoying together the beauty of a sunset, a walk on the beach, a well-prepared meal, are examples of the "us" that make a partnership desirable. "I am enhanced when I have me—you have you—and we also have us."

A healthy relationship creates an environment where you can grow. In this climate of support, you also encourage your partner to do the same. Through the directions of your individual growth, you develop together as a couple.

A couple also grows together by developing mutual goals and working together on ways to achieve them. Interestingly, it is the journey toward the goals, and not necessarily the goals themselves, which help the relationship grow. Whether or not you attain a goal is part of the process toward the next shared experience.

Intimacy means that you have a love relationship with another person where you offer, and are offered, validation, understanding and a sense of being valued intellectually, emotionally and physically.

The more you are willing to share, and be shared with, the greater the degree of intimacy.

A healthy relationship is not a power struggle. The two of you don't have to think the same way about all things.

A healthy relationship is not symbiotic. You do not have to feel the same way about all things.

A healthy relationship is not confined to a sexual relationship which must end in orgasm, but celebrates the sharing and exploring.

8

8

Relationship Issues Shared by Adult Children of Alcoholics

You have been living with many myths generated and perpetuated by your family system. Because of this, you put such enormous pressure on yourself that you wonder whether having a healthy, intimate relationship is worth paying the price.

You are torn apart by push-pull issues which may be illusionary to others, but are very real, and sometimes paralyzing, to you.

"I want to become involved. I don't want to become involved."

"I want to meet someone. I don't want to meet someone."

"I want to get to know you better. Please, simply go away."

These issues interfere with your ability to get what you want out of relationships.

Your first step is to take a good, hard look at these myths. Acknowledge them. Reject them. Then replace them with what exists in the real world. This is by no means a small task, because you have been living with these myths for a long time. They will not vanish overnight. Simply becoming aware of them is the place to begin.

ACOA MYTH

"If I am involved with you, I will lose me."

TRUTH: In the real world, healthy relationships enhance the self and do not absorb it.

Fear of Loss of Self

This fear is present because you never clearly established your sense of self while you were growing into adulthood. The early messages that you received from your parents were very confusing. The lack of clear messages forced you to create many of your beliefs and values, rather than learning them through example.

Because your parents didn't consistently care for you in all the ways that a child needs care, you have had to do a lot of self-parenting. This has left you with an inconclusive sense of who you really are. Your selfhood is still in the state of evolving and is easily influenced. Ideally, by the time one reaches adulthood, the inner messages are much stronger than the outside influences. In other words, your decision making evolves out of what your knowledge and instincts tell you, rather than depending upon what you are reading or being told at the moment.

For ACOAs, this state of confidence in your ability to make decisions and act upon them is not reached so easily. Someone (anyone) else's opinion often influences yours. So, if you have been working on being your own person, and having confidence in your decision-making skills, you may feel threatened by the idea of involvement with another person whose opinions and ideas will be important to you—and may influence you in ways you don't want.

Feeling this sense of insecurity does not automatically mean the "loss of self." What it does mean is that you will "check out" many of your perceptions, opinions and responses more carefully, to see where they are coming from. This provides valuable information for you. Your next step is to not automatically dismiss your opinions in favor of new input. Think it over. Give yourself a little time to assess and consider the situation.

This gives you three choices in every situation: You may maintain your original position, change your position or adopt an entirely new position which incorporates both your thinking on the subject and that of others. You will feel much more confident about the decisions that you make, and less threatened by other people's opinions.

ACOA MYTH

"If you really knew me, you wouldn't care about me."

TRUTH: You probably aren't as good an actor or actress as you think you are. Your beloved probably *already* really knows you. And cares about you anyway!

Fear of Being Found Out

Many ACOAs constantly worry that the person they love would want nothing more to do with them if he or she really knew them. Although it's a little vague to you about just who that real and horrendous person may be, you still feel the anxious feelings very strongly.

You try to stave off this possibility by acting out your fantasies of how a perfect person would act. You try to behave as though you have your entire life in order and are totally problem-free. After all, the simply human, real you with human frailties will never be good enough for someone you love.

This belief is not something you made up. Since childhood, you have been told overtly and covertly that you are the cause of family difficulties. Getting close to a loved one will expose your dark side and cause that person to negate the positive side of you that they have loved until now.

Changing this belief as an adult begins with hard, cold logic. Think about it. Were you really powerful enough as a child to cause your family problems? Truthfully, you will have to answer "no."

ACOA MYTH

"If you find out that I am not perfect, you will abandon me."

TRUTH: Nobody is perfect. And perfection does not exist.

Fear of Abandonment

Fear of abandonment is very strong in ACOAs and differs from the fear of rejection. Adult children of alcoholics seem to be able to handle rejection and adjust to it. Fear of abandonment, however, cuts a lot deeper because of childhood experiences.

The child who experiences living with alcoholism grows into an individual with a weak and very inconsistent sense of self, as we have already discussed. This is a very, very critical self which has not had the nurturance it needed. It is a hungry self and, in many ways, a very insecure self.

This is caused by the fact that you never knew when, or if, your parents would be emotionally available to you. You expected unpredictability and inconsistency. Once the drinking began, you simply did not exist. Your needs would not be met until the drinking episode and any accompanying crises were over. There was no way to predict when this would occur. What a terrible, terrible feeling. No matter what you did to try to prevent it, it would happen anyway.

Some children living in this situation continue trying to get their needs met, and others give up entirely. Those children who give up entirely are not as anxious to enter into adult relationships as are those who still hold onto the fantasy that maybe, just maybe, this time things will be different.

The constant fear, however, is that the person you love will not be there for you tomorrow. In an attempt to guard against losing your beloved, you idealize the relationship and idealize your role in the relationship. Your safeguard against being abandoned is to try hard to be perfect and serve all the other person's needs.

Whenever anything goes wrong (and in life, things go wrong), and when there is conflict (and in life, there is conflict), the fear of being abandoned takes precedence over dealing with the pertinent issue which needs to be resolved. This fear is so great that it is not unusual for ACOAs to completely lose sight of the actual problem.

A typical example of this is illustrated by the argument that Mary A., aged twenty-six (one of six children whose father is still actively drinking), had with her boyfriend. It erupted because he was paying attention to other women, and Mary got angry. The boyfriend responded defensively, told her that she was being paranoid, and the argument continued.

When he left, Mary's anger soon turned into a sense of panic.

"Oh, my God! I'm sure I was wrong. Maybe I was overreacting. Maybe he doesn't care about me anymore. Maybe he's going to leave me now. After all, if I weren't so insecure, his behavior wouldn't have bothered me." It was a classic example of feeling abandoned.

Within three hours, Mary A. drove to her boyfriend's home, gave him a red rose and apologized for her behavior. He accepted her apology, and they made love.

As she was recounting the story to me later, I asked her, "How did you resolve the issue?"

She looked puzzled at first, and then said, "Oh, that!"

Her terrible fear of abandonment had erased the issue from her mind. The problem itself was lost when the panic set in. Reducing the pain of her fear of abandonment became her primary goal.

In cases like this, the problem doesn't go away just because it is being ignored. It will recur—maybe in the same form and maybe in a different form—until it is dealt with, or until it becomes a significant underlying issue with the couple. Repressing the problem does not cause it to be truly forgotten.

Mary's problem also illustrates the fears of "loss of self" and "being found out."

Mary starts placing all her emphasis on his reaction to the experience. Then she begins to wonder and worry about his reaction to other experiences. She thinks about him constantly, particularly at times when he is not being attentive to her. She focuses entirely on him, what he thinks of her and how she can keep from losing him.

What about Mary's needs? What about the fact she simply did not want to experience the way he was ignoring her to flirt with other women? She starts judging herself harshly for reacting to his behavior. And the woman who felt that reaction begins to disappear, something Mary recognizes and hates in herself. The next time I saw Mary she commented, "I tend to lose myself in every relationship when I am involved. Maybe I should end it now."

Mary does not believe she is worth very much, and is fearful he will discover that. She believes she can fool him, if she is on her best behavior. This creates heavy tension in the relationship, but she is afraid to be open and honest. Now she begins to wonder whether she reacted appropriately, and says, "This is really my fault. If I were more secure, I wouldn't have been so upset when he paid attention to other women. My insecurities are getting in the way.

"If he knows how insecure I really am, he may not bother with me anymore. Perhaps it is just as well that we ended the argument the way we did. I want him to see me as a 'together' woman, not as a scared little girl. He wouldn't have anything to do with that scared little girl."

How long can Mary pretend to be somebody else? The truth of the matter is that he probably already sees the "scared little girl" aspects of her personality, and is attracted to the whole complex person that she is. She probably doesn't hide her fears as well as she thinks she does—or would like to!

It isn't important whether Mary reacted to her boyfriend's behavior because of her own insecurities, or because he was being somewhat obnoxious. It probably is a combination of both. What is important is that the couple can discuss the issue.

If she is insecure, she won't become more secure by denying these feelings. She needs to acknowledge these feelings, and then have the relationship develop to the point where she feels more secure. If he cares about her the way he says he does, he will attempt to accommodate her feelings. It is just as important for her to recognize if he is not interested in accommodating her feelings and prefers to play. Lack of accommodation on a relatively minor issue may signal lack of accommodation on more significant issues which will arise in the future. If this is the case, this relationship may not offer Mary what she is seeking.

ACOA MYTH

"We are as one."

TRUTH: In the real world, you are you, and I am me. And then there is us.

Bonding

Chances are that you did not experience the bonding in your early years that children in more typical homes did, especially if your mother was the alcoholic. You could not depend on your parents taking care of your needs in a consistent way. You could not depend on being held and loved to solve your fears and calm your hurts. You could not trust that your mother would nurture you when you felt badly, whether you were right or wrong.

This affects the way you become involved, and the intensity of that involvement today.

Chris L., aged thirty-three, whose mother is an alcoholic, was taking a course in group dynamics at a local college. She reported that she didn't fit in with her classmates because they were concerned with their struggle to *break* the bonds with their parents, while her lifelong struggle was in trying to *develop* bonds.

It is important to understand the difference and recognize the implications for the early stages of a relationship. Adults who had many of their needs satisfied at home (many to an unhealthy degree!) are able to let an involvement develop slowly. The investment can take place slowly, along with the growth of trust.

Those who are products of homes where bonding never took place, if they invest at all, invest at once, heavily and on a deep emotional level. They seize the opportunity for bonding and are deeply involved before they know what is happening.

In the early stages of a relationship, there is great intensity of feelings. The body chemistry that attracts you to each other is activated, and both parties are superattentive and superinvolved. You understand this degree of intensity because it feels to you like the energizing you experience in a crisis.

This is the time when both parties greatly desire fusion. You are on each other's minds all the time—the phone calls are frequent—the desire to be together is great. Emotionally, it is a very powerful time.

The early stages are probably more an "involvement" than a "relationship." It is the playing out of a fantasy. You cannot sustain this intensity which is so appealing. This is just a dynamite beginning, and not what a healthy relationship is all about.

Initially, this is flattering to the new partner, and the closeness feels good. Often, the partner gets pleasure out of feeling needed and in fulfilling the needs of the love object. But after a while this begins to feel suffocating, and starts to become a drain. Your partner, if healthy, will stop wanting to be devoted completely and exclusively to the relationship. Life holds other priorities, as well. The aura of the ideal love evaporates as a result, and things begin to be put into perspective.

When life begins to normalize, the intensity decreases. The telephone quits ringing all the time, and you feel let down and rejected. You feel that your partner no longer cares because he no longer desires to spend every moment with you. From your point of view, this feels like abandonment. It's the drunk versus sober parent scenario once again. You feel the gaping hole inside you even more deeply than before.

Clutching at your partner will force her into the "I love you, go away" stance, even though your beloved still cares. If you continue to play out your script, you will set yourself up for what you fear the most: rejection and abandonment. Then you will feel very confused because all you wanted was a loving relationship, and you will think once again you picked the wrong person. The truth may be that you were asking unrealistic things of your relationship. It is important that you be very clear about what you want your relationship to fulfill within you so that you avoid this situation.

On the other hand, you may react by deciding you no longer care, and leaving the budding relationship. This may mean you are "hooked" on intensity, and have fooled yourself into equating intensity with the relationship itself. Or, it may mean that you are terrified about beginning the process of getting to know and being known by another person. It probably is a little of both.

ACOA MYTH

"Being vulnerable always has negative results."

TRUTH: In the real world, being vulnerable sometimes has negative results and sometimes has positive results. But it is the only route to intimacy.

Vulnerability

Early on you learned that you were the only one who could be responsible for your happiness, and that other people could make you angry only if you permitted it. You learned that you were in charge of your feelings. This was essential and critical to your being able to survive emotionally in an alcoholic household. But now you need to open up your feelings to others if you want to participate in a healthy, intimate relationship.

It seems to me that the *idea* of being vulnerable is really more terrifying than actually *being* vulnerable. This was underlined for me by the discussions which took place one Monday night in one of our ACOA group meetings. Jimmy opened it up by telling how intensely sharing his feelings in the previous group meeting had affected him all week. "I left feeling so vulnerable," he said, "and the vulnerability lasted all week. I tried to be alone most of the time, because I was afraid of what would happen if I were with others while I felt so open to devastation."

The other group members understood what he was saying and agreed with him.

"Hey, wait a minute!" I said. "What does being vulnerable mean to you people? And what are you talking about when you say that you are afraid to be vulnerable?"

One by one, every person there defined "allowing themselves to be vulnerable" as being out of control of their lives. They felt that someone else would then take control of their lives and do them damage. To them, there seemed to be no other way. Vulnerability meant loss of self, devastation, being powerless to prevent these negative things from happening.

"When I was a child," Malone shared, "I was afraid that I would be killed if I let my guard down for even one minute." Allowing vulnerability, to her, meant potential death. Although it didn't mean the possibility of death to the others, it did mean something terrible. It represented being left out, being hurt.

Just talking about feeling vulnerable created a very tense and somewhat depressing climate within the group.

"This is a very important thing for us to examine," I said. "If we are to develop healthy intimate relationships, we must allow our partner access to our feelings. There is no other way to do it. If you are too terrified of being vulnerable and its consequences to take a risk, you are automatically saying that you are incapable or unwilling to have a healthy, intimate relationship.

"Have you ever considered the possibility that many of the feelings you are defending against are feelings which would actually enhance your life? Have you considered the fact that there are many aspects of love feelings that you haven't felt? That there are feelings of excitement about being in your presence that you don't feel? That there are supportive feelings that you don't allow yourself to feel? Have you considered that there is a whole spectrum of feelings you have denied yourself because your terror about being vulnerable takes control of your life?"

Leslie shared that after three years, she is able to be emotionally accessible to the man she loves. "I no longer have any secrets, emotional or otherwise," she said. "I tore down my walls little by little. Sometimes I've rebuilt a piece of them because I became afraid or because he didn't react the way I had hoped he would. But, slowly and gradually, I was able to let down the barriers as our relationship grew and our trust developed.

"I don't know many others whom I would trust in this way, but I do know that it has not been harmful to me to be vulnerable in this relationship. It has, in effect, made me stronger. Once I really allowed him into my life, he could begin helping me feel things about myself which had been a struggle to feel before. And that helps me feel more solid, more secure as a person.

"It hasn't been easy, but it has been worth the struggle!"

This reinforced for the group that the idea of being vulnerable may be more terrifying than the actual experience. In reality, you wouldn't even be reading this book if you were not interested in personal growth. Growth does not take place unless we allow access to new thoughts, feelings and ideas. And this access is gained only by being open to it, which means allowing ourselves to be vulnerable.

ACOA MYTH

"We will never argue or criticize each other."

TRUTH: In the real world, couples argue from time to time, and are critical of each other's behavior.

Anger

Adult children of alcoholics believe that in an ideal relationship there will be no conflict and no anger. Although they recognize intellectually that this is impossible, emotionally this is what they want. Anger is very complicated and very much misunderstood by them. Historically, anger needed to be repressed. Children growing up with alcoholism live in a very angry climate, where it is never resolved. Expressing anger is never useful and only tends to make life worse. It never did anyone any good.

Therefore, ACOAs learn how not to be angry. Instead they rationalize, explain things away and finally become depressed. The words they use to describe their depression are words of anger. Since anger is repressed, the only time it comes out is when it is no longer containable and has turned into rage. Rage is frightening to ACOAs because they don't know what they might do. It is not unusual for one to say, "I am terrified of allowing myself to be angry because if I lose control of my anger, I might kill." Many turn this anger inward, and since they would never harm others, have suicidal thoughts.

They also fear another person's anger being expressed toward them. Anger may cause physical violence, which must be avoided at all costs. This is another submerged issue which comes into play in a relationship. Yet, there is no way to have a good relationship without resolving conflict. If two people are healthy and alive, and have thoughts and ideas, there will be times when they disagree. There will also be times when one person does something that irritates the other and makes him angry. It is impossible to know in a developing relationship where all the sensitive spots are. The ideal is to talk it over when anger surfaces, learn where it comes from, and how not to repeat it.

ACOAs often translate anger into something that it is not. It goes something like this: "If I am angry with you, I don't love you. If you are angry with me, you don't love me. Since I do love you, then I can't allow myself to be angry at you. If you really love me, you will not be angry at me either." On an emotional level, this is the message that adult children give to themselves. Though not a valid message, it plays out just the same: "If I cannot contain my anger at you, I must reject you. If you do not contain your anger at me, then you must reject me." Once again, the issue that made the couple angry has been forgotten. Why even bother to deal with it if the outcome will be rejection?

In addition, because adult children have no experience in problem solving with another person, they don't know how to resolve the angry feelings. They don't know how to work with their anger in order to dissipate it. Anger needs to be expressed, in one way or another. It needs to be recognized, acknowledged, talked over, understood and dissipated. It is important to realize that anger is an ever-present, hidden issue in the relationships of ACOAs.

Part of what made Mary believe her boyfriend was going to abandon her, or that she had to reject him, was her anger. Since she did not understand how to resolve anger, these were the only alternatives she saw.

In addition to being terrified at the depth of their anger, ACOAs are also uncertain about its appropriateness. "Would that make a normal person angry?" is the question I often hear. It is asked in reference to both their own anger and that of the people with whom they are involved. "Just what is okay to be angry about?" they want to know. Recently, I gave a lecture on ACOAs which a client and her boyfriend attended. He said, "I came because I want to know as much as I can about the things that have affected Carol, because I love her." I was most impressed.

They sat on the right side of the room, and most of the rest of the students sat on the left. About one-half hour into the lecture, a security guard walked into the room and turned out the light. I made a comment to him, and he turned it back on and left the room. I made light of my annoyance and went on with the lecture. The next time I saw Carol, she told me how furious Bill had become. "How could anyone walk into a room, look directly at you and turn out the light? The discourtesy was outrageous!" She said, "You know, it didn't bother me at all. I guess I'm used to being treated as if I don't exist."

For them, Bill's anger was an important learning experience. It was clear to her that she needed to work on her own self-worth. And he learned how deep the lack of validation is for ACOAs. Asking the question about whether the reaction was "normal" prompted the insight. Who is to say what is normal? You react according to your history, and when your reactions are put into perspective, you decide what is normal.

ACOA Myth

"Anything that goes wrong is my fault. I am a terrible person."

TRUTH: In the real world, some things that go wrong are your fault. Some things are not. Terrible things happen, but you are not terrible.

Guilt and Shame

Guilt and shame emerge in any relationship with someone who has grown up with alcoholism. They are issues which need to be worked on. Ernie Kurtz, in his booklet, *Shame and Guilt: Characteristics of the Dependency Cycle*, describes guilt as "a feeling of wrong-doing, sense of wickedness, 'not good.'" The child is taught that what goes wrong is his fault. Even if it wasn't his fault, he hears, "If you were not such a rotten kid, I would not have to drink." The guilt that many ACOAs have is on a level so deep that they believe that their very existence caused the problem.

Shame, although somewhat different, is very closely linked to guilt, and one tends to feed off the other. Dr. Kurtz describes shame as "a feeling of inadequacy, sense of worthlessness, 'no good.'" Guilt is associated with behavior, while shame relates to the essence of the person, the self, which is even more basic to the person. It is very hard to overcome these feelings. It is a lifelong struggle to feel that your behavior is not "no good"; it is also a lifelong struggle to believe that you are not "no good."

In a relationship, anything that goes wrong becomes, to some degree, your fault. You feel it is your fault because the things you do are no good, and because you are no good. It is your fault, because in growing up it was the only means of control you had. If you were responsible for what happened, then you believed you could do something to change it. It was, of course, futile because you were not responsible, but the struggle to try made you feel that you were not completely out of control. In a relationship, if something occurs about which you feel responsible, you think you can do something to change it. You can apologize, or you can do something different. If you are guilty, then you can do something. If you are not guilty, then you are, because of your mind-set, in a very real sense, stuck.

The idea of saying to your partner, "Why don't we take a look at this, regardless of whether I'm at fault, or you're at fault? I'm okay, and you're okay, and you and I need to find out what's going wrong," does not enter your mind. Because, essentially, you do not believe that you are okay. Even if what you did was okay, you don't realize it. Therefore, every interaction gets extremely complicated. Also, you do not want the person with whom you are involved to find out how inadequate or worthless you are. This, in turn, creates a climate in which you are less than totally honest. It goes back to the fear of "being found out."

ACOA Myth

"In order to be lovable, I must be happy all the time."

TRUTH: In the real world, sometimes people are happy, and sometimes they are not.

Depression

Many ACOAs are what we call "chronically depressed." This means that there is an edge of sadness about them. As I discussed earlier, it results, in part, from the anger they have turned inward upon themselves. It also has to do with the experience of loss.

The adult child never got to be a child. He did not have the experience of being spontaneous, foolish, childlike—of doing the things that children normally do. He did not have an opportunity to experience fun, or even to know what fun is. Although he knows what it is to be worthless or impulsive, the experience of having fun is something that, if experienced at all, was negligible. This causes a degree of sadness, which makes it harder to feel free and spontaneous in any relationship. This causes depression. The adult child will fight against depression, because he tries to be pleasant in an attempt to be "the perfect partner." But, for many, the feeling of depression is always present beneath the surface.

Loss is also a major issue with ACOAs. They have, in effect, lost their childhood, and therefore many of the experiences other children have. For them, any change involves a loss of what they had before. Change is difficult because, psychologically, change means anarchy. With the fear of abandonment comes the fear of loss, accompanied by the ever-present fear that the relationship will not last. Once again, then, loss will have to be experienced. This fear causes a tremendous conflict. "I know it won't last, so I wait for the bomb to drop, and I panic at having to experience the loss, so I hold on tight." This kind of behavior tends to drive the other person away, which sets the dreaded fears in motion. Unfortunately, the feelings are not discussed, so there is little opportunity to begin to solve them.

The typical attitude is: "So that you do not see the level of my pain and how close it is to the surface, I will put on a 'happy face.' The song from *The King and I* about whistling a happy tune is my way of life."

ACOA Myth

"We will trust each other totally, automatically and all at once."

TRUTH: In the real world, trust builds slowly.

Trust

It is natural for children to trust others. From infancy, they trust that their needs will be met. If this early trust is denied, they die, as they are completely helpless, and depend on others for nurture and care. Trust is so natural to children that, even in a typical family, they must be taught when not to be trusting. Children must be taught not to go with strangers, that it is not safe to run into the street, nor to touch the stove. Children, in their naivete, want to love and trust all people and all things.

In a home that has been affected by alcoholism, the child's needs are not totally unmet, but they are inconsistently met. This means that trusting people will mean being hurt, and therefore that trust is inappropriate. It means that the child must learn how to take care of himself. In order to survive, the child learns how not to trust . . . that he can depend only on himself. If someone is trustworthy, it is the exception rather than the rule. When there is an expectation, it is most often met by frustration and disappointment. "Don't trust" is something that the child learns very early and very well. However, contrary to the child's nature, it is an adaptive response to a mal-adaptive situation.

The discussion here is about how to build a healthy relationship. A major element—a necessary prerequisite for a healthy relation-ship—is trust. Without it, the relationship cannot prosper; it simply will not develop and grow. Trust is not easy to accomplish, because you have to unlearn many negative responses and feelings. You have to go all the way back to your early childhood, and once again begin to trust.

In a group of adult children, one young man said, "I have just started a new job. I like everyone I have met so far, but I am not going to trust anybody just yet. They are going to have to earn my trust." The group agreed with him. I said, "Why not trust everyone and then discount those who violate your trust? It will take much less energy. It doesn't mean you have to act in any particular way. If you decide to trust, you don't have to behave any differently than if you decided not to trust. It would just make it easier for you."

The group was fascinated and wanted to learn more about this approach, which was a new one for them. "It costs you nothing to trust automatically," I said. "You end up at the very same place. If you don't trust, and someone behaves in a manner that is untrust-worthy, then you have affirmed and reinforced the fact that you can't trust anybody. If you do trust someone and he turns out not to be worthy of it, yes, you will be disappointed, but you will not be devastated. Disappointment is something that you have learned to handle very well. Affirming the fact that it was a good idea not to trust in the first place does not mean you will not be disappointed. That is the reality of it." This was a very curious idea to them—something that, given their backgrounds, they could not have thought of on their own.

What does trust mean in a relationship? There are several compo-nents. First, trust means that your partner will not abuse your feel-ings, and that you will show your feelings. Right there you are stymied, as you are entering into an arena outside your range of expe-rience. Trusting others is one of the primary things you have guarded against since childhood, and now I am telling you that it's not going to work anymore.

One of the things that makes a good, healthy relationship so scary is that trusting is the opposite of what you have learned to do. You must trust that the person you care about will not want to hurt you, and you must show some of yourself. This is the beginning of getting to know someone in a very real way. Trust also means that you will not abuse your partner's feelings and that she will be able to show them to you. It goes both ways.

Second, trust means honesty: The other person will say what he means and mean what he says, and you will do likewise. Honesty allows you to trust the other person not to deliberately lie to you. When you reciprocate, this helps give substance to your relationship. You will know when you reach out that your hand will touch a solid arm, belonging to someone you can depend on. Your relationship won't be "fly by night," and you won't be confused.

Third, trust means that your partner will not willfully hurt you, and that you will not willfully hurt her. If it does happen, you will want to discuss ways to make sure it doesn't happen again. We cannot always know, when getting to know another person, what will be hurtful. It is extremely important to be able to say, "It hurt me when you said that," and for the other person to say, "It's important for me to know that; I don't want to hurt you. I will try hard not to let it happen again."

For many, trust means the promise of no physical abuse. I get angry every time I hear that an adult had such terrible childhood experiences that when we talk about trust, it automatically means they want to be rid of this fear. Physical abuse is inexcusable in any relationship. Therefore, it is non-negotiable.

Fourth, trust means the freedom to be yourself without being judged. It means that you do not have to walk on eggshells, that you can be who you are, and that the other person can be who he is. You are both okay. Not judging yourself and not being judged is a whole new experience, glorious and exhilarating. It is also scary as hell.

Fifth, trust means stability. There is certainty about the other person and about the relationship. It means that tomorrow's behavior will be similar to yesterday's, that you can count on things, and you can plan. It means you know that if you have plans to go somewhere on Saturday, when Saturday comes you will be able to do it. Stability, being very inconsistent with your childhood experiences, may be difficult to learn and to accept in another person.

Sixth, trust means commitment to the relationship, to the degree that the couple has agreed to be committed to the relationship. If your partner has said, "I will see only you; you are the only one with whom I am going to bed," you need to be able to believe it. Likewise, if you have offered the same thing, you need to behave accordingly.

Last, trust means that confidences will be kept. You won't have to worry about anyone else knowing your secrets. Neither will you share the secrets of your partner. It is especially important, when you have an argument, to know that these confidences will not be used against you.

Because trust is different for different people, it can mean whatever a couple decides it means to them, individually and together.

The facets of trust I have discussed here, although essential to a healthy relationship, are difficult to build. Trusting another person doesn't happen overnight, and you needn't criticize yourself because you find it difficult. Perhaps one of the easiest ways a couple can begin to trust each other is to discuss the difficulties they have with trust and acknowledge that it is something to aim for. They need to commit themselves to working on trust on a step-by-step basis as the relationship develops. It is very important for you to recognize that trust is not something you can automatically give to another person in the depth that has been discussed here. It is important for you to know that developing trust is an essential part of the process of building a healthy relationship. At this stage, you may only hear the words and not have any idea of how to put them into practice. This is not unusual, but eventually you will learn to trust.

ACOA Myth

"We will do everything together—we will be as one."

TRUTH: In the real world, couples spend time together, alone and with friends.

Boundaries

Adult children of alcoholics have difficulty respecting the boundaries of others, and recognizing what their own boundaries are.

You grew up in an environment where boundaries were very confusing. It was difficult to identify the respective roles of mother and father. It was hard to know if you were the child, or the mother or the father.

This confusion raises many questions. Whose pain did you feel? Was it yours? Was it your mother's? Was it your father's? Where did you end and somebody else begin?

What about privacy? What things belonged to you and could not be violated? Was your privacy invaded, even in the bathroom?

What were the limitations of good taste? What is appropriate behavior? What is inappropriate behavior?

Now that you are an adult, how do you decide if you are doing something reasonable or violating someone else's rights?

Perplexing statements and questions often come up in discussions with ACOAs.

"He hugged me. I felt violated. Am I wrong to feel that way?"

"I let myself in because her door was unlocked. Why did she get so bent out of shape?"

"I enjoyed the evening and invited him in for coffee. What right did he have to move in on me on the first date?"

"I worry that I will offend you. I always say the wrong thing."

"I clutch when I'm asked something personal. Isn't that my business?"

There is much confusion about what is intimacy and what is an invasion of boundaries. A lot of checking out is in order before you act. For example, don't do me a favor by cleaning my room unless you know I would consider it a favor. Don't insist on paying the bill after I've offered to split it, unless you know I am not invested in paying my own way. So many serious misunderstandings arise from not knowing where the other person's boundaries are. They are different for different people, and ACOAs, who tend to have rigid boundaries, don't understand this.

In a healthy relationship, partners try to let each other know what their boundaries are. They discuss them before the fact whenever possible, but if not then, later. For example, "I knew you meant well when you cleaned my room, but I felt enraged. That is my space, and although I would prefer it neat, it has to be my problem if it isn't."

A simple act for one person can be a major issue for another. Respecting and understanding boundaries is part of the process of becoming closer.

Boundaries and barriers are different. There is a private space that belongs to me and me alone. It is not that I choose to shut you out. It is rather that my space needs to be respected, if I am to be fully myself and fully functional.

For many, violation of that space causes irritability and a variety of physical symptoms. I develop symptoms of suffocation if my private space is violated. Others have different reactions. Some have a greater need for space and privacy than others. The issue needs to be talked about, in order to be respected and not misunderstood.

ACOA Myth

"You will instinctively anticipate my every need, desire and wish."

TRUTH: In the real world, if needs, desires and wishes are not clearly communicated, it is unlikely they will be fulfilled.

Expectations

You have learned in the process of growing up with alcoholism that it is not in your best interest to have expectations. If you have an expectation, you will, at the least, be disappointed or, at most, devastated. It depends on what the promise is and how much it means to you. Unfulfilled promises run all the way from, "I'll buy you an ice cream cone," to "I'll send you to college."

You learned that the only way to protect yourself is not to expect anything from anybody. It's a rough way to live, but it's safe. You cut your losses.

But—that ever-present "but"—you also cut your gains.

Healthy relationships involve expectations. Not only do they involve expectations, they involve a shared commitment to fulfill them. The shared part is very important, because it means that you have to tell your partner what you want, and there is an agreement to attempt to meet your needs. To want flowers for your birthday and then become devastated if you don't get them is not fair to your partner, if he had no idea you expected flowers. If he knew and didn't fulfill your expectations, it is important to talk about it, because it may be a signal of difficulty in the relationship.

Many people want their partners to please them by being mind readers. That is a setup, and comes out of your fears and your questions about whether you are worth anything. If he anticipates your desires when you don't ask, you don't have to suffer over the issue of your value. If he doesn't and you don't ask, you can then put yourself down and lock in your negative feelings about yourself.

If you decide that you will express your desires and they are fulfilled, that is wonderful. But you will probably find the situation stressful, because it is unfamiliar. The body does not differentiate between distress (bad) and eu-stress (good), and you, as a result, may be inclined to sabotage the relationship if it is going too smoothly. That is a response to reduce the stress, but there is the risk that you will once again begin to judge yourself negatively. After all, if you were a good person, you wouldn't do that. Good things take getting used to. Give yourself a break by allowing some time for the adjustment.

If you make your wishes clear and they are not met, it is important to understand what is going on. If the desire seems reasonable to you and it was not met, you need to find out why. You need to check it out. You may not have been clear. Your partner may not be listening to you. Your partner may be caring about you in terms of himself and not in terms of you. You may have made a demand that he could not fulfill. You might say: "If you care about me and do not express it in ways that are meaningful to me, your caring is not useful to me. It does not enhance me; it only enhances you." Once this is understood, if there is no attempt to accommodate your needs, it is a sign that the relationship is not developing in a healthy way. Either your demands are too great for your partner to meet, or your partner is too self-centered to accommodate you. This is important for you to know regardless of how the relationship is progressing. If you require a lot of nurture, you will not be satisfied in a relationship with someone who is aloof. It simply won't work.

Mutually agreed-upon expectations are essential to a healthy relationship. Explaining away continual disappointment will not get you what you want. People do disappoint those they care about, even in healthy relationships. But it does not happen often.

Many ACOAs do not know what a reasonable expectation is. *Is it reasonable for me to ask him to come to my door, rather than sit in the car and wait for me to come out? Is it reasonable for me to want him to wear a tie if we go out to dinner? Is it reasonable for me to ask her to share some of the expenses?* A typical reaction is: *Since I don't know what a reasonable expectation is, and since I don't want to look like a jerk, perhaps I should just keep my mouth shut and see what happens.*

That attitude may have some validity, but it is also a way to avoid confronting an even bigger fear. Confronting the discomfort is a big step toward developing healthy intimacy. Couples develop their own norms and fulfill mutual expectations. But first, they need to be expressed and discussed.

ACOA Myth

"If I am not in complete control at all times, there will be anarchy."

TRUTH: In the real world, one is in charge of one's life and takes control of situations as needed, by conscious decision and agreement. There are also times to share control and times to give up control.

Control

"If I am not in control, everything will fall apart." You learned that lesson very early. You controlled your life as best you could, because without some order there would be anarchy.

What are the implications of this approach to control in a relationship? Healthy relationships are not power struggles. They involve give-and-take, and shared responsibility. They also involve not having to do everything all by yourself.

To you these are just words. "I moved without asking for help from anyone!" Ann says emphatically. "Many of my friends offered to help, but I was determined to do it myself. I don't want to owe anybody anything. And nobody would care for my things the way I do."

She feels that if she accepts help, she loses control of her life. Her possessions will be ruined, and she will be forever obligated.

There is also the fear of being dependent. "If I let him help me this time, and he doesn't disappoint me, when something else comes up, I may ask him again, and pretty soon I'll become dependent on him to take care of me. Then I will no longer be able to take care of myself and I'll be stuck." This attitude implies that not being in charge at all times will lead to devastation when the inevitable abandonment occurs.

She also does not know how to share: "I know how to do it all," or, "I don't know how to do anything. Balancing responsibility is unfamiliar to me. I don't know how to do it. It may look as if I want to run everything, or as if I run away from doing my part, but it may have to do with not understanding how to work out a balance."

This is something else that needs to be talked about in very specific terms. When your partner says, "It upsets me that every time you say I can do something for you, I know you have a backup in case I let you down," an answer might be, "It has nothing to do with you. I need a little time to accept the idea that I am not in this alone, and can give up a little control without being devastated."

An exchange such as this is double-edged, because the need for approval and fear of abandonment are so strong in ACOAs that they give up emotional control. They fight for situational control, but give up their emotional selves. While declaring, "I don't need you," they don't sleep if they don't hear from you.

This kind of conflict is exhausting and requires a lot of discussion and time to process within the relationship. With work, however, it can be eased.

ACOA Myth

"If we really love each other, we will stay together forever."

TRUTH: In the real world, people stay together and people separate for many reasons. You can love someone and still terminate a relationship.

Loyalty

ACOAs are very loyal people and offer it in all relationships. Loyalty, while an integral part of a healthy relationship, has some limitations. Loyalty is best based on a mutual decision about the limits of the relationship. Both parties decide together whether or not they want a monogamous relationship. They discuss the areas in which they feel insecure, so that the other person will not carelessly push the wrong button.

For example, if you panic when someone is five minutes late, and your partner has no sense of time, an accommodation must be worked out. If both parties respect the needs and wishes of the other, accommodations can be found. "I'll call if I'm running late," or, "Give me fifteen minutes leeway."

ACOAs tend to carry loyalty to an extreme. They remain in relationships they know to be destructive to them. If problems cannot be worked out, it is not a good idea to stay in the continuing fantasy that they can be resolved. That is replaying the childhood wish that life will be wonderful if only. . . . It didn't work then. It won't work now.

Loyalty in ACOAs is also a modeled behavior. Families enmeshed in alcoholism rarely break up until some semblance of sobriety is achieved. They stay together through thin and thinner. As a result, it is easier for you to stay with someone, even after the relationship is no longer working, than to walk away. "How can you be so callous as to hurt another person?" you ask yourself. But you dismiss the ways in which you are being hurt. You invalidate yourself.

Another aspect of this extreme loyalty comprises a strong desire not to experience the pain of loss. Very often, an ACOA will have resolved all of the issues involved in ending a relationship that has become toxic. All the air has been taken out of the fantasy balloons on both the intellectual and emotional levels, and yet they do not act. "I'm still stuck! I can't move. What is wrong with me? I'm not afraid of being alone. I know I can manage. Why can't I get unstuck?"

You will have to go through a mourning period after a relationship ends. Entering into a new relationship immediately only puts it off and interferes with the new relationship. There is no way to avoid experiencing the loss. There is no way to avoid the pain. It is a part of the growth process.

In a relationship, you need to understand and be willing to work on appropriate limits to loyalty. Decide in advance what the limits are and commit yourself to remain aware of them. Recognize when you exceed them, and when something else is operating that is not in your best interest. When you start rationalizing, be aware of what you are doing; remember, it goes back to your early tapes. But, with work, you can change.

ACOA Myth

"My partner will never take me for granted, and always be supportive and noncritical."

TRUTH: In the real world, things do not always go smoothly, but you always have a right to your feelings.

Validation

One of the things an ACOA needs most is to have his feelings validated. In your alcoholic family, your feelings were never validated. On the contrary, they were discounted with "You don't really feel that way. It's not okay to feel that way." So you start feeling peculiar about whether it is okay to feel this way or that way. You need someone who will validate your feelings—not necessarily your behavior, but your feelings.

You need someone to whom you can say, "Gee, that really made me angry. I really wanted to act like that. I really wanted to do this." And you need someone to reply, "I can appreciate those feelings. They are valid." Nobody comes into counseling, nobody goes for help, who has been validated. So it's extremely important, whatever feelings are expressed, for a partner of an ACOA to validate them. "Sure, you feel that way. Absolutely. That's the way that you feel. You might want to look at it, you might want to feel differently about it. I see it differently, but it's okay to feel however you feel, and it's good for our relationship to let me know what that feeling is. The sharing makes us closer."

The sharing of feelings helps make you closer if you have established a safe climate where sharing feelings is okay. In some circumstances, the validation of feelings is critical to the development of a healthy relationship. That is, lack of validation by a partner can get in the way.

A rather extreme example of this occurred recently. A client of mine, the daughter of an alcoholic mother, is in her second marriage, to a man who has been in recovery from alcoholism for about eight months. She is not an alcoholic herself, but she is addicted to sugar. This was a difficult time in her life because her mother was dying of cancer, a long and difficult process. In addition to brain tumors and generalized cancer, her mother was suffering from advanced alcoholism. Joanie wanted to help her mother.

Although her mother had never consistently served her needs, in order for Joanie to feel good about herself, she needed to be there for her mother. If this meant visiting her mother in the hospital every night, or visiting her regularly when she was at home, it was important to Joanie that she do it. For her own sense of herself, she could not walk away from what she considered her responsibility at that time.

Joanie's husband reacted negatively to this situation. Before her mother became ill, she was a constant thorn in their sides. She did everything she could to destroy their relationship, and even her daughter. Not only that, now she was taking away the precious little time the couple had together. He was very hostile about it. "I don't like you going to visit your mother every night," he said. "We never see each other. What kind of relationship do we have?" He was very angry and jealous. You might even say he was behaving like a selfish little boy.

Her response to his behavior was very defensive. "Your attitude really stinks," she said. "My mother will be dead before long, and I need to do this for her. You and I have the rest of our lives to spend together. It is unfair of you to begrudge me this time. Your lack of understanding of my needs is absolutely appalling."

The yelling went back and forth. They were in constant conflict. She felt justified in her position, and he felt justified in his. Neither one was validating the other.

The reality here is that they do not really disagree, and that the situation was terrible. The mother's illness did take away the precious little time they had together, and it was unfortunate and uncomfortable for all of them. Joanie was spending a great deal of time with her mother, and still not getting validated. The fact that her mother was dying did not serve any of Joanie's needs. So, once again, Joanie was giving and giving.

It would be ideal if her husband were in a stage of his own development where he could be supportive to her, but he was not. It would also be ideal if Joanie were in a stage of her own recovery where she did not have to devote herself totally to her mother, but she was not. If this couple were able to validate each other, the friction that existed between them would virtually disappear.

Joanie needed to say to her husband, "I agree with you. You are absolutely right. My mother is a pain in the ass. You and I are not spending enough time together, and she is taking away from the precious little time that we have together. Yes, I am resentful that I need to do this for myself, and that I haven't reached a point where I can be more reasonable in serving my mother's needs." If she were able to validate his feelings instead of defending her mother and defending her right to be there for her mother, they would not be in conflict. She would not have to behave any differently. She would be capable of saying, "I wish I were able to be less compulsive about this, and that I could serve both our needs and my mother's needs. I wish I were further along in my growth."

Once she had validated his feelings, he would no longer have to feel as defensive and then neither would she. He could then validate her feelings with something like, "I am glad you understand how I feel. It really makes me angry, but I can also understand how there will be no living with you if you do not do what you see as your responsibility right now."

Validation can be the key to getting through a crisis. Without validation, it is quite possible that the damage done to the relationship will be irreparable. She won't be able to forgive him for his "stinking thinking," and he won't be able to forgive her for abandoning him when he wanted and needed her.

This story does have a happy ending. They did validate each other, and the pressure on their relationship eased. One afternoon, when Joanie was visiting her mother but unobserved by her, she overheard her mother tell the nurse things she had never told Joanie. She told the nurse how much she loved Joanie, how proud she was of her, and how appreciative she was of her care and attention.

When Joanie told her mother she had overheard the conversation, they cried together, shared the depth of their love, and her mother was then able to die well because she had finally begun to live well.

Validation does not mean agreement. It means respect for similarities and differences. It is the cornerstone of good, solid communication. Without validation, communication is merely a power play.

9

Issues of Sexuality

Same-Sex Relationships

ACOAs' concerns about having healthy, intimate relationships are the same in same-sex relationships as those in opposite-sex relationships. These concerns, however, are compounded because of the difficulties involved in being homosexual in a culture that is largely homophobic. Though the issues are the same for those involved in same-sex relationships, they are exaggerated by the larger culture. The ability to share oneself openly, honestly and freely, without fear of the consequences, is impaired by living in an alcoholic home. Learned defensive behaviors have to be turned around in order to have a healthy relationship, especially for the homosexual, whose need for defenses has been reinforced in the mainstream.

Clients I see who are involved in same-sex relationships fall roughly into three categories. First, there are those who have been aware of their sexual preference for as long as they can remember, and have spent time and energy dealing with, and coming to grips with, what that reality means to them. For these people, the struggle is the same as for those involved in opposite-sex relationships, except that the struggle may be more pronounced.

The second group consists of those who are just becoming aware of their sexuality. They are people of all ages, who have just admitted on a conscious level that they have a same-sex preference. Many of the symptoms they have carried with them during their lives begin to disappear. One symptom is depression, which, for many, once they have acknowledged their sexual preference, begins to abate. This group is very similar to the blossoming adolescent who is becoming aware of himself as a sexual being for the first time and is excited about it, afraid of it, and has to test it out by going through many experiences to find out how things work. This person experiences the great joy and great pain of the adolescent extremes. The age may seem inappropriate, but one must go through all of these stages, regardless of when the awareness hits. An additional complication may arise from the fact that many of these people are married, have children and have complicated lives in the heterosexual world. They need to make decisions as to how best to handle the rest of their lives.

The third group consists of those who have decided that, because they have had such horrendous relationships with the opposite sex, starting invariably with the parent of the opposite sex, that they do not want to repeat the experience. As a result, they decide they will become involved only in same-sex relationships. Needless to say, this does not work. Whether or not an individual has or does not have a penis does not mean that he will not have the same personality type as that of those you have been involved with before, or as your mother or father. It has been my experience that people who run to same-sex relationships as a way of avoiding repetition of the horrors of their past run the risk of picking the same personality type they picked in heterosexual relationships.

The important consideration here is that they come to grips with the underlying issues from which they are fleeing. A healthy choice of a partner is possible, regardless of sex.

The essentials for intimacy for lesbians and gay men who are ACOAs are no different from those in opposite-sex relationships. The difficulties are compounded by society, but the struggle is the same.

General Sexual Issues

What happens to a couple in the sexual part of their relationship is symptomatic of everything else that is happening. The issues present here show up in other places, as sexual intimacy is one means of communicating and sharing oneself.

The questions I hear are endless: What's normal? How long does it take to be in synch sexually? Is it a good idea to be honest about sexual experiences and attitudes? Am I any good? Am I good enough? Can sex be fun? Is there a lot to know? How do I keep from holding back? If I'm free, will I be more vulnerable? Am I seen only as a sex object? Do I have to give up control?

Ask the questions. Read the literature. Talk about sex with your partner. Find out what works for you. The couple decides what is normal, and it is a shared learning experience. Discuss the things that get in the way. Some are easily resolved, while others that are historically based will take time to overcome. The parental relationship you saw in your childhood was distorted in many ways, including the sex life. It may have influenced you in ways that make your sexual adjustment difficult, and leave you with questions about your sexuality. You may be as confused about your sexuality as you are about other aspects of your life.

Celebration of yourself in any aspect of your life is difficult. So you need to take a look at what sex means to you. One client said, "My parents fought. Then they had sex, and everything was fine. I always understood sex was a way to end an argument, but I knew there had to be something wrong with that." The missing piece is that there was no resolution of the conflict. Sex was used as a way to avoid problem-solving, rather than to enhance the relationship.

Here is another example: "My mother told me having sex was a woman's duty. It wasn't pleasurable, but it put men to sleep. I don't want that for myself, but I feel guilty if I don't perform when asked."

To resolve these feelings, a couple should talk about their sexual relationship, especially their expectations.

Again, "Sex was always a control and power issue in my house. It was linked to physical abuse. I am so afraid it will happen to me that I remain celibate."

This is a deep and serious problem that needs to be worked out with a therapist. A caring partner can help, but more is probably necessary in a case like this.

Many men and women have reported an inability to climax. When explored, it becomes clear that there is a holding back in other areas of the relationship as well. It is a fear of being vulnerable, because being vulnerable has always meant pain. It is a very clear demonstration of how the lack of risk-taking can limit an experience.

Alcoholism results in even more complex problems. Martha related the following: "My father cheated on my mother, and my two alcoholic husbands cheated on me. As a result, I don't want to get sexually involved with anyone, because I don't think I could go through that again. I think that's probably one of the reasons why I have gained all of this weight."

A discussion of alcoholics, and the need for alcoholics to have enablers, will not work with this lady. She has decided on a deep level that it is her own lack of desirability that caused her husbands to be unfaithful. Somehow she also finds herself responsible for her father's philandering. Putting on a lot of weight is a way to avoid the issue: If no one finds her sexually desirable, then she does not have to deal with the issue. Fortunately, she is working with a good therapist who will help her discover her sexual self, and recognize that the difficulty lies not in her lack of desirability, but in her selection of a partner. As she changes and grows, her choices will be more compatible with what she really wants.

In healthy relationships, decisions about monogamy evolve as the relationship progresses. When people are first getting to know each other, it is not unusual for them to be involved with others, too. As the relationship develops, they make decisions about exclusivity. When alcoholism is involved, the rules get shifted. Early on, there is monogamy, but as the disease progresses, it is not unusual for the alcoholic to seek out other partners.

Another problem I hear is, "The only place that I feel powerful and in control is in the bedroom. I begin to believe that that is the only thing that I have to offer another person. It makes me very sad." Take heart. If you are capable of being a good partner in the bedroom, you are capable of being a good partner in other aspects of the relationship. What goes on in the bedroom generalizes to other places.

Being technically good is something else again. If you are merely technically good, we are not talking about a relationship. In a relationship, emotional investment and caring are primary. You have probably not given yourself enough credit for being able to express your feelings. The bedroom may be a place where you can do that. Somehow, you have used your freedom in this area as another means of beating yourself rather than using it to celebrate yourself. The opposite is also true. "I love my husband very much. He is very dear to me, and we are good friends as well as being man and wife. I want to share my entire life with him, but I don't want to make love to him. In my house, lovemaking was like violation. I am terrified that this is what it will evolve into."

When I talked to Lynn about lovemaking, it became clear that she was talking about intercourse. When I asked her if she enjoyed having her husband say affectionate things to her, or having him put his arms around her, she said, "Oh, yes." When I asked her if they just ever held hands when they went for a walk, she said she enjoyed that, too. The reality here is that they make love in a variety of ways. Because of her childhood experience, she mistakenly equated intercourse with lovemaking and was not able to see the larger picture. As she became aware of the many aspects of lovemaking that she shared with her husband, she was free from the notion that she would repeat her parents' negative relationship.

The variations on these themes are endless. The underlying problem is, "I am afraid of being close." As you work out other aspects of allowing yourself to be close, the sexual part will work out, too. If you find that this area still presents difficulties, it may be time to work with a professional who can help you overcome them. Sex is only one aspect of a relationship. Yet, the shared closeness can be very important and very significant. Overcoming the distortions resulting from your childhood is important to your personal growth. Remember, here, too, you do not have enough information to answer all of your questions. This is probably a large part of what is getting in your way.

Take it easy on yourself. Take it easy on your partner. Once again, the message is—go slowly. In fact, no aspect of a healthy relationship happens overnight. The potential may be immediately obvious, but a relationship is a day-to-day developing experience.

Incest

Although incest is not necessarily part of a family system affected by alcohol, it is present frequently enough to warrant discussion.

Incest is a much more widespread manifestation of dysfunction in families than we have yet begun to explore. The family system where alcoholism is present is a fertile ground for it to occur. There is no doubt that ACOAs who are survivors of incest have an additional dimension of great difficulty in establishing healthy, intimate relationships.

Although incest occurs between mothers and sons, fathers and sons, and among siblings, the most common form is between fathers and daughters. The latter will therefore be the focus of discussion here.

Incest can be overt or covert. Overt incest is defined simply as sexual contact within the family. Though not necessarily actual intercourse, it involves sexual contact in one form or another. The most usual forms involve fondling of breasts and genitals, use of the child to masturbate and oral sex. Covert incest involves many of the same dynamics, but there is no actual physical contact.

Many of the conditions present in other incestuous families are also present in the alcoholic family system. Certainly the taboo against talking about what is going on exists, as does isolation of the family. In many incestuous families, as in many families where alcoholism is present, one of the daughters, usually the oldest, has taken over many of the responsibilities of running the household and looking after the younger children. Fulfilling her father sexually may be looked upon as an extension of the role of "little mother." There is a greater likelihood that this behavior will occur if there is a role reversal between mother and daughter. This role reversal happens often when the mother is chronically ill or alcoholic.

How does incest relate to later intimate relationships? First, the ability to trust, which has been discussed earlier, is destroyed. The most outrageous aspect of an incestuous relationship precludes a "safe harbor." The child has no one to run to.

I have asked many clients who were incest survivors why they didn't tell someone. "Why did you wait until your late twenties or early thirties to let someone know that you were abused as a child?" Invariably, the response is, "What good would it have done? If I had told my mother, it would have made no difference. She would not have believed me, or dealt with it. It would only have made circumstances worse. I certainly could not have gone to anyone outside the family." These children had no place to turn, no one to help them.

So here is a circumstance where you found out at a very early age that there was no one to trust. You certainly could not trust the parent who was sexually abusing you, nor the other parent. So you learned that the only one you could trust was yourself. Because of this early and generally continuing experience, what you learned is quite clear. First, you learned from living with alcoholism that you cannot trust, because if you do, you will be hurt. Moreover, you learned that there is no one to trust. This early experience greatly exaggerates the difficulty you have later on in trusting someone in an intimate relationship.

Second, incest affects your present sexual behavior. It is not unusual for incest survivors in a sexual relationship with another person to flash back on the horrors of their childhood. They will flash back while in a loving relationship to the experiences of childhood, and this causes problems.

Third, some survivors of incest believe they can only obtain love and affection through sex. If the sexual experience with the father was pleasurable, they see themselves as having tremendous sexual powers. This fantasy distorts the development of a healthy, intimate relationship. It also leads to idealizing men.

Fourth, many decide to involve themselves in same-sex relationships, because they never again want to face the dreaded penis. However, the other distortions and difficulties continue to come into play. The difficulty of trusting does not go away because you are involved in a same-sex relationship. Neither parent could be trusted. So this, in and of itself, is not a solution to the problem.

When incest is covert, rather than overt, some of the same circumstances apply. The father treats the little girl like his wife or his love object. He is jealous of her suitors and makes subtle sexual innuendoes. She does many of the things that, in other circumstances, his wife might do. The result here is somewhat different. The child doesn't feel abused: She feels idealized. She also idealizes the parent, which makes it extremely difficult for her to relate to other men. Because her daddy is the perfect love object, she seeks out men who are like her father in an attempt to replace him.

This is a very difficult bond to break. How can you want to pull away from someone who makes you feel so special? How can you find someone else who will adore you unconditionally? The pain of working this through is excruciating. Although your sexual fantasies have not been experienced in the real world, they may be powerful enough to keep you from appreciating someone else. It is a mistake to underestimate the hold of a covertly incestuous relationship.

The child's reaction to the violation of incest is on a very deep level and must be addressed on that level. With many of the issues concerned with living in an alcoholic home, the mere flushing them out by discussion with people who understand, who have had the same experiences, goes a long way toward resolving them.

However, this is not usually the case with incest, so it is very important to work this out with a professional. You must come to grips with the guilt and shame that incest survivors feel. Somehow there is always the sense that "I am responsible." "Why does it happen to me and not to my sister?" Or, "If it happened to both my sister and me, why didn't I do anything to prevent it?" Since children are compliant in an alcoholic family system, when they reflect back, they see themselves as going along with it, as being willing, as not fighting against incest. They feel responsibility, which is neither valid nor true.

Today, you would not permit this kind of behavior, but the adult you are now did not exist when you were a child. Take a look at yourself as a small child, and tell her she is guilty for what happened. It is not possible. Relieving the guilt, however, is not as easy as intellectually understanding that you could not have been responsible. For many who have taken over the role of the mother, it is even a protection of her. This is similar to a child taking a beating for other siblings or the mother, so the others will not have to endure it. At any rate, you were not responsible. The guilt you feel because you were powerless to stop incest from happening is inappropriate. You had no choice, because you knew no alternatives.

The shame you feel is also inappropriate. The sense of yourself as a disgusting person, as someone who experienced incest because you were disgusting, is not true. You were not disgusting. You were a victim, and you were trapped. You need to work out these feelings of shame in order to feel good about yourself. Otherwise, your shame will get in the way of developing a healthy sexual relationship, where you can celebrate your body as wholesome and good.

Do not try to do this alone. Today there are many therapists who specialize in working with incest survivors. It is important to work with someone who is not only sensitive to the alcoholic family system, but sensitive to what happens to children who have been sexually abused. I cannot emphasize this strongly enough, because the pathology of sexual abuse is deeper than the results of alcoholism. I am not, however, minimizing the pain and struggle that one has for the rest of one's life, as a result of living in an alcoholic home.

You are not alone. You will be flabbergasted, once you begin to share your experience, at how many others have also been through it. Just as keeping the secret of living with alcoholism was not to your advantage, keeping the secret of incest works against you. Sharing this secret can be the start of setting you free. It is in no way a reflection on you that you had a parent who was sick enough to use you in this way.

10

So You Love an ACOA

It is not surprising to me that you have fallen in love with an ACOA. ACOAs are the most loving and loyal people around. They offer more than any other group of people I know. I am certain that you, too, are impressed at what they are able to offer in a relationship, or you would not be involved with an ACOA.

A relationship with an ACOA is also very confusing to you, I am sure. Just when you think everything is fine, just when you think that the relationship is the most fantastic, beautiful, intense, intimate, exciting experience of your life, your ACOA will back off. You will not know what hit you. When you think you have a thorough understanding, he or she will do something contrary. Many times your ACOA will react in ways that seem peculiar to you, in ways that make absolutely no sense. Naturally, you will find yourself confused. This section is designed to help you better understand what goes on in your partner's mind. More often than not, your partner's peculiar behavior has nothing to do with you, although your behavior may trigger it.

I am not telling you to behave differently unless it is useful for both you and your partner for mutual behaviors to be modified. This discussion is to let you know what is going on, so that your reactions in a given situation will be more responsive to what is really happening to your ACOA.

Understanding what makes your partner tick will be very useful. When ACOAs respond peculiarly to situations, it is often because they do not know how to react differently. They do not know that there are other options, and they do not know what is appropriate. Many times I hear, "How could I do the right thing, if I don't know what right is?" It may be that there are no "rights." But there are certainly responses which are appropriate.

For example, people who have typical backgrounds can more easily confront others than those who come from alcoholic homes. If you are in a restaurant and the person at the next table is smoking, which is offensive to you, it is natural to ask him to put out the cigarette or blow the smoke in another direction. Your ACOA, on the other hand, may start squirming in the chair or become terrified. Your ACOA has many feelings that would never occur to you. Depending on the history, there might be a great deal of fear, along with a sense of protection toward you, and an overwhelming sense of gratitude to you for taking care of the situation.

Confrontation is never easy for ACOAs. And it is especially difficult for them to confront you in an intimate relationship. It is also not easy for them to observe you confronting someone else, regardless of how insignificant the confrontation is. I am not saying don't do it. Simply be aware of the possibility that the reaction may be something different from what you anticipate.

Several bottom-line fears children of alcoholics have will affect their responses to you. Your understanding can help alleviate them. I am not suggesting that all ACOAs have all of these fears, but they probably have one or more of them.

Fear Number 1: "I am afraid that I will hurt you."

This fear results from the fact that ACOAs are not taught how to speak and behave appropriately. The behaviors they develop result from watching others. Although many of them do behave appropriately, and many are very clever, charming and articulate, they don't really believe they are. They are afraid they will violate your boundaries. They are afraid that, without meaning to, they will say something or behave in a way that will be hurtful to you. If they do these things, it is not deliberate, but because they don't know there are alternatives. As a result, ACOAs tend not to be spontaneous, and you may frequently sense that they are holding back. This is something worth checking out. You might say to the ACOA you are involved with, "Let's take the risk. If you do or say something that hurts me, I will tell you, just as I want you to tell me if I do something that hurts you. This is the only way we can really get to know each other and be attentive to each other's feelings."

Fear Number 2: "The person you see does not exist."

Adult children of alcoholics are so concerned with trying to look and behave normally that, in many ways, they fabricate the person they would like to be, or the kind of person they think you would like them to be. Chances are, this mask does not work as well as they think it does. You are probably able to see who he or she really is, and that is who you are attracted to. This is difficult for the ACOA to believe. The outside looks good. While outside behavior is exciting and interesting, however, inside there is fear and trembling. Although both parts of the person are valid and true, the ACOA feels that the outer side that looks confident is not real, and the inner self that is frightened is the real self. Therefore, you have been fooled into believing the inner self does not exist. Ideally, it would be good for the ACOA to express fears and have self-confidence. Though both parts of the person exist, the ACOAs are not sure you see them as they really are. Worse yet, if you did, you would no longer find them interesting and attractive. The desirable, interesting, attractive, intelligent, charming, sexual person with whom you believe you are involved does not really exist in the ACOA's mind.

Fear Number 3: "I'll lose control of my life."

"My mother was out of control; my father was out of control; and they were in control of me. What a terrible thought! What a horrible memory! I cannot let it happen again. Since I am so unsure of myself, I am afraid that if I get close to you, I will defer to you in all things. I will let you make all the decisions, because I am afraid I will make the wrong ones. I really don't want to do that, but I am uncertain I will be strong enough not to give in. Therefore, I will back away from you, or make preposterous demands that you cannot possibly fulfill in order to prove to myself that you want control."

To counteract this problem, you have to sit down as a couple and work on decision making. ACOAs do not have a strong sense of what alternatives and consequences are. Discuss the options involved, and come to some mutual agreements. Your impatience at indecision, although certainly understandable, will not help your partner make a decision. You may have to allow time to work things through together, and find out if the ACOA has all of the information necessary to make the decision. You might need to say to your partner, "I am making this decision, because there is a time limit. However, that does not mean I am trying to control our relationship. It means only that a decision has to be made." Things that are shared up front are less frightening and can be viewed more realistically.

Fear Number 4: "It doesn't matter anyway."

This is a very defensive position. It comes from a depressed atti-tude learned in the alcoholic family system, which develops into a depressed lifestyle. When one is depressed, one feels that nothing really matters. This attitude is also somewhat protective: "If I decide that it doesn't matter anyway, then I will be less hurt if something goes wrong. If I allow it to matter, then I will be devastated if some-thing goes wrong." It is also a way of testing. An ACOA who has this attitude will test you repeatedly to be sure that you will not leave. You may have to confront your partner, saying, "This is a game. I care about you. You do not have to continue to test me." If you don't say anything, and the testing continues, eventually you will leave: You won't be able to handle it.

The testing, however, is not selfishness or wanting to put you through your paces. It comes from insecurity and a rather poor self-image, which only time can cure. Gradually, the defenses will ease up. "It doesn't matter" is akin to "I don't exist," and "If I am not around, you will forget all about me." This is a setup for you to con-tinue to prove that you care. Once you see it as such, you might ask, "How many times do I have to tell you?" "How much more do I need to show you?"

Fear Number 5: "It's not real."

Your ACOA may have said to you on many occasions, "This is not real. This is not really happening." He makes these statements when things are going well—when the relationship you share is something that you find so wonderful and so fine and so rare that you can hardly believe it. Not believing it is different from not seeing it as real. Not believing it involves real excitement and a sense of incredulousness:

"How lucky I am to have found this person with whom I can share and experience so much!" That's probably what you mean when you say, "This is not really happening to me. How fortunate I am!"

When your ACOA says, "This is not real," it means something different. For many ACOAs, growing up was so traumatic that this is the only reality they know. When life is going well, the circumstances are so unfamiliar they have a sense of unreality about them. So the effect is unsettling.

When you are walking on clouds and believe that your partner is right there beside you, he or she may do something to sabotage the relationship. All of a sudden, out of the blue, your ACOA will pick a fight with you or not answer your phone calls. This kind of thing makes absolutely no sense to you, and you feel pushed away. If things are that wonderful, they cannot be real, so the ACOA, in order to make them real, will use sabotage.

Since you now know this, you can feel a little less punched in the stomach. You can recognize that an unpleasant reaction does not have to do with you, but with the ACOA's learned responses. You might simply say, "I have not done anything. Things are good. Just try and relax and go slowly." If your ACOA runs away, chances are he or she will be back. You will probably need to do something in order to protect yourself, but realize that the rejection is only temporary. Your understanding will help keep the situation from getting more complicated.

When ACOAs realize what they have done, they feel very guilty and remorseful, and decide that you couldn't continue to love them anyway, because they are terrible people. If they weren't so terrible, they could enjoy things going well, and wouldn't get in the way of their own happiness, etc. If you can just roll with it, chances are you can ride this one out, too.

Fear Number 6: "You'll see how angry I am."

ACOAs learn to repress their anger. They learn as children that if they express anger like other kids do, it will only create more difficulty. As a result, many are filled with unresolved anger. There is a real fear that the anger felt towards their parents and their backgrounds will leak out in a relationship. They are afraid that their anger will be directed at you in inappropriate ways. They are also afraid that if you see the extent of that anger, it will frighten you away. This may or may not be true, according to your own reactions to anger, and to what degree you are concerned about other people's reactions to you.

Things happen in a relationship that will trigger off early experiences. It is important for you and your ACOA to know each other well. Then, when something happens which you don't understand on the face of it, you will realize that it relates back to childhood. When your ACOA reacts with inappropriate anger to a situation, chances are that the degree of anger does not relate to what is going on in the moment.

Sarah asked Tommy if he would move some branches that had fallen off her tree from her front yard to her backyard. They were too heavy for her to carry, and it was not difficult for him. He said he would be very happy to do it for her. When she returned from work and saw that it had not been done, she went into a rage. He was flabbergasted at how angry she was, but said, "I'm sorry. I forgot all about it, but I will get it done for you." It is clear that since she was ready to end the relationship over such a minor thing, she was overreacting. But, if you look at Sarah's reaction in the context of her being an ACOA, the incident has a great deal of meaning.

First, it was a struggle to ask him to do her a favor. It was very hard for her to say, "I need help with the work." She has learned not to ask for favors, because they were never granted. But, since she is working on this important relationship, she made a conscious decision to ask.

She is also overly concerned about what her neighbors will think if her yard is messy. This consciousness of other people's opinion of her indicates she is not yet secure with her opinion of herself. When Tommy forgot, she felt completely invalidated by him. Her reasoning went like this: If he really cared about me, he would recognize that I would not ask him to do anything that was not important to me, and he would not forget. Not forgetting to remove the wood means that he cares about me. Forgetting to remove the wood means that I am not as important to him as he pretends I am.

Certainly, the extent of her anger at him is inappropriate. There is cause for annoyance, but not for the rage that she feels. He was insensitive to her needs in taking her request so casually. He was responding to his own history, to the fact that he procrastinates.

This couple needs to discuss this incident thoroughly in order for the relationship to remain healthy. She needs to understand that every request will not automatically be responded to, even though it is difficult for her to ask. She also needs to understand that his procrastination is not a reflection of his feelings for her. If his behavior continues, and it is something that she cannot live with, then she may need to reassess the relationship. But, on the face of it, her reaction seems more powerful than the circumstance called for.

Tommy will have to learn that if he agrees to do something, he must do it on the terms of the person who asked him to do it. If he tells her, "Yes, I will do it for you," and understands her urgency, then it is unfair of him not to fulfill the request as it is asked. If he is not certain that he can do what is asked immediately, it is important for him to say, "I will do it for you, but I cannot promise that I will do it right now."

Communication and discussion of feelings are critical for ACOAs, and the people with whom they are involved. It is the only way to have a healthy relationship.

Fear Number 7: "I am ashamed of who I am."

You may be shocked when you become aware of how low an opinion the ACOA with whom you are involved has of himself. It may be nearly impossible for you to understand how this bright, charming, capable, lovable person can see himself as such SHIT! Though it makes no sense to you at all, it is real and a deep, dark secret.

The reason for this level of shame is that many ACOAs believe they were responsible for the dysfunction in their families. Many were told from the beginning, "Life was great until you came along." "If you weren't such a brat, I wouldn't be drinking." Not only did many believe that they were responsible for the alcoholism, but as they grew older and understood that alcoholism was a disease, they became disgusted with themselves because they were still angry with their parents and humiliated by their behavior.

The message they gave themselves was, "I must be a very disgusting person if I feel this way about a person who is sick."

It may be that your ACOA has not invited you to see her family, and you wonder why. This could be part of the reason. Your ACOA might be humiliated, while judging herself for feeling this way. At the same time, she is very concerned about what you think—whether you will continue to care if you know what the family situation is like. Although these feelings of responsibility and shame are inappropriate, that does not mean they don't exist. This lovely adult whom you have come to know and care about is still beating herself for childhood experiences over which she had no control. Your discovery of this secret causes fear in ACOAs. Once the secret is out in the open, it may lose some power. But the attitude is so deeply rooted, it perpetuates a sense of "If you really knew me, you wouldn't want to have anything to do with me."

Fear Number 8: "You will get to know me and find out that I am not lovable."

This fear is closely allied to shame. The feeling of not being lovable was learned in early childhood.

The child wanted to find a way to make things okay, to fix them. No matter what he did, it was not good enough. No matter how hard he tried, it did not matter. The child, a powerless victim of the situation, believed that there was something wrong with him because he could not find a way to fix it. If he were truly lovable, he would find a way to make life fine and happy once again. Many ACOAs have cried in my arms: "I tried to stop it, I tried to make it different, but I just couldn't. And the worst thing of all is that sometimes when my parents were fighting, I didn't even get in the middle of it, because I was terrified that I would be next. How could I be lovable if I was thinking about myself first?"

The truth is that the person you care about is lovable.

It will be hard for him to accept that. You will need to be patient. It takes time for a self-perception to change.

Fear Number 9: "I want to be comfortable."

The person you care about may back away from an involvement with you by using the argument, "I want to be comfortable." This may make absolutely no sense. The rationale goes something like this: "My whole life has been one series of emotional crises after another. I'm tired of it. I don't want it. I don't want to feel any more. Feelings are very disruptive to me. If I get involved with you, I'm bound to feel. I'm bound to feel ups and downs, and right now I have my whole life in order, and don't want to risk screwing it up. Getting involved with you would not allow me to maintain the even keel I'm on now. I will begin to care, and then I'll feel upset. I'll begin to feel a whole variety of things. I don't want that right now! I want to feel comfortable."

This attitude won't last long. It is a fantasy that many ACOAs have when they go through a level period. It won't last, not only because they are active, vibrant people, but because they have no frame of reference for it.

Being comfortable will become extremely boring, and they cannot sustain it. The reality is that the development of a healthy relationship will afford them a level of comfort that has not been experienced before. But that is a long process, requiring much hard work.

Fear Number 10: "You'll leave me anyway."

Your ACOA may be afraid to get involved because of fear of abandonment. The fear that the person with whom she is involved will walk out on her is absolutely terrifying. This fear is different from the fear of rejection. Fear of abandonment is much deeper: "If you abandon me and I am left all by myself, I will die."

This, too, has its roots in childhood, and not in the real world. It results in an initial fear of getting involved at all. But once the decision is made to become involved, you may find that your ACOA is very possessive, jealous and insecure where you are concerned. This disconcerting behavior comes from fear of abandonment. It is a big problem, because if this possessiveness gets out of hand, you may be forced to do exactly what your partner fears the most. It is therefore important for you to continue to reassure your ACOA that you do care, that you are not going to leave, but that it's important for you to have other people in your life. It is also important for your partner to have other people in her life. Rather than harming a relationship, other friends enhance it. You may need to reinforce this idea many, many times, at the same time being aware that the possessiveness comes from a very basic fear of abandonment.

You also need to be careful not to disappoint your partner. Other people react much more casually when you forget to call, or are an hour late. But ACOAs tend to overreact to this kind of behavior; they begin to panic. You need to understand this, so your relationship can develop, flourish and provide the security necessary to both of you.

You may be wondering at this point whether or not it's worth struggling with all the fears I have outlined. Try to bear a few things in mind. First, not all ACOAs suffer from all of these fears. Second, not all people are free from these fears, even though they did not grow up with alcoholism. Third, ACOAs' greatest difficulties are in the area of their relationship with themselves. Their greatest difficulty is the lack of ability to experience themselves as valuable and worthy and lovable. Their greatest assets are a capability of offering *you* the sense that *you* are valuable and worthy and lovable. There is much to be gained from being involved with an ACOA. The difficulties you face can be overcome if both members of the partnership are willing to work on them. With awareness and understanding come the potential for resolution of most difficulties.

Knowing the characteristics shared by many ACOAs can help give a direction to effect change. Being able to pinpoint areas of difficulty makes it easier to offer options to make the struggle for a healthier relationship that much easier.

11

Getting It All Together

1. Adult children of alcoholics guess at what normal is.

You have probably decided that you are not going to have the kind of relationship your parents had. Whatever else you do in your life, that is a no-no. However, you won't get off that easy!

Since you have decided that you will not have what you experienced at home, what will you have? Where will you get your role models? You got it! The media—*The Brady Bunch*—*Eight Is Enough*—or *Father Knows Best!* You might have picked a family down the block that does everything together and that you think is ideal. All of these are fantasies. If you have any of these notions about ideal family relationships, you have set yourself up for failure. At the very least, you will be disillusioned.

First, no woman can, for a sustained period of time, bake the bread, be an ideal mother, keep an immaculate house, maintain a career, be a sex object and helpmate, have no problems of her own, and always lend a willing ear. Neither can a man be a perfect father, pursue a career thirteen to fourteen hours a day, keep all the repairs up to date, be attentive and appreciative at all times, and pay the bills without a word of worry or complaint.

Because you decided this is the opposite of what happened at home, you try to be "perfect." The result of behaving this way is not sainthood and appreciation; it is burnout and resentment.

What is normal in a relationship is behavior that is reasonable and comfortable for you as a couple. Normalcy means discussing and working through behaviors that cause discomfort. People have different strengths and weaknesses, so there is no mold into which one must fit. A couple defines their own norms, according to what works for them.

Outside stresses will intervene and upset the balance, but you, as a couple, will address those issues as well. If you know couples who have relationships you admire, talk to them: Find out what works for them—then decide if any of it is useful to you.

2. Adult children of alcoholics have difficulty following a project through from beginning to end.

A relationship is very much like a project in that it involves a process. For the same reason that you have had difficulty following through on a project from beginning to end, you will have difficulty in developing a relationship. Keep in mind that healthy relationships develop slowly; they do not happen overnight. Remember the alcoholism in your family. It, too, developed slowly. Things that are good for you develop slowly as well.

It is important to recognize that in a relationship the critical part is the journey. The Alcoholics Anonymous slogans "Easy Does It" and "One Day at a Time" apply to relationships as well as to everything else. Though it is very hard to be patient, there is no other alternative. You cannot know everything about each other in a short time, no matter how intense you were in the beginning. It doesn't matter that you spent all day and all night together over a weekend. You cannot know what a long-term day-to-day relationship is like until you experience it. You need time to develop a healthy relationship.

When you were a child, you were completely vulnerable, trusting, and you gave all. That is what children do. As you got a little older, you learned how to hold back a little of yourself. That was important for your own survival. Now you say, "I will no longer give 100 percent. I will give maybe 80 percent or maybe 75 percent, but I am incapable of giving 100 percent." It is important for you to change your usual style of making a great emotional investment in the beginning. Instead, decide ahead of time on some limitations.

Other people do not have to make this kind of decision. It comes naturally to do it slowly; in the initial stages of the relationship, they invest 10 percent or 15 percent. As the relationship develops, the investment grows as well. It grows according to what both people put into it.

Do not start out at the end of the scale, where you give all that you have. Let your investment in the relationship develop naturally over time. During this process, you will reach a decision about how much is appropriate for you to give.

3. Adult children of alcoholics lie when it would be just as easy to tell the truth.

It is important to realize that you may lie automatically. This is not going to be useful if you want a healthy relationship. Chances are that you hold back on the truth with respect to your feelings, and not much else. Be careful that you don't set yourself up so your partner is suspicious of everything that comes out of your mouth. You might simply say, "Sometimes I am not honest in reporting the way I feel, but when I realize it, I want to be able to tell you at a later time that I didn't say what I meant." It could be helpful to write down the things you want to say. If you tend to be defensive and dishonest in situations where you want to be honest, write down what you want to say and then read it to your partner. "This is what I want to tell you. Let me just read it and we'll take it from there." You may be able to trust written communication more than the spontaneous words that come out of your mouth. As you become more comfortable and secure in the relationship, it will be easier to change your habit of not saying what you mean.

4. Adult children of alcoholics judge themselves without mercy.

Be aware of the fact that your inclination is to automatically find fault with yourself. Rather than finding fault with yourself or with your partner, try to look at issues and circumstances and make decisions on the basis of them. If you or your partner behave in ways that you are unhappy with, step back, take a look at the behavior, and try to understand what it means. If you can be objective, you will be able to look at the situation differently and judge it less. This will be a struggle, because your automatic inclination is to judge. Become fascinated with yourself and your responses. You are a very interesting person. The more you look at how you behave, the more skilled you will become in getting to know yourself. Of course, there is always the risk when you do this rather than judge, that you may really get to like yourself.

5. Adult children of alcoholics have difficulty having fun.

6. Adult children of alcoholics take themselves very seriously.

Playing and having fun are wonderful goals to strive for. In a relationship, it may be important for you to say, "I am learning how to play and how to have fun. I want to do this a lot, because as a child I never learned how. If you will initiate, I will follow. I do not even know how to think of fun things to do, but I will do my best to go along with the things you suggest. Maybe in relatively short order, I will be ready to come up with some ideas, too." Having fun in a relationship is a superb priority to work on. But learning to have fun is serious business—for you.

Socializing is part of what many people in the "adult world" consider fun. You may even have to learn how to survive at a party.

Here's how some of my clients have expressed themselves on the subject of socializing.

"I have recently moved to a new city," John said. "I want very much to meet some people and make new friends. Although I want mainly a female, I would be satisfied right now if I could even meet a couple of guys to hang around with. I feel more lonely and isolated than usual, and I know it is up to me to do something about it. Last Saturday night there was an AA party in Boston, which is about half an hour away. I decided to go. I made the half-hour drive—pulled into the parking lot—parked my car—felt immediately depressed— turned on the ignition and drove home. When I feel depressed I am useless to myself or anyone else. It was not as if I could have bitten the bullet and went in anyway. I was finished."

Connie stated, "The anxiety I feel before I go somewhere is so overwhelming that I continually ask myself if it's worth going. I carry a complete makeup kit, manicure set and hair blower in my car, just in case I need to make one final stab at making myself look decent. If one hair is out of place, I know I will not be acceptable."

"When we were at that party last Sunday, you stayed pretty close to me most of the evening." Marie asked Jim, "Did you do that because you felt sorry for me?" She went on, "I would rather stay at home than go out socially. My own anxiety increases at a party, and by the end of an hour it overwhelms me, and I know I have to get out of there."

These are fairly typical ACOA reactions to a social situation. "Let's have a party" or "Let's go to a party" is met with enthusiasm, but with varying degrees of terror. Where does the terror come from? What does it mean? Can one learn to react differently? First, let me explain that ACOAs are not the only ones who experience anxiety when entering social situations, particularly those where they will encounter unfamiliar people. "What will I say?" "Will I be accepted?" "Do I look okay?" are universal concerns. I have never heard anyone say, "I adore cocktail party talk," or "It's great to go to a singles group," or "The bar scene is a boon to mankind." The reality is that social encounters are work for most people. Some enjoy them, some get by, but many just barely get through them. People who fortify themselves with chemicals are not usually capable of a realistic assessment until the following day. Certainly their anxieties were reduced, but their hilarious behaviors of the night before look different in the light of day.

ACOAs tend to react more strongly than others. Why is that? Back we go to those thrilling days of yesteryear. Parties—celebrations—holidays were all variations of the same theme. Going to a social event with your family generally caused embarrassment. You prayed that your alcoholic parent wouldn't get drunk. You tried to make yourself small enough so others wouldn't think you were with him or her. You worried about taking care of your alcoholic parent. You were desperate to leave before you even got there. Eventually, your family stopped going to parties. You became isolated.

Holidays were always a nightmare. You got all excited about Christmas or Thanksgiving and it would end up in a fight. You would be disappointed and upset. It was inevitable that something bad would happen. Your birthday might have been ignored; or if you had a party, you were in a panic. You could never be sure it would go okay. Having your friends visit your home was an unusual event, so the mere idea of it automatically produced anxiety.

Because of your increased isolation, you did not have much practice at social situations. Your parents were not available to teach you social skills. They did not show you how to dress, how to be comfortable or how to talk to strangers. So no matter how appropriate and charming you appear to others, inside you feel you are fooling them all.

You believe that the attractive, well-dressed, charming, intelligent, warm person others see exists only in their imagination. This is what causes the depression or extreme anxiety over going to a party. It is a throwback to childhood and those traumatic, early experiences.

There are ways to make it easier if you decide to go:

1. Don't go alone. Go with a close friend.
2. Drive your own car.
3. Plan your exit before you get there.
4. Read the day's newspaper.
5. Find out if alcohol will be served.
6. Give yourself permission to be anxious.
7. Promise yourself you will meet one new person.

8. Be useful. Pass around the potato chips or help empty the ashtrays.
9. No matter what happens, congratulate yourself for making and following through on the decision to go.

Next time will be easier. All you need is some practice.

7. Adult children of alcoholics have difficulty with intimate relationships.

Recognize this as a truth. It is almost a universal truth. You are not the only one who has difficulty. Accept that fact. Intimate relationships are difficult for others, too; otherwise the number of divorces would not be so great.

Recognize the difficulty and make the decision that this is a hurdle which you are willing to work at to overcome. It sounds very simple, but it is not. Acceptance is never simple, but it gives you the freedom to change and enhance your life.

8. Adult children of alcoholics overreact to changes over which they have no control.

Harriet has been furious with Arthur for days and cannot contain her anger at him. When they attended a dance a few nights ago, she put a lot of pressure on herself to have a good time, to participate and to become involved. When the disc jockey called out "Ladies' choice!" she said to herself, *Okay, I am going to be assertive and pick someone to dance with.* Just as she had made this decision, Arthur came over and asked her to dance. She rudely turned him down and walked away. This incident took her back to her childhood, when her father had taken away her opportunities to do things for herself, her own way, and to make her own mistakes. Because he was very dominant and domineering, she felt oppressed. These feelings surfaced when Arthur asked her to dance.

Since Harriet is an ACOA, in many ways she is compliant and will do as she is told. She makes the assumption that other people are also compliant and will behave in the same manner. When the disc jockey said, "This is Ladies' Choice," she assumed that for everyone there it would be ladies' choice. However, Arthur was not compliant; he wanted to dance with her, and was not going to let the disc jockey decide for him.

Harriet had overreacted to a change over which she had no control. Arthur had taken it upon himself to change the rules. She, because of her overreaction, could not simply say to him, "Later. I want to do this differently right now."

It is important for you, as an ACOA, to recognize what you do to yourself when you react so strongly to a change. It does not mean that the person with whom you are involved is out to get you. It may simply mean that he does not follow the rules as you do, or that he is more spontaneous than you are. It is important for you to explain that you do not shift easily. That way, he will know that his ideas will not always be received by you in the way they are intended.

Developing flexibility is something you may want to work toward. You must realize that the desire and the ability to effect that change are two different things. Find out what is in your partner's head when she changes a rule. What you see as a personal affront may have a very different motive. It is only fair that you discover what the motive is, and clearly recognize that your response is not to the present incident, but to your past. Only then can you begin to reconcile these two things.

You may never be the easygoing, flexible, roll-with-it kind of person you would like to be, but it is a direction worth spending some time and energy on.

9. Adult children of alcoholics constantly seek approval and affirmation.

It is important that you recognize the excessive approval you seek from your partner. This can be a real trap for you in a relationship. Yet it is equally important for you to be involved with someone who affirms, validates and supports you. A healthy relationship involves two people who give each other the right to their feelings and the sense that they are of value. If your partner's approval becomes paramount, you will begin to lose yourself in the relationship. If it is necessary to your feeling good about yourself, you will be very easily manipulated whenever that approval is withdrawn.

What you need is to seek your own approval. This does not mean you do not want to please your partner, nor that you won't feel wonderful when you do get approval. But if you rely on another person for your sense of value, you are no longer involved in an adult relationship. You have allowed your partner to become a parent to you, and say, "Yes, you are good, no, you are bad." For adults this is not desirable.

When you find yourself in this situation, try to remember that a parent-child relationship is not really what you want. If you desire your partner to affirm you and tell you that you are wonderful, that is different, as that is part of any healthy relationship. It also helps you to approve of yourself more. Primarily, you need to learn that the wonder of you exists regardless of another person's acknowledgment.

10. Adult children of alcoholics usually feel different from other people.

Feeling different from other people seems to stay with you throughout life. The sense of difference, aggravated by your isolation as a child, is very hard to overcome. But feeling different does not have to continue to be a big deal, to carry with it components such as, "I am different because I am unworthy." You are different because you are unique, and you are developing your own personality.

In a relationship, don't pretend that you are not different, but begin to recognize your individuality, and also encourage your partner to celebrate his. This will enhance your own uniqueness as a couple. Though you may always feel different from other people, decide that it makes you more, and not less, interesting.

It is also time for you to realize that difference does not automatically mean worthless. We are all different. Growth enhances one's uniqueness, which does not mean that you are destined to be alone or lonely. It simply means that you are an individual in your own right.

11. Adult children of alcoholics are extremely loyal, even in the face of evidence that their loyalty is undeserved.

Your loyalty is one of your greatest assets, and one of your greatest liabilities. Anyone involved with you is very fortunate, because she can depend on you. You may run away from certain issues, but the loyalty you have for the people you care about knows no bounds. Although this is a wonderful quality, it needs to be tempered with rationality. You may continue to be loyal to someone whose behavior is inexcusable. Because of this unacceptable behavior, you may have to end a relationship or a friendship. It is critical to recognize the point at which you need to draw a line.

Loyalty to another person does not take precedence over everything else. Loyalty to yourself must come first. Ask yourself these questions: *Am I getting out of this relationship what is good for me? Am I receiving to the degree that I am giving? Am I fantasizing that this relationship, because of my loyalty, will work out the way I want it to?* This is a very important question. If, when you look at it realistically, it is less than you want, and the two of you are not willing to work out problems together, then you need to reassess. Walking away without trying to look at solutions is not a good idea. But neither is staying put because it's the only thing you know how to do. Your family was very loyal. However, the road to recovery began when that loyalty was tempered with reason and responsibility to each individual. Your loyalty to yourself must come first.

12. Adult children of alcoholics are either superresponsible or super-irresponsible.

One of the joys of being involved in a healthy relationship is that you don't have to handle everything by yourself. You can do your part and your partner can do his part. When problems arise, the two of you can sit down and work out a solution. It is important for you to recognize that you are not alone. Planning with another person is something new to you, but it takes a great deal of weight off your shoulders. No matter what is going on, there is someone you can discuss it with, someone you can include in finding ways to accomplish what you want to do. This is also true for your partner, who will include you in things that he wants to accomplish.

You are not alone. For example, if you are fixing a meal or running an errand, you can get help. If you have to figure out something which seems unsolvable, you can get help. You do not have to take all the responsibility. You can begin to balance your life. While you take care of some things, your partner can take care of others. You can participate, which is what a relationship is all about.

It will not be easy for you to trust that someone will be there for you, or to accept the fact that her word is good. It will not even be easy for you to believe that a problem is not wholly and completely yours. Yet, shared responsibility is essential to a healthy relationship.

If you are among those who are super-irresponsible, letting someone else do all the worrying and caring, another set of problems arises. You can probably find someone who takes pleasure in doing things for you. There are people who enjoy giving and who don't consider receiving important. Many of them, of course, are adult children of alcoholics. What will happen eventually is that if you don't become more responsible, your partner will learn to resent you. There is a limit to how much giving a person can do without getting anything in return.

So consider working on becoming more responsible. This, too, has its pitfalls. If you are involved with someone who has decided to take care of you, you have entered into a parent-child role. When you decide to be more responsible, you may meet with resistance and resentment.

However, being irresponsible and having a healthy relationship are incompatible. You need to work on this trait, but you don't have to do it alone. If you are in a developing relationship and want to assume more responsibility, which has not been your style, talk it over. You can say, "I want to do more, to be an active participant, and I need your help." Relationships involve give-and-take. They are not one-sided.

13. **Adult children of alcoholics tend to lock themselves into a course of action without giving serious consideration to alternative behaviors or possible consequences. This impulsivity leads to confusion, self-loathing and loss of control over the environment. As a result, much energy is spent cleaning up the mess.**

Your impulsivity is one of your biggest enemies. If you feel compelled to make a phone call, fly to Europe, get married, end a relationship—put it off for a while. Call in an hour, decide on the European trip tomorrow, wait until the middle of the week to get engaged or to end a relationship. Once you have bought the time, force yourself to consider the alternatives and the consequences. If you cannot do that by yourself, find someone who can help you. Once you have considered the variables, you can make a reasonable decision (which may or may not be the one you had made impulsively). This is the only way you will be fully responsible for your actions. Later on, if things don't work out well, you won't say "if only." If things do work out well, you will know it was not the result of fate, luck or chance, but of your own reasoning ability.

12

Conclusion

The family system affected by alcoholism is dysfunctional. Dysfunctional family systems have dysfunctional relationships. Your behavior is based upon what you learned as a child, but you don't want it for yourself. Knowing what you don't want does not mean you know what you do want.

You need to learn what a healthy relationship is. You need to learn how to achieve one. You need to change habits that do not work. Struggle is inevitable. Mistakes are inevitable. Discouragement is inevitable. However, so are—sharing, loving, enhancement, joy, excitement, companionship, understanding, cooperation, trusting, growth, security and serenity. The choice and the challenge are yours.

PART THREE

At Work:
The Self-Sabotage
Syndrome

A Message from
DR. JANET WOITITZ

Preface

When I wrote the book *Adult Children of Alcoholics*, it was with children of alcoholics in mind. Since its publication in 1983, it has become clear that what is true for children of alcoholics is just as true for children growing up in other types of dysfunctional families. If you did not grow up with alcoholism, but lived, for example, with other compulsive behaviors, such as gambling, drug abuse or overeating, experienced chronic illness, profound religious attitudes, were adopted, lived in foster care or in other potentially dysfunctional systems, there is a good chance that you will identify with the characteristics described for adult children of alcoholics.

That is why I have used the term *adult children* in the subtitle of this book without being more specific.[7] The term adult children has come to indicate those adults who grew up in a variety of dysfunctional families and need to improve the relationship they have with the child part of themselves. This problematic relationship causes

---

[7] *The book referenced here is* The Self-Sabotage Syndrome: Adult Children in the Workplace, *which constitutes this section of* The Complete ACOA Sourcebook.

difficulty in all aspects of their lives. The workplace is no exception. The cluster of symptoms that relate to difficulties in the workplace is described in this book (formerly titled *Home Away from Home*). I define these symptoms as the Self-Sabotage Syndrome.

Introduction

The impact of growing up with alcoholism pervades every aspect of adult life. It influences feelings of self, relationships and one's ability to get things done, regardless of whether one is looking at the home, social or work environment.

Since a large portion of one's waking hours is spent in the workplace, the way one feels and behaves in that environment, whatever or wherever that setting may be, is a significant part of one's life.

The same dynamics that cause difficulty at home may serve one in very good stead in the workplace: A secretary's family may go nuts with her compulsive need for order and attention to detail, but her boss probably values it greatly. Your friend may be very grateful that you are driving him to work while his car is in the shop, but your supervisor may see your lateness as a hostile act.

Similar traits manifest themselves differently depending on the environment. These examples of issues—issues involving control of environment as a reaction to growing up with anarchy and the inability to say no for fear of rejection—are fairly common to children of alcoholics. This study evolved in order to satisfy my own curiosity as to how these issues play out in the workplace.

Regardless of the degree of success that you achieve in the world of work, if you are an ACOA, there are questions that continue to plague you. These are the result of feelings that get in the way of your finding the satisfaction appropriate to your job performance or finding the courage either to assert your needs or make necessary changes. This is not only confusing to you, but damaging to your self-image. You end up very angry at yourself. *Why do I . . . when I know better? Why don't I . . . when I know how? Why can't I accept praise? Why does criticism devastate me? Why do I sabotage success? Why am I overwhelmed so much of the time? Why is everyone else better able to cope than I? Is there any end to it? Could my parents really be responsible?* And on and on this seemingly endless list of questions goes.

Adult children of alcoholics (ACOAs) are among any company's most productive and valuable employees. You will find them in high management positions as well as in unskilled jobs. They are dedicated, conscientious, capable, loyal and will do everything in their power to please. These qualities are brought to whatever they do, regardless of status or pay scale.

If ACOAs are so desirable as employees, what are their problems? One goal of this book is to encourage Employee Assistance Programs (EAPs) to pay particular attention to addressing them.

1. ACOAs are prime candidates for burnout. The excellent performance you admire and want has a limited life span.
2. ACOAs tend not to know how to handle stress and lose more days due to illness than other employees.
3. ACOAs are prone to depression, especially around holiday time, so performance may lag at those times.
4. ACOAs have difficulty with separation and change so are prone to quit impulsively or do poorly with new opportunities.
5. ACOAs run a higher risk of developing their own substance abuse problems than other employees.

Enlightened Employee Assistance Program personnel are able to identify ACOA issues when they surface and, as a result, are able to treat many right in the workplace. More and more EAP programs are reporting that large numbers of their caseloads are ACOAs. Early intervention with ACOAs in the workplace is cost-effective.

Models developed for identifying and treating adult children of alcoholics may be applied to adult children from other dysfunctional families as well. Many similarities exist between ACOAs and those who grew up with other compulsive behaviors such as gambling, drug abuse and overeating; those who experienced chronic illness; or those who were subjected to extreme fundamentalist religious attitudes. Compulsive behaviors can also be seen in those who were adopted or lived in foster care. The patterns are not exclusive so the benefits of workplace awareness carry even greater significance.

This book is designed to answer questions for the ACOA employee and to develop a perspective for EAP personnel to include in designing their programs. The goal is to make the work experience more satisfying for the person who has grown up in a dysfunctional system and make the work environment more effective for all concerned. Samples of different work environments and how they reflect the old life at home are included. How and why these set up a work environment that is all too reminiscent of the family of origin becomes clear.

Also included are the myths held by ACOAs in the workplace and how these perpetuate a poor self-image—leading to workaholism, subsequent burnout and the inability of many ever to get started at all.

The toxic interaction of these elements among peers and supervisors—the inevitability of it—will become apparent.

Ways to effect change from the point of view of the counselor, the ACOA and the corporation are dealt with in the second half of the book. It is designed to be used by the employee for self-help and by the Employee Assistance person as a counseling tool.

SECTION ONE

ACOAs on the Job

13

The Overview

Adult children of alcoholics have a number of characteristics in common. And regardless of the kind of work they do,
whether they are bookkeepers or bus drivers, librarians or lawyers,
they bring these characteristics with them into the workplace.

Adult Children of Alcoholics
Guess at What Normal Is

The significance of this statement cannot be overestimated, as it
is the ACOA's most profound characteristic. Adult children of alcoholics simply have no experience with what is normal. If you are an
ACOA, you will recognize what we're talking about here.

After all, when you take a look at your history, how could you
have any understanding of normalcy? Your home life varied from
slightly mad to extremely bizarre.

Since this was the only home life you knew, what others would
consider "slightly mad" or "extremely bizarre" were usual to you. If
there was an occasional day that one could characterize as "normal,"

263

it certainly was not typical and therefore could not have had much meaning.

Beyond your chaotic day-to-day life, part of what you did was to live in fantasy. You lived in a world that you created, a world all your own, a world of what life would be like *if* . . . what your home would be like *if* . . . the way your parents would relate to each other *if* . . . the things that would be possible for you *if* . . . and you structured a whole life based on something that probably was impossible. The unrealistic fantasies about what life would be like if your parent got sober probably helped you survive, but they added to your confusion as well.

You have no frame of reference for what it is like to be in a normal household. You also have no frame of reference for what is okay to say and to feel. In a family that is not dysfunctional, one does not have to walk on eggshells all the time. One doesn't have to question or repress one's feelings all the time. Because you did have to be careful, you became confused. Many things from the past contributed to your having to guess at what normal is.

What this means in the workplace is that ACOAs . . .

1. Are ideal candidates for exploitation because they don't know when to say no.
2. Very frequently become scapegoats because they ask a million questions.
3. Will pick inappropriate role models because they make assumptions and don't check them out.

Adult Children of Alcoholics
Have Difficulty in Following a Project
Through from Beginning to End

The topic one evening in an Adult Children of Alcoholics meeting was procrastination. When I asked the group members to talk about what it meant to them, the opening response was either, "I'm the world's biggest procrastinator," or "Somehow I just don't seem to be able to finish anything that I start."

These comments are fairly typical and it's not too hard to understand why a difficulty exists. ACOAs are not procrastinators in the usual sense. The great job was always around the corner. The big deal was always about to be made. The work that needed to be done around the house would be done in no time. . . . The toy that will be built . . . the go-cart . . . the dollhouse . . . and on and on.

I'm going to do this. I'm going to do that. But this or that never really happened. Not only didn't it happen, but the alcoholic wanted credit simply for having the idea, even for intending to do it. You grew up in this environment. There were many wonderful ideas, but they were never acted on. If they were, so much time passed that you had forgotten about the original idea.

Who took the time to sit down with you when you had an idea for a project and said, "That's a good idea. How are you going to go about doing it? How long is it going to take you? What are the steps involved?" Probably no one. When was it that one of your parents said, "Gee, that idea is terrific! You sure you can do it? Can you break it down into smaller pieces? Can you make it manageable?" Probably never.

This is not to suggest that all parents who do not live with alcohol teach their children how to solve problems. But it is to suggest that in a functional family the child has this behavior and attitude as a model. The child observes the process and may even ask questions along the way. The learning may be more indirect than direct, but it is present. Since your experience was so vastly different, it should be no surprise that you have a problem with following a project through from beginning to end. You haven't seen it happen, and you don't know how to make it happen. Lack of knowledge isn't the same as procrastination.

What this means in the workplace is that ACOAs . . .

1. Are shortsighted.
2. Will operate superbly under pressure.
3. Will be unable to complete long-term projects.

Adult Children of Alcoholics Lie When It Would Be Just as Easy to Tell the Truth

Lying is basic to the family system affected by alcohol. It masquerades in part as overt denial of unpleasant realities, cover-ups, broken promises and inconsistencies. It takes many forms and has many implications. Although it is somewhat different from the kind of lying usually talked about, it certainly is a departure from the truth.

The first and most basic lie is the family's denial of the problem, so the pretense that everything at home is in order is a lie and the family rarely discusses the truth openly, even with each other. Perhaps somewhere in one's private thoughts there is a recognition of the truth, but there is also the struggle to deny it.

The next lie, the cover-up, relates to the first one. The nonalcoholic family member covers up for the alcoholic member. As a child, you saw your nonalcoholic parent covering up for your alcoholic parent. You heard one parent on the phone making excuses for the other one for not fulfilling an obligation, not being on time. That's part of the lie that you lived.

You also heard a lot of promises from your alcoholic parent. These, too, turned out to be lies.

Lying as the norm in your house became part of what you knew and what could be useful to you. At times, it made life much more comfortable. If you lied about getting your work done, you could get away with being lazy for a while. If you lied about why you couldn't bring a friend home or why you were late coming home, you could avert unpleasantness. It seemed to make life simpler for everybody.

Lying has become a habit. That's why the statement, "Adult children of alcoholics lie when it would be just as easy to tell the truth," is relevant. But if lying is what comes naturally, perhaps it is not as easy to tell the truth.

In this context, "It would be just as easy to tell the truth" means that you derive no real benefit from lying.

What this means in the workplace is that ACOAs . . .

1. Second-guess the person who asks so that they can give the answer they *think* the person wants.
2. Will agree to perform tasks they cannot perform because they assume that they *should* be able to do them or they would not have been asked.

Adult Children of Alcoholics
Judge Themselves Without Mercy

When you were a child, there was no way that you could be good enough. You were constantly criticized. You believed that your family would be better off without you because you believed you were the cause of the trouble. You may have been criticized for things that made no sense. "If you weren't such a rotten kid, I wouldn't have to drink." It makes no sense, but if you hear something often enough, for a long enough period of time, you will end up believing it. As a result, you internalized these criticisms as negative self-feelings. They remain, even though no one is saying them to you anymore.

Since there is no way for you to meet the standards of perfection that you have internalized from childhood, you are always falling short of the mark you have set for yourself. When you were a child, whatever you did was not quite good enough. No matter how hard you tried, you should have tried harder. If you got an A, it should have been an A+. You were never good enough. A client told me that his mother was so demanding that when he was in basic training, he found the sergeants loose. So perfectionism became a part of you, who you are, a part of the way you see yourself. The "shoulds" and "should-nots" can become paralyzing after a while.

Your judgment of others is not nearly as harsh as your judgment of yourself, although it is hard for you to see other people's behavior in terms of a continuum either. Black and white, good or bad, are typically the way you look at things. Either side is an awesome responsibility. You know what it feels like to be bad and how those feelings make you behave. And then if you are good, there is always the risk that it won't last. So either way, you set yourself up. Either way, there is a great amount of pressure on you all of the time. How difficult and stressful life is. How hard it is to just sit back and relax and say, "It's okay to be me."

What this means in the workplace is that ACOAs . . .

1. Will assume that they are responsible for anything that goes wrong.

2. Will not accept strokes if the task was easy to accomplish.
3. Will downplay any credit they receive for completing a difficult task because "It's all a part of the job."

Adult Children of Alcoholics Have Difficulty Having Fun; They Take Themselves Very Seriously

These two characteristics are very closely linked. If you're having trouble having fun, you're probably taking yourself very seriously, and if you don't take yourself all that seriously, chances are you can have fun.

Once again, in order to understand this problem you need to look back at your childhood. How much fun was your childhood? You don't have to answer that. Children of alcoholics simply don't have much fun. One child of an alcoholic described it as "chronic trauma." You didn't hear your parents laughing and joking and fooling around. Life was a very serious, angry business. You didn't really learn to play with the other kids. You could join in some of the games, but were you really able to let yourself go and have fun? Even if you could have, it was discouraged. The tone around the house put a damper on your fun. Eventually, you just went along with everyone else. Having fun just wasn't fun. There was no place for it in your house. You gave it up. It just wasn't a workable idea. The spontaneous child within was squashed.

Having fun, being silly, being childlike, is to be foolish. It is no wonder that adult children of alcoholics have difficulty having fun. Life is too serious.

You also have trouble separating yourself from your work, so you take yourself very seriously at whatever job you have to do. You can't take the work seriously and not take yourself seriously. You are there-fore a prime candidate for burnout.

One night a client turned to me with a very angry face and said, "You may make me laugh at myself, but I want you to know I don't think it's funny."

What this means in the workplace is that for the ACOA, the intensity from childhood carries over into the workplace and every-thing is taken *very* seriously.

Adult Children of Alcoholics Have Difficulty with Intimate Relationships

ACOAs want very much to have healthy intimate relationships, but doing so is extraordinarily difficult for a number of reasons.

The first and most obvious reason is that they have no frame of reference for a healthy intimate relationship because they have not seen one. The only model they have is their parents' relationship, which you and I know was not healthy.

They also carry with them the experience of "come close, go away," a parent-child relationship that is inconsistently loving. They feel loved one day and rejected the next. They grow up with a terrible fear, the fear of being abandoned. If the fear isn't over-whelming, it certainly gets in the way. Not knowing what it is like to have a consistent, day-to-day, healthy intimate relationship with another person makes building one very complicated and painful.

The fear of abandonment gets in the way of developing a rela-tionship. The development of any healthy relationship requires a lot of give-and-take and problem-solving. There is always some dis-agreement and anger for a couple to resolve. A minor disagreement gets very big very quickly for adult children of alcoholics because the issue of being abandoned takes precedence over the original issue.

These overwhelming fears of being abandoned or rejected prevent any ease in the process of developing a relationship. These fears are coupled with a sense of urgency—"This is the only time I have; if I don't do it now, it will never happen"—that tends to put pressure on the relationship. This sense of urgency makes it much more difficult to evolve slowly, to let two people get to know each other better and to explore each other's feelings and attitudes in a variety of ways.

This sense of urgency makes the other person feel smothered, even though smothering is not the intent. I know a couple who have tremendous problems because whenever they argue, she panics and worries that he is now going to leave her. She needs constant reassurance in the middle of the argument that he's not going to leave her and that he still loves her. When he is in conflict, which is difficult for him as well, he tends to want to withdraw and be by himself because he is fearful of being aggressive. But if he tries to be alone, she panics even more. If he can't be alone, he feels smothered. Needless to say, this makes the issue at hand more difficult to resolve than if it were only the issue itself needing to be confronted.

The feelings of being insecure, of having difficulty in trusting and questions about whether or not you're going to get hurt are not exclusive to adult children of alcoholics. These are problems most people have. Few people enter a relationship fully confident that things are going to work out the way they hope. They enter a relationship full of hope, but with a variety of fears.

The things that cause you concern are not unique to you. It's simply a matter of degree; being a child of an alcoholic caused the ordinary difficulties to become more severe.

What this means in the workplace is that . . .

1. ACOAs have trouble with boundaries, so they don't know how much and what information about themselves to share with fellow workers and supervisors.
2. They will not know how to assess what is a compliment and what is exploitation—be it sexual harassment or a personal favor.

Adult Children of Alcoholics Overreact to Changes Over Which They Have No Control

As a young child of an alcoholic, you were not in control. The alcoholic's life was inflicted on you, as was your environment. In order to survive when growing up, you needed to begin taking charge of your environment. This became very important and remains so. As a child of an alcoholic you learned to trust yourself more than anyone else when it was impossible to rely on someone else's judgment.

As a result, you are very often accused of being controlling, rigid and lacking in spontaneity. This is probably true. It doesn't come from wanting to do everything your own way. It isn't because you are spoiled or unwilling to listen to other ideas. It comes from the fear that if you are not in charge, if a change is made abruptly, quickly and without your being able to participate in it, you will lose control of your life.

When you look back on your reaction and your behavior later, you feel somewhat foolish, but at the time you were simply unable to shift gears.

What this means in the workplace is that for the ACOA . . .

1. Any change involves some loss of one's identity.
2. Adjustment to change involves experiencing the old fears of inadequacy and discovery.

Adult Children of Alcoholics Constantly Seek Approval and Affirmation

We talk about an external and an internal locus of control. When a child is born, the environment pretty much dictates how he is going to feel about himself. The school, the church and other people all have influence, but the most important influence is what we call "significant others." In the child's world, this usually means his parents. So the child begins to believe who he is by the messages that he gets from his parents. And as he gets older these messages become internalized and contribute significantly to his self-image. The movement is toward the internal locus of control.

The message that you got as a child was very confused. It was not unconditional love. It was not, "I think you're terrific, but I'm not too happy about what you just did." The definitions were not clear and the messages were mixed. "Yes, no, I love you, go away." So you grew up with some confusion about yourself. The affirmations you didn't get on a day-to-day basis as a child, you interpret as negative.

Now when affirmation is offered, it's very difficult to accept. Accepting the affirmation would be the beginning of changing one's self-image.

What this means in the workplace is that . . .

1. Since ACOAs cannot affirm themselves, they look for affirmation from supervisors and coworkers.
2. They will overwork in order to get strokes.
3. They become convinced that the next promotion will provide personal validation.

Adult Children of Alcoholics Feel That They Are Different from Other People

ACOAs also assume that in any group of people, everyone else feels comfortable and they are the only ones who feel awkward. This is not peculiar to them. Never, of course, does anyone check it out to find that each person has his own way of trying not to look awkward. Is that true of you, too?

Interestingly enough, you even feel different in a group of adult children of alcoholics. Feeling different is something you have had with you since childhood, and even if the circumstance does not warrant it, the feeling prevails. Other children had an opportunity to be children. You didn't. You were very much concerned with what was going on at home. You could never be completely comfortable playing with other children. You could not be fully there. Your concerns about your home problems clouded everything else in your life.

What happened to you is what happened to the rest of your family. You became isolated. As a result, socializing, being a part of any group, became increasingly difficult. You simply did not develop the social skills necessary to feel comfortable or a part of the group.

It is hard for children of alcoholics to believe that they can be accepted because of who they are and that this acceptance does not have to be earned.

What this means in the workplace is that ACOAs will comply with any requests and demands, regardless of how appropriate or inappropriate they are, because they don't want to be discovered as being different.

Adult Children of Alcoholics Are
Either Superresponsible or Super-Irresponsible

Either you take it all on or you give it all up. There is no middle ground. You tried to please your parents, doing more and more, or you reached the point where you recognized it didn't matter, so you did nothing. You also did not see a family whose members cooperated with each other. You didn't have a family that decided on Sunday, "Let's all work in the yard. I will work on this, and you work on that and then we'll come together."

Not having a sense of being a part of a project, of how to cooperate with other people and let all the parts come together and become a whole, you either do all of it, or you do none of it. You also don't have a good sense of your own limitations. Saying no is extraordinarily difficult for you, so you do more and more and more. You do not do it because you really have a bloated sense of yourself; you do it (1) because you don't have a realistic sense of your capacity or (2) because you are afraid that if you say no, they will find you out. They will find out that you are incompetent. The quality of the job you do does not seem to influence your feelings about yourself. So you take on more and more and more . . . until you finally burn out.

What this means in the workplace is that . . .

1. ACOAs have difficulty sharing responsibility since they have no experience with operating in a cooperative atmosphere; they take it all on or back away entirely.
2. They find it difficult to trust that others will do what they have agreed to do.
3. They may judge the performances of others and the organization in the same merciless way they judge themselves.

Adult Children of Alcoholics Are Extremely Loyal Even in the Face of Evidence That the Loyalty Is Undeserved

The alcoholic home appears to be a very loyal place. Family members hang in long after reason dictates that they should leave. The so-called loyalty is more the result of fear and insecurity than anything else; nevertheless, the behavior that is modeled is one where no one walks away just because the going gets rough. This sense enables the adult child to remain in involvements that would be better dissolved.

Since making a friend or developing a relationship is so difficult and so complicated, once the effort has been made, it is permanent. If someone cares enough about you to be your friend, your lover or your spouse, then you have the obligation to stay with them forever. If you have let them know who you are, if they have discovered who you are and not rejected you, that fact, in and of itself, is enough to make you sustain the relationship. The fact that they may treat you poorly does not matter. You can rationalize that. Somehow no matter what they do or say, you can figure out a way to excuse their behavior and find yourself at fault. This reinforces your negative self-image and enables you to stay in the relationship. Your loyalty is unparalleled.

What this means in the workplace is that . . .

1. "If they were kind enough to hire me, I owe them my loyalty."
2. The ACOA will give loyalty immediately and automatically.

Adult Children of Alcoholics Are Impulsive

They tend to lock themselves into a course of action without giving serious consideration to alternative behaviors or possible consequences. This impulsivity leads to confusion, self-loathing and loss of control over their environment. In addition, they spend an excessive amount of energy cleaning up the mess.

As a child you could not predict the outcome of any given behavior, so you don't know how to do it now. Also, there was no consistency at home. As a result, you haven't the following framework of "When I behaved impulsively in the past, this happened and that happened and this person reacted in that way." Sometimes it would go okay and sometimes it wouldn't. Essentially, it may not have really mattered. Nor did anyone say to you, "These are the possible consequences of that behavior. Let's talk about other things that you might do."

What this means in the workplace is that . . .

1. ACOAs have difficulty with decision making, so they will behave impulsively.
2. Since separation issues are so difficult, they will tend to move on quickly rather than deal with them.

14

The Home
Away from Home

Regardless of the nature of their work or the status of their occupation, adult children of alcoholics have similar feelings about themselves on the job and about their work. In a study of 236 ACOAs, 30 percent of the men and women interviewed reported that they feel inadequate. There is no indication that these feelings have a basis in the rational world.

Feelings of inadequacy and of being unappreciated, of boredom and of perfectionism, create stress. That stress comes primarily from using energy to repress these feelings and from keeping others from discovering them. The stress is worsened when ACOAs lack an understanding of how to deal with these feelings in constructive ways.

As a result, issues out of the past get played out in the workplace just as they do everywhere else. It is not unusual for the ACOA to find that his workplace home is a lot like his childhood home.

Duplicating the Family of Origin

In many ways the workplace is a home away from home. Coworkers become siblings and those in authority take on the role of parent. The work environment is set up like this.

Where the workplace differs from the home is the degree of intimacy one experiences there. Since ACOAs have difficulty with boundaries, they have difficulty maintaining an appropriate and comfortable social and emotional climate with their supervisors and peers. The relationships are unclear because the ACOAs swing between trying to "parent" their superiors and being enabled by their peers.

As a result of this swing, unresolved anger and dependency needs will be played out in their work relationships.

Another dynamic that surfaces is covering up for those who exhibit alcohol and drug problems. ACOAs also enable coworkers by picking up the slack for those who don't do their part. This behavior is encouraged by the system. "We all pitched in" is a fairly common attitude that management likes to foster among its employees.

Once the codependency begins, conditions invariably worsen, regardless of the job situation; the ACOA will take on total responsibility—or give it all away. The reality is that once the codependency takes over, reason leaves and is replaced by fantasy. This happens very slowly so it is most difficult to realize when it is happening. Eventually, anger and fear alternate as the prevailing responses to the work environment, with the occasional plateau where the ACOA believes that everything is fine—until the next time. It is a repeat of childhood.

Ruth is someone I know well. She is a very capable, conscientious professional who is very much aware of her codependent responses. I mention that so you can keep in mind that the awareness is only the first step. Without awareness, growth is impossible, but awareness without action is of dubious value.

I am an ACOA and an alcoholism counselor. I am one of ten children. My mother is the alcoholic. She is a periodic binge drinker, the standard Jekyll-and-Hyde alcoholic. When sober, she is beautiful, brilliant, caring and responsible. When drinking, she is ugly, sick and unavailable for a week or two weeks at a time. Father is a textbook coalcoholic. He is himself the son of two alcoholic parents. He abstains from alcohol. He is a self-made man, the breadwinner of the family, the one who takes over as much as possible when mother is drinking. My brothers and sisters all have at least one of the identified roles adopted by alcoholic children. Growing up, I assumed the roles of mascot, lost child and family hero.

I am twenty-seven years old, three years recovering from my own alcohol and drug dependency, two years in ACOA and Al-Anon, and a year and a half in therapy with a wonderful, very skillful therapist. Severe depression, anxiety and a problematic marriage brought me to therapy. The process of therapy for me was hard and painful. As I moved through the muck, the depression lifted and I gained a perspective on where I came from, how it affected me and what I need to be doing in the present. I began to not feel guilty about taking care of myself. This new perspective changed my behavior, my thinking and my feelings. I finished the necessary course work for certification and my master's degree program. When I separated from my husband, I had no job and no money. But I kept going to meetings and therapy and I got a job.

The agency where I work is an outpatient treatment center. The clientele is primarily alcohol and chemically dependent. The staff is basically trained in chemical dependency. The organizational structure is an executive director, three program supervisors, four full-time therapists and four part-time therapists. The similarities between being one of a staff of twelve and being one of a family of twelve never crossed my mind. I was hired at the same time as two other full-time therapists. Our primary supervisor is Bob. Bob is attractive, witty and well-versed in therapeutic interventions. During the first three months of this job, I divorced my husband and developed very intimate relationships with my coworkers. The work schedule was extremely difficult. I worked mostly in the evenings and I was expected to carry twenty-five individual clients, as well as families and groups, in a forty-hour workweek. It is a community agency, so no one is turned away.

I was feeling good about myself as an individual and with what I was doing with my clients and coworkers. During this period I was not alone in wondering what was happening in my life. The other therapists were also working to get acclimatized and settled.

Relatively early on, I started asking questions, sometimes getting answers to my questions, sometimes not. My supervisor would tell me he would get back to me and would forget or not attend to the question asked.

The staff brought new skills, new ambitions and new energy into this agency. We presented our ideas, thoughts and feelings on new programs, new groups and new treatment to the supervisor and to the administrator. They'd agree; they'd acknowledge that all of these ideas and programs were needed and necessary. They encouraged us to go on.

When we asked for what we needed to carry out this work, they would tell us that they would get back to us and didn't. The months continued and the frustration grew. We began to notice that the supervisors would play ball with responsibility. They would toss responsibility from one to the other, back to the administrator, back down to the supervisors and come back to the staff with nothing—no concrete answers to the questions, no materials or support for the therapists to do their jobs. When I got in touch with my frustration, I initially would try to use one of my three programs by reminding myself during these moments to let go and let God. I found out that I could no longer let go and let God when there wasn't a chair for the client or somebody to answer the phones that were constantly ringing.

All of the line staff identified feelings of abandonment, anger and frustration. As a group we supported each other and helped each other to get through the moment. As individuals we would go back to the supervisor and ask again for what we needed. Sixty percent of the time we didn't get what we needed, 20 percent of the time he wouldn't be there to ask and 20 percent of the time we got what we needed.

I tried to respect the supervisor and his authority, until I realized that he was not worthy of my respect. The staff then consulted with the administrator on the problems we had in dealing with the supervisor. She would console us and tell us it was wrong and that she would do something about it.

She would then meet individually with the supervisor and let him know that she expected a change. There would be a brief period of change and then the supervisor would relapse to his old behavior, irresponsible and unpredictable.

As this pattern continued, the frustration began to feel familiar. I knew it from somewhere else as well. At a staff meeting one day I sat at the end of the table and looked at the faces. I looked at the administrator and I looked at the supervisors. There were twelve people there. I knew that what I was reacting to was my family of origin. My supervisor was my alcoholic mother. The administrator who consoled and worked hard and wished that things would change was my father. Several of the other staff, the quiet ones, were the lost children. There were also mascots and family heroes on the staff.

I had developed a new role here that I never had in my own family. I was a scapegoat. The supervisors felt that I was stirring up trouble. If it weren't for my complaints and my demands, everyone would feel better on the job. There were statements being made during the staff meeting, but I couldn't hear them. I kept looking around the table. I identified which staff person behaved like one of my brothers or sisters. I clearly saw what I was reacting to and it made me more angry.

I was enraged that a treatment facility working with sick individuals and families could let this happen.

When I gained this insight into my anger, I experienced hope; hope that now that I knew what was going on, now that the problem was identified, changes could be made.

I met with the administrator and shared my thoughts with her. Ironically she is the ex-wife of an alcoholic. I told her that I thought she was enabling the supervisor by allowing him to continue his destructive behavior patterns. Again I let her know that his behavior was affecting me and other staff members. She turned to another supervisor who was more responsible to clean up the mess. That worked for a week. My resentment continued to grow.

The administrator created problems because she didn't want to hurt anyone. Her answer to the problem of Bob was to change his position from supervisor to public relations.

I never saw Bob do his job as a public relations person either. I was relieved with this insight. I could see so clearly what I was reacting to. Once I saw that there would be no change, I felt empowered. I had to leave to take care of myself. This I did. I had left home once and I could do it again. At least this time, having done my best, I recognized my powerlessness and knew I had to move on.

Another example of an alcoholic family system involved Jean. Jean is a keypunch operator and has been for twenty years. Her company is installing a new machine and she is terrified that she will be unable to learn the system and will lose her job. She gets paralyzed at the training sessions.

The person in charge of the training explains things quickly and leaves out important information. Those who know her say she does this because she is frightened that if others get too good, she will lose her authority.

When someone asks a question, she makes the person wait for the answer while she does makeshift work. The trainee is sitting in the office doing nothing while everyone else is busy. The trainee feels awkward and awful and becomes certain they are all aware of the fact that she is stupid. When the question is finally answered, it's answered in such a way as to imply that anyone with half a brain would have understood the first time.

A typical response to this behavior would be anger, not paralysis. It therefore becomes important to discover what the paralysis means.

When growing up, Jean was always told by her alcoholic father how stupid she was, and she believed him. She was also told to do things around the house, but never told how and then got yelled at if she asked. She would then be beaten if she didn't do it right. She knew it had to do with her because she didn't think the same thing happened to her twin sister. She found out later that it did happen to her sister, but her sister suffered more silently.

It is no surprise that Jean would become frozen when placed in a situation that is so much like her childhood. It is a replay of the same scene.

The difference here is that with this insight, Jean no longer has to be the victim and can take action to ensure that she will be treated in a more respectful manner.

Codependency in its simplest terms is a loss of personal power. It is characterized by giving over control of one's ego to another.

If codependency is loosely defined as the giving away of personal power, the answers lie in how to be personally powerful and maintain that power; how to be active and not reactive; how to take appropriate responsibility but not allow others to induce guilt.

In the first case, the answer lay in leaving the job; in the second case, the answer lay in being more confrontational.

Functioning within the first system became impossible. In the second, when the training is complete, the contact with the person who precipitates the codependent response is also over.

The context in which the bad feelings emerge is relevant to the resolution.

15

The ACOA

One of my assumptions when I began researching this book was that adult children of alcoholics are found predominantly in stressful occupations. But it became apparent to me that ACOAs are represented in all job categories. The occupational choices seemed to follow those of the general population. In a survey of 238 people, eight were clerical workers and eight were managers; four were lawyers and four were bus drivers.

The accounts you will read here demonstrate that, regardless of occupational choice, the qualities inherent in being an ACOA predominate. It appears that stress is created by the ACOA, even when it is not inherent in the job description. The ACOA teacher, technician, religious worker, foreman, airline employee, administrator, nurse, athlete, soldier or officer, waitress and medical student all have much in common.

The ACOA Teacher

Since I see myself as typical of ACOAs who have entered the teaching profession, the best way for me to describe "them" is to let you know me.

287

It is only in the past five years or so that I have realized the impact of my parents' alcoholism on my life and how I have led that life, including decisions that I have made. Both of my parents are active alcoholics and probably have been for at least the last thirty of my forty-two years.

The only career aspiration I ever had was to be a teacher. I programmed myself to like school before I ever entered. My efforts to do well and to gain recognition paid off in terms of teacher acceptance and personal achievement that continued throughout my academic career. By my own choice, I attended Catholic schools from first grade through college . . . sixteen years. I was elected to the National Honor Society, graduated magna cum laude *from college and always received exemplary grades in conduct.*

Making my parents proud was my expressed reason for my need to excel, although I was deeply shamed by the occasional lower grade and/or teacher dissatisfaction. I often made deals with God (and with St. Joseph Cupertino, patron saint of test-takers) for inspiration to do well with papers and reports and on tests. Having achieved success, I was convinced that my decision to be a teacher was a good one.

I liked the sense of control I had in the classroom. I was in charge! I made the rules and, most important, people did what I wanted them to do. A big fish in a little pond, I believed that my life would have the order and purpose that I was unable to make happen at home with my parents.

And such a teacher! I prepared with zeal—not content to have one source, I researched many, to leave out nothing. I wonder now if those early lessons made much sense to those fourth-graders, chock-full as they were with all of that researched information. This need to be a Super Teacher points out the other side of that control issue: my personal feeling of lack of control accompanied by my fear of exposing the fear and inadequacy I was experiencing.

I felt an urgent need for my classroom to be a place where youngsters felt safe and appreciated. No "What the hell happened with Science, you only got an A-" in my class! I worked very hard to reach every youngster, feeling guilty when I thought about those youngsters who remained shy or ignorant of a subject/chapter/lesson in spite of my hardest efforts to inspire and to educate. Actually, I was angry with them for not coming along. I was frustrated with my lack of success with them. I was hurt that they did not like me. It never occurred to me then that those children and I might have something in common—a dysfunctional, if not alcoholic, family.

When, equipped with my fear of close relationships and my unfamiliarity with emotional intimacy, I reached out to those youngsters, I was asking of those children what I was unwilling to share: feelings, fears, worries, "secrets." I was very sensitive to what I perceived as their rejection of me.

I also appreciated the isolation of the classroom. There I could attempt to be all things to each student without a peer audience. In addition, I prided myself on never asking anyone for help. "I am capable" was my façade. Only I knew the scared little girl behind it.

To pretend that all was not only well but excellent, and certainly under control, I decided—the first year that I taught—to have my fourth grade present a play during the day for the other students and in the evening for parents. (At the time, I was several months pregnant with my first child and determined that none of this would affect the Super Wife I presented to my husband.) Not content to settle for anything prepackaged, I wrote the play . . . and the songs (after a self-taught crash course in piano-playing) . . . and planned and executed the elaborate scenery and costumes (it involved the illusion of descending beneath the ocean and finding an underwater kingdom). . . .

One day as my class was working on various tasks related to the play (painting, drawing, sewing, singing, rehearsing), the principal entered the room. Walking to a cabinet on her sweep of the room, she came to me and informed me that there was dust on the cabinet. I had managed to find a principal with my father's ability to remind me that I would never be good enough. Fascinating how the fear of being found out was tied in with the need to prove myself, which led to my overextension. Incidentally, the play was a great success but I can only truly appreciate and remember it as such within the recent past.

Ultimately I decided to return to college for a master's degree in counseling, again with a dedication to achieving As. When I got that degree, I became a junior high school guidance counselor. I made it a point to understand the master schedule and its planning; I reminded the director of guidance of deadlines; I excelled at the efficient expedition of necessary paperwork, which was not the forte of the two men with whom I counseled, so I often did all the paperwork myself and usually at home so that my time with students would not be impeded. Throughout this period, I was striving to enhance the image of the Guidance Department and to fulfill my prime purpose of being available and helpful to students and concomitantly to parents and staff. This meant no coffee breaks except at my desk while working. It meant no regular lunch times or departure times. This began to change five years ago when I faced up to my problems as the adult child of an alcoholic and began to really live my own life.

The ACOA Manager

A manager of the Employee Assistance Program at a high-tech research firm has this to say about ACOAs on the job:

The composite profile I have observed is that of an individual with good credentials who is very capable, who, however, lacks self-confidence. ACOAs have used the high-technology environment to avoid dealing with people. They see themselves as different, on the outside looking in, and not really part of the group. They often become so isolated that they can no longer communicate in other than technical terms.

ACOAs do not expect anything from relationships beyond technical support and they don't get anything. Their isolation grows until they find themselves in a situation in which they can no longer function. They reduce all human tasks to analytical terms, seen through technical paradigms. The smallest task becomes a major technical issue. Because the interpersonal world is not always logical in technical terms, they feel more and more like failures, using human fallibility as evidence for their lack of self-worth.

By the time these people come to me, they actually do look different. They often dress very plainly, are poorly groomed and seem to have simply dropped out of the social mainstream. These folks are wonderful employees as long as they do not have to interact socially or get involved with what they see as "political games." A serious problem is that sometimes they are promoted and they make awful supervisors.

As supervisors, they are demanding and sometimes unrealistic, but they don't delegate authority. They do not trust their subordinates and ask to have every assignment repeated over and over. Sometimes they seem very pleased and the next moment they are screaming at the subordinate in public. Later they may return tearful and apologetic. They can't be pleased.

Some indicate that they feel like frauds and know that they will be fired if the company finds out what they are really like, even if they are actually very competent. Their victims are their subordinates who come to the Employee Assistance Program feeling abused, terribly confused and often ready to give up.

The ACOA Medical Student

Professional schools have always been very stressful places, but they are particularly stressful for ACOAs. The system is designed to teach humility and confidence, to make students work to the limits of their endurance—just what the ACOA doctor ordered, as Tom tells us of his experience in medical school:

In the dysfunctional family I grew up in, we were expected to do two things perfectly—schoolwork and being nice to other people. Perfectly meant straight As, always having adults compliment your behavior and doing this all apparently without effort and without mistakes.

I was "perfect" up through college when I just had to learn and take tests, and no one had to know me. But medical school was different; I went into medical school thinking I'd be a hero who would do something wonderful for people that no one else had ever done. It seems silly, but what else could I do? I'd been taught to get my self-esteem from being better/smarter than everyone else and by making myself liked by everyone.

The first two years were more books and tests—only now there was more work than I could do perfectly. Besides, medical school is full of people who'd been top students and I was no longer effortlessly best in my class. I got average scores and tried to tell myself I could have been tops if I'd worked at it, but that never satisfied me. No longer being the smartest punctured my self-image.

Medical school is training for novices and, in truth, we have to learn from our mistakes and from seeing that we need to learn more. But if an attending physician pointed out a mistake I'd made, or something I didn't know (but should have), or just didn't seem interested in me, I felt imperfect, bad and at fault. I didn't want people to see that.

Unfortunately medicine is traditionally taught by taking a top student, giving him more to learn than he can, giving him no priorities as to what to learn—"Everything is important; I wouldn't expect you to learn it if it weren't"—and then ridiculing and demeaning him and telling him he's useless until he thinks he got into medical school by mistake.

My perfectionism, people-pleasing and readiness to accept blame made me an ideal setup for this system. Throughout most of my medical training I felt guilty about becoming a doctor. I thought I didn't want it enough to deserve it, that I'd never learn enough to be competent. At the same time I was expected to exude confidence and authority with patients.

The next two years I had to deal with individuals—the doctors (attendings) who were my teachers and my patients. In retrospect, I see that these people were not out to make me miserable, but what I'd learned in my family made these close relationships painful. Growing up I'd been told I was smart and kind. These were the positive attributes I identified with and I needed to keep hearing them.

Attendings rarely had time to teach, needed us to do some of their work, and trusted us to do things only if they thought we already knew how. The only way for us to get experience was to pretend we already had it. This didn't fit with my idea of perfect patient care but I did it, got the experience I needed, and felt guilty and phony.

On the other hand, my patients liked me, listened to me, wanted to see me and told me I was important to them. I was taught that I should look at patients clinically, but I didn't. I needed some positive strokes. This led to even longer hours as I spent more time with patients. I felt guilty when I went home because I always felt that there was some patient's need I'd left unattended. I had been taught this, as well, by attending staff who often sacrificed their personal lives to their patients. And I found myself becoming at ease with the role of caretaker but not *enjoying the rest of my life. Since my personal relationships and free time had never been fun or satisfying, it was easy for me to become a workaholic, even though I started to hate medicine.*

The ACOA Priest

The workplace is not exclusively the office, the store or the factory. It can also be the religious community, where the ACOA experiences the same problems that occur anywhere else on the job—and then some!

A counselor who deals with religious communities writes:

The ACOA in the religious workplace has all the traits of the typical ACOA but there are some added complications. Certain elements in the training of priests, religious sisters and religious brothers seem to be harmful to the ACOA unless they are honestly faced. For instance, religious training frequently has given statements such as . . .

- *You are called to be a person for others.*
- *You must be all things to all people.*
- *Service to others is its own reward.*
- *The needs of the community must be addressed before personal needs.*
- *You must strive to be perfect.*

The religious ACOA has little or no understanding of the need for personal boundaries within the ministry. There is a real difference between religious life and the life of a person who has a secular occupation. When you have an occupation, you can try to separate your work life from your personal life. The religious ACOA is unable to do this. Thus, it is more difficult to understand the place of boundaries and clearly defined limits in one's work.

The religious ACOA is given strong religious motivation to put others first. Scriptural statements like, "The Son of Man has not come to be served, but to serve and to give his life as a ransom for many," are frequently applied in ways that are harmful rather than helpful. ACOAs in general put others first and themselves last, but the religious ACOA is given a powerful theological motivation to do this as well. So when the religious ACOA goes into therapy, there can be tremendous resistance to placing himself first. It is perceived as not simply a matter of personal well-being. It is seen as a direct contradiction of the message that the religious ACOA is supposed to be following.

There are several different reactions that the religious ACOA may have to criticism. One reaction is simply that the religious ACOA is a bad person. However, another reaction is directly related to the religious calling. If you are criticized for what you do in your ministry, you are not only letting down another person, you are letting down God. Thus, rather than realizing that we often can and do make mistakes, we come to question the whole foundation of our religious commitment.

Statements like these come into the mind of the religious ACOA:

"If I have done this, then I must not be a good priest."

"I am a fraud in my religious vocation."

"I help no one."

"People can see through me."

ACOAs can feel that they are frauds as people. The religious ACOAs believe they are frauds as people and as the type of person they believe God has called them to be.

Loneliness is a particularly acute phenomenon for the religious ACOA. While the idea of living within a religious community theoretically means that sharing can take place, this is often the last place where the religious ACOA can share. When others appear to be striving for perfection, the religious ACOA may feel that he or she is *really trying to admit imperfection. This builds up the isolation and creates yet another complication for the religious ACOA.*

Intimacy and sexuality are different issues for the religious ACOA who is celibate. The reason religious ACOAs are celibate is that celibacy enables them to be loving and open with all and to truly serve all in the community. The negative side of this for religious ACOAs is that they need to share their deepest feelings and thoughts. They need to share their past experiences and admit their present inadequacies. But sometimes the religious life may not foster this type of experience, so the sense of loneliness and isolation increases, the ability to be intimate and loving decreases. Obviously, people who are married or in relationships frequently are unable to be intimate and loving. But it seems that the nature of religious life provides a greater sense of loneliness and isolation than other vocations.

The ACOA Foreman

As children, we were often told, "Work very hard and you'll be rewarded." Companies sometimes support and reinforce this message. Hank is a case in point—a guy who worked so hard that he almost lost his job.

I've worked for a public utility for about fourteen years now, and of those fourteen years, I spent approximately twelve at a power plant. I began with the company as a laborer, working very hard, long hours outside in the field. Then I went "inside" to the power plant.

I was always taught that if you work very hard, you'll be rewarded by a job, so to speak, or a promotion. I've now found out that it's a little different. When I went into the power plant, I began as a stockman. What I did in this position was off-load trucks, along with various kinds of paperwork, until I moved up into my position as a material clerk which consisted of controlling forty thousand or so spare parts.

My job was to see that each part was classified and broken down into subsystems and defined as either mechanical, electrical or instrumentation parts; then to assign each part a particular six-digit catalogue number which referenced that part to the part number and established a minimum/maximum for the part; then to find it and store it in one of eight warehouses. There was also a ledger system and an index so that when employees came in, they would be able to locate the part they wanted. This manual system was also transferred into a computer. I worked very hard and very long (ten hours a day, seven days a week). In fact, I averaged 550 to 575 hours of overtime per year. My travel time to and from work was an hour's drive, so I would get up at 5:30 each morning to go to work and would leave work about 5:45 to go home.

This still wasn't enough work for me. I spent four and a half years building a house and I would sometimes stay up until 3:00 A.M., sleep on my way to work (I carpooled), sleep on my lunch hours, catch another couple of hours of sleep after work then get up around 9:00 P.M. and work most of the night on the house. I was always taught that if you want something, you have to work for it.

I went through a marriage; I just came out of a relationship; and I find at age thirty-five that I really don't know who the hell I am! Everybody looks at me and idolizes me because I can do everything.

Like I said, I built that house—designed it, framed it, did all the plumbing, the electrical work, insulated it, dry-walled it, spackled it, sanded it, wallpapered it, did the outside stone work (with the help of some friends), etc. The house is approximately thirty-five hundred square feet, it has thirteen rooms and I'm the only one living there! This sounds funny but it's true. I found out that my lifelong dream was actually more like my coffin.

On my job I never refused overtime. In fact, for nine of those eleven and a half years on my company rating report, I was described as a very loyal employee, never refusing overtime and always willing and available for work. I thought that was good. You work for a company, you're a responsible individual. It was part of your job assignment to be responsible when something happened in that particular operation—which ran twenty-four hours a day, seven days a week, holidays included. I worked many Easters, Thanksgivings and double shifts. I would go home, be called back out and off I'd go again. I had it good there. It paid well and I had many good benefits. I had a stove at work, a Crock-Pot and a blender; but I found out that when my job was done (eleven other people left that job because it was "crazy" or "not worth it"), I was the only one who had stuck it out because I had confidence in my ability.

But this got me into a lot of trouble. It caused my divorce because I would never say no to overtime. I got into many arguments with my immediate supervisor because I carried things too far at times in trying to be perfect.

I was always too serious. People always tell me I'm too serious— I never laughed. It got to the point where I wouldn't even socialize with my friends because I felt my job was more important. I wanted to get ahead so I worked very hard for this. I even went to school for three years to get a purchasing degree. I joined the Purchasing Management Association (none of the company buyers, other than the head buyer, belonged to this association), and this cost me money for which I wasn't even reimbursed. I even took personal vacation time to attend a seminar so I could get one point toward my certification at the university.

I felt this was good. I was gearing myself toward a better position. I attended a meeting of the PMA every week and made a point of having lunch with one of the buyers to discuss work. When the job *was done, though, the system was functioning and I was bored!*

When I got bored, I got into trouble. I was picked to join the Activities Committee, the Safety and Health Committee, Plant Betterment Committee, Fire Protection Committee. I belonged to all of these! I started running company bus trips, at first once a month, then once every weekend, then twice and even three times every weekend. People were calling me at work constantly and this caused problems with my immediate supervisor and his supervisor. They thought I wasn't doing my job because they considered this a sideline, even though it was company-oriented. I was told I would only be given an hour per week for these activities. But I kept on doing it until I was reprimanded and told to either stop or be removed from the committee. At the time I was VP of the committee for approximately one thousand people. When I took over the position, the "kitty" was almost in the red, but at the end of the year we were one thousand dollars in the black.

I was doing a good job in that respect. I was neglecting my duties on my full-time job, but the job was done and everything was running smoothly. Even so, this was a problem for the company because I didn't seem to be there. My supervisor was very upset over having to answer my phone all the time. I finally decided to take a voluntary demotion, and I left that installation to be closer to corporate headquarters.

My voluntary demotion was a mistake. I lost $153.00 a week and went from a B-8 status down to a B-2, just so I could be closer to the corporate office, figuring they would recognize that I have so much experience under my belt, my certifications, membership in the PMA, etc. I had bid on several jobs and was turned down for various reasons.

My former boss of nine years retired and I put in for his position. I didn't hear anything for approximately two months and then I got a letter. I didn't even open it right away because I was so confident of getting an interview for the position. I even went out and bought a new suit, new shoes, etc., for the big interview. Well, lo and behold, when I opened the letter I found that, out of thirty applicants, I was placed on a level where I wouldn't even be considered for an interview.

This was the reason I went to see the counselor, and she said I looked like somebody had taken a knife and cut me in half. I felt, boy oh boy, I had put all my eggs in one basket and look what happened!

Of course, I was told not to be discouraged because something would eventually come my way and I believe it will. The day I got that rejection letter, I walked and walked and walked for at least five miles on my lunch hour, and I wasn't even going to return to work. I was going to say "BS" to the company. But the bottom line is that the company really doesn't owe me anything other than forty hours' pay for forty hours' work. I guess I'm obsessed with being a perfectionist and thinking that if you work hard for a company, you go down with the company—like the captain of a sinking ship.

The ACOA Airline Employee

Another EAP counselor, working this time in the airline industry, says this about his ACOA workers:

ACOAs who come to me for help often have a very strong work history and are often self- and supervisor-described as very conscientious. For those whose job performance was deficit and who were referred by supervisors, I noticed that I was able to trace a historical point when excellent performance was interrupted by a progressive decline. ACOAs often report that their performance on the job and the company are very important to them.

The advent of deregulation has resulted in a change from a nurturing paternalistic management style to one that is demanding and results-oriented, and a more pressured work environment. Some ACOAs adjust well to these changes and appear to identify with the needed company changes as a survival need. Some experience an anxiety and pain related to being unable to please passengers and respond to their demands or not being affirmed by supervisors, as in the past.

ACOAs appear more likely to assume a special caretaking relationship with troubled employees. This is reflected in supervisors and coworkers who invest energy in helping and taking responsibility for the maintenance of their jobs. They have often sought help in the past that did not address their needs.

It appears that many of their problems are related to interpersonal difficulties which often escalate and cause a great deal of anxiety. This is often connected with family difficulties that have become unmanageable. Often the loss and abandonment themes seem to be connected with this issue and result in either job deterioration or a great deal of energy expended on the job to no effect.

The ACOA Administrator

Bureaucracy often provides the firm guidelines adult children of alcoholics need to have—where they stand in relation to their fellow employees, what they are supposed to do—but these boundaries can often mean nothing to a hardworking ACOA. ACOAs have the ability to turn a part-time job into a full-time occupation, as Bill shows here in his account of the work he did to support his graduate studies.

I was involved in the dormitory administration of a big university on the west coast, first as a front desk staffer, later as a front desk *supervisor and finally as an acting front desk manager. I achieved this in the space of only three years, during which I also worked full-time on my graduate studies, participated in residence hall politics and worked on behalf of the students in my department on the Graduate Fine Arts Council. Somewhere in there, I was also trying to conduct a "meaningful" relationship with a fellow student.*

From the start, I was very hard-working and conscientious. In part, it was out of gratitude for having a job where I lived—just a hallway away. And it had come at a time when I was still waiting for my student loan and had no money at all, so I also felt indebted to the people who hired me. I worked all kinds of shifts—daytime and late night. I did all kinds of special jobs and projects that demanded a great deal of attention to detail and I know that I did them well. I was pleasant to work with, pleasant to the hall residents and the rest of the staff. I was popular and eager to solve problems.

After being on the staff for a year and a half, working both the Christmas and summer breaks, I was offered the supervisor position. Despite the fact that I was in the middle of preparing for my comprehensive exams, I took on the job.

From the start as supervisor, I began to do more and more at the front desk. It wasn't just a matter of the added responsibilities of the job; it was a matter of picking up on everything that was happening there. Nothing could happen without my supervision, without my approval. I was on call twenty-four hours a day, and I had a real sense of anxiety every time I left the building. One time, I jokingly told a friend that if the dorm sank into sea, I would be standing at attention on the bridge. Some joke!

I began to feel that I was overextending myself, so I dropped the residence hall and campus politics over the summer. But then I had too much time on my hands—too much for the front desk, although I was working about thirty hours a week; too much for my papers and academic work, although that was taking up another forty or fifty hours; too much for trying to make the relationship work. As a result, I took on a research assistantship to fill in the quiet hours.

As supervisor I took tremendously good care of my staff. Since I was taking several independent study courses, I spent less time in the classroom, so when one of the staff had an exam to prepare for, I would take over her shift. When a resident was having a problem with a roommate, I would talk with him about it and help him to resolve it.

The one thing I did not play by the book when I was supervisor was the huge amount of paperwork. It was my conviction that the purpose of bureaucracy of that sort was to lay blame, and I wanted my staff to know and feel that I had trust and confidence in them, even though I was spending so much time down at the front desk that trust wasn't really an issue—I would always be there for them, quite literally.

The manager retired after I had finally passed my exams and, since I knew the job so well, I thought I was the logical successor. But the university was in the midst of a hiring freeze, and all I could do was assume the role of the manager but not the title or the pay. I felt, in a sense, that I had to take on the added responsibilities because the general manager of the dorm was new on the job and didn't know how it worked. I was told, in any case, that a special exemption might be made for our dorm and that I would get the position very soon.

The soon was at first two months, then three. I spoke vaguely to my boss about getting some kind of pay raise, but pay scales had been frozen, too. I asked him about filing for the exemption and he said that he "would look into it." I began to get a little restless as three months dragged into six.

Then I decided to take action. I wrote to the university ombudsman, the residence halls administrator and the dean responsible for university housing. I said nothing about any of this to my boss, but I was getting tired of working at the front desk, tired of the hassles with

my girlfriend and generally tired of the university. I started to smoke
a lot of dope and work on my music. I took no classes at all in my
final term and worked at the desk only during the days. I was waiting for something —anything—to happen.

And things did happen in quick succession. The first was that the
ombudsman's office had called my boss, not me, and I was brought
into his office.

"How could you do this to me?"

I responded that I felt I had no choice, that he wasn't doing anything for me.

He replied that he had assumed responsibility for the work I was
doing and that I was making him look bad. I apologized, then fumed
around and fired off a memo to the residence halls administrator saying that I was still doing all this work and enclosed the job descriptions
of the front desk supervisor and the front desk manager.

Nothing more happened after that, although I did have another
unproductive meeting with my boss. A week later, my girlfriend, sup-
posedly in the middle of summer classes, asked me to put something
in her room during the day. I went in that morning and found her in
bed with someone else. I couldn't believe it and even now I wonder
if it wasn't some kind of hallucination. Whatever the case, I immediately went down to the desk and wrote up my resignation. I finally
had the excuse I needed to get away.

The ACOA Nurse

Adult children of alcoholics very often find themselves in human
service occupations, as this nursing supervisor describes:

Nurses are very proud of the fact that they are caretakers; they
tend to the suffering and deal with death on a regular basis. As a

nurse, I felt good to assist in relieving another's pain. With this in mind, the sense of responsibility that I carried in the name of my patients was overwhelming. I shouldered this responsibility to the point of believing I could hold back death itself.

The small successes and experience of another's joy in the painstaking process of recovery encouraged me to want more. These experiences, combined with the expectations that others had of me, compelled me to demand more of myself. I thought nothing of trying to fill simultaneously the roles of counselor, healer, wife, mother, technician, manager, transporter and M.D. assistant. Denial is evident: I was far removed from the impossibility of what I expected of myself.

Guilt is a wonderful motivator for nurses. Viewed by others as an angel of mercy and self-sacrificing, I learned that saying no was just not an acceptable way for me to deal with my limitations. Consequently, I became a skilled manipulator, deal maker and controller of my environment. If these methods didn't work, my temper flared up: martyrdom and excuse-making would.

Generally, an ACOA nurse will readily give up her own instincts and thoughts about her work, a patient or a situation in the presence of an M.D. This surrender by the nurse occurs less frequently with supervisors, but nonetheless it does happen. These people were intimidating to me, for they represented authority. They were all-knowing and had power.

Among my peers, I occasionally released my emotions—most often in the form of anger. Wittiness and humor also worked well to relieve my load. Resentment, self-pity and resignation weighed me down. When asked about my feelings I quickly deflected the question, gave excuses or flatly denied their existence. Clearly I was uncomfortable, quite possibly because I was out of touch with my feelings. I met thoughts of changing my situation or expanding my *abilities with an air of sadness. As an ACOA I offered excuses or simply resigned myself to my plight.*

It is not surprising that the ACOA nurse takes pride in creating calm out of chaotic situations. I was a true artist, a magician in seeming to perform the impossible. I returned each day to meet the challenge, for I knew it well; it was a place that felt like home.

The ACOA Waitress

Ever see a waitress carry five plates (four on one arm and a plate in the other hand), take orders on the way to the table for two cups of coffee and a glass of water, and still give the right food to the right customer, all from memory? That may be enough for most people to handle, but with an ACOA on the job there's always something more to be done.

When I was thirteen, I worked as a waitress for a man who owned a pizzeria. Much of the time we were in the restaurant alone. His business was a bomb, from the food to the wallpaper; he was a very unhappy man. I wanted to make his business an overnight success and solve all his personal problems. I shared my ideas with him and began to make arrangements to help him remodel. I thought that if I could help his business flourish, then his personal problems would be solved, too. I cared so much that he tried to bang me in the kitchen. My mother found out about this through a careless slip of my tongue and promptly called him on it, scaring the man to tears. He called me, crying and apologizing. Had my mother not intervened, I would've gone back to work although I was scared out of my mind. Confronting my boss was more terrifying to me than going back.

When I was sixteen, I worked in a "fine dining" restaurant that was also a bomb. I remained there loyally for about eight months, *although I was being exploited in several ways. At times I did the work of a manager and cashier at waitress wages ($7.95 per hour) just to "keep busy." My employer once charged me over $100 for cashiering mistakes on credit cards, in spite of the fact that it wasn't my job to handle money and that no one had ever trained me. Naturally, I paid him and reprimanded myself for making the mistakes. My employment there ended after a few such incidents when the Board of Labor and Department of Health became involved.*

Most of my restaurant jobs have had similarly dramatic endings. I tend to get so emotionally involved in my work that there is no separation between my job and my personal life. In the beginning my employers like me because I compulsively overwork. Then I begin to get resentful and emotional because no one is considering my feelings and I usually get fired shortly thereafter.

At present I waitress at a restaurant that is very poorly managed. When I first started working there, I worked much harder than humanly possible. If I was the only waitress on and the dining room was jammed, I panicked about trying to take care of all 1 million customers. The thought never entered my mind that maybe they should hire an additional waitress.

The ACOA Athlete

Nobody knows better than an ACOA how to turn play into work. Because ACOAs have difficulty in simply having fun, the games others enjoy in childhood become much more serious. Mark describes his experience and the experience typical of ACOAs who have made a career of something that others do for fun, whether it's in sports or some other field. While other people dream of having a career they can enjoy, an ACOA, in following such a career, puts a lot of effort into making sure he gets no joy out of it at all.

The ACOA Super-Achiever-Athlete (ACOA-SAA) will sacrifice many childhood activities in order to excel in athletics. He may pass up playing with his friends in order to spend time practicing. He may also give up soft drinks, sweets and more, in order to perfect his body.

The ACOA-SAA goes to school to compete and succeed in sports and bring worth to his family and himself. College and pro scouts don't recruit players from the local Boys Club or YMCA, so school is an important institution in which to participate. He studies enough to maintain his 2.5 GPA and continue competing for the school. (If his grades are higher, it is a bonus.)

Like other children of alcoholics, he also spends a great amount of time daydreaming. He will be daydreaming about the winning basket, touchdown or home run, just as his teacher asks him a question. It is important to him to see himself as a winner because he has to battle constantly with an inner voice that tells him he is worthless, unlovable and a failure.

The ACOA-SAA is loyal to his school and coaches. No one wears the school colors louder or prouder. He brings prestige to the school via the media and community acknowledgment. He is usually the team captain and demands the respect of his peers. He sometimes thinks of himself as a player/coach. He will push himself and his teammates to their physical limits in order to prepare for competition.

Some people may say, "It's not whether you win or lose, but how you play the game," but this is blasphemy to the ACOA-SAA. He lives for game nights. He lives to win, win, win, because games are his only opportunity to gain recognition and self-respect. If his team wins, he cannot sleep that night because he cannot stop wondering what good things the newspaper will say the following morning. His sense of self-worth depends solely on reported statistics and the printed article.

But the ACOA-SAA is not an impenetrable fortress in the heat of competition; he is actually the most likely to crack under the stress of a game because of the inner voice of failure. There is nothing more awful for him than to hear that voice while attempting to shoot the winning free throw, toss the winning pitch, catch the winning pass or sprint the winning lap. The voice speaks inconsistently but always in the key moment of the competition. When he hears it, his concentration breaks and he makes crucial mistakes.

He interprets losing a game as his individual responsibility and not the team's. The inner voice of failure echoes loudly in his mind, "You are a failure. You blew it again!" He has brief suicidal thoughts. He thinks there is nothing to live for since he has failed everyone who depends on him. He might put his thoughts into action because his self-worth, which was strictly rooted in athletic success, has been shattered. However, he will not display his depression outwardly because he must maintain his stable public image to please others.

He does not compete well at home in front of everyone he knows because he is trying too hard to please the crowd and is rarely relaxed. If he goes away to college and returns to compete against a local school, he will not play well; the inner voice is too loud.

Because he is a people-pleaser, he will allow his peers at school to control his life in the hallways and classrooms. He would rather be alone, though, because he knows he is really a loser.

The ACOA-SAA is most prone to injuries during stressful periods of the season. Consciously, he prepares himself to be in the best physical shape possible for the season, especially for the very important games. Subconsciously, his mind (if under a great deal of internal/external stress) may cause his body to be susceptible to injury. The injury will occur prior to or in the middle of the competition. It will give him a safe excuse not to face the inner voice of failure. Therefore he won't have to take the chance of losing and blaming himself once again. No one else could possibly blame him for the team's loss if he was physically incapable of competing.

The ACOA-SAA's choice of which college to attend is also affected by the inner voice of failure. Though he has the ability to compete at a large university, he will more likely select a smaller school. It is much safer to be a big fish in a small pond. However, this does not guarantee success at the collegiate level. Only if he can continue to fight the voice and if he gets enough exposure, might he make it to the professional level of competition.

The voice follows the ACOA-SAA into the professional arena, bringing the same emotional havoc he's always known. The inner voice will affect his contract negotiations, his ability to compete and his emotional stability. This is when he is most likely to use alcohol and drugs on a steady basis.

The ACOA in the Military

Not all jobs present the ACOA with boundary problems. Sometimes, as Alan says in his description of military life, they can provide the ACOA with all the rules he needs to get by.

As an adult child of an alcoholic, where better could I find approval and affirmation than in the military? I received instant and lasting recognition for my accomplishments. I spent twenty years in the navy, the first twelve as a practicing alcoholic, the remainder in recovery. The military offered the perfect atmosphere for this rule-bound ACOA. The system encourages workaholism, unquestioning loyalty, super-responsibility and no questioning or doubt of superiors. The system is rigid and demanding. It dictates what normal is. . . . I was home.

My uniform set me apart and I achieved instant status. I wore many of my accomplishments on my chest—awards and ribbons ranging from combat action and achievement to foreign decorations.

My gold wings further enhanced my position. On my collar and sleeve you could see my status in the hierarchy and my length of service. In the navy after twelve years of good conduct (what else?) the red service stripes are replaced with gold ones.

In my personnel record there are numerous letters of commendation, achievement and appreciation. Also in this file are my semiannual performance ratings. They are excellent. Of course, I wrote my own evaluations for six years. My record also contained six job specialty codes and thirty-five correspondence courses I had completed.

I loved crisis, and there was a lot of it in military medicine. My twenty years as a hospital corpsman was a rush! I worked in emergency rooms, drove ambulances and flew helicopters doing search and rescue work—this in addition to managing clinics and supervising others. My approach to management was to give 150 percent and "I'll do it so the job is done right." I was rewarded for my workaholism by being assigned more tasks.

Other ACOAs I knew behaved in much the same manner as I. There was a pilot who flew three combat sorties per day when he could have flown two, the acceptable standard. There were many who survived on three hours of sleep or less for days on end in order to meet the can-do edict of the command.

In my drinking years I looked for a boss who had a drinking problem or another ACOA. I was enabled for years by both. There were many chances to confront me—yet what problem drinker or ACOA would or could violate the no-talk rule?

During my last year in the service I experienced abandonment. I was transferred from the navy to the marines. I had spent nineteen years being a good sailor and I felt devastated by this turn of events.

It was also at this time that I first discovered an article concerning adult children of alcoholics. It talked about issues that I had been living with but had not recognized. Once I began to understand *them, I could deal with all the other issues in my life. This made my transition from the military to civilian life much easier since I could understand the feelings I was encountering.*

16

Boundaries

One of the legacies of growing up in a family affected by alcohol is that there is a blurring of boundaries. This leads to confusion in virtually all areas of adult life. In the workplace it affects relationships with supervisors and peers.

The interaction with parents will transfer to the interaction with supervisors. If you grew up with alcoholism, it was hard to tell who was the parent and who was the child. The child not only had to self-parent but also, in many cases, to parent the parents in order to keep the peace so that things would not get out of control and someone get hurt.

As a result, the ACOA's feelings toward authority are ambivalent at best. Anger and fear, the need to protect the self and to anticipate trouble—these feelings arise regardless of the personality of the supervisor. ACOAs will interpret behaviors of supervisors in this framework with evidence that may or may not be related.

I got a call from my friend Bob, a vice president of our local bank. "You may like working with these ACOAs," he said, "but, frankly, I don't know if it's worth all the energy. I just had a meeting with my branch manager and I'm still spinning. John came into my office

313

and, out of the blue, announced that he was upset with me. He said, 'You know how strongly I felt about the schedule changes and you don't care about my feelings!'

"I said, 'Wait a minute! That simply isn't true. I supported the schedule changes you wanted *because* I care about your feelings. I don't happen to agree with you, but I can understand your point of view and I'm willing to go along.'

"I was completely thrown by what he said. For me, it was a business decision. I was not emotionally invested in it. I can respect points of view other than my own even if I disagree. For me, it was uncomplicated and frankly unimportant in terms of other things that I'm dealing with right now.

"Obviously, it was a big deal for him. He wanted not only my support of his idea, but for me to agree that his was the only way to go."

The problem relates to lack of boundaries. The boundaries between him and his idea no longer existed. If Bob didn't agree with John's idea, he didn't care about John.

Bob had also become the parent whose approval he always sought and never got. He was playing out his childhood tape of: *Do whatever you want—just leave me alone.*

Even if the employer is aware of all this, it is not his role to *fix it.* If he does that, then he plays into the boundary confusion. His role is to be clear, supportive and consistent. As it happened, Bob got angry because he would not allow himself to be abused, and pushing down his feelings would be destructive to him.

Since John sees Bob as a parent, Bob's anger has meaning beyond the interaction. Was he now going to be fired? Did he have to keep a low profile so things wouldn't get worse? Did he have to confront him now about it?

Since the boundaries are so confused, no attention is paid to Bob's position, feelings or reactions and what they mean. The person with boundary confusion gets so caught up in his own feelings and reactions that it is a real struggle to get past them and be aware of what is going on with someone else.

If he can get outside of himself, the branch manager needs to let go of it at this point, because a minor situation is starting to get out of hand. He needs to look at the stuff of the conflict—a change in scheduling design. He wanted the change. The VP was satisfied with the way things were and saw no need for change but would go along with the changes.

The way it progressed was that the situation was not allowed to die. The branch manager wrote Bob a letter about how he reacted to his anger. The VP chose to ignore the letter, but couldn't help questioning his judgment as to whether this person's value to the organization was as great as he had believed originally. Managers are supposed to put out fires, not start them.

In families affected by alcohol, sibling relationships get distorted as well. Siblings tend to live side by side and, although older kids may take care of younger ones, feelings are not shared and meaningful interaction does not take place. There is not a sense of closeness. They live alone together.

Similarly, the peer relationship in the workplace tends to get confused. The desire to get close along with the fear of discovery results in ambivalence. The role playing (because of the risk of being rejected if you show yourself as you really are—whatever that is) leads to distancing. The question of what is safe to talk about and what is not safe to talk about creates confusion. Too much or too little ends up being said. Wanting to be liked will make the ACOA overly sensitive to disagreeable coworkers or sexual innuendos. The ACOA will also be prone to covering up for slackers and does not know how much to help a fellow worker who is behind.

♦ ♦ ♦

Julia was upset and confused. Her office mate, Sandy, was always late coming back from lunch and coffee breaks. "I'm furious! I end up answering her phone and taking her messages. It's like I'm *her* lousy secretary. I haven't said anything to her yet because I'm afraid I'll lose control or cry. It's like my family. I'm the only one who ever does anything."

The overwhelming nature of the problem exists because of Julia's lack of understanding of boundaries. Her statement about being *the only one who ever does anything* is the clue. Once again, she is taking over as she did as a child. It's the role she knows. If she had a better understanding of boundaries, she wouldn't have a problem. She simply would not answer the other phone. It is not her problem unless she takes it on as her problem. If the phone goes unanswered, it is Sandy's problem. Sandy then has to deal with the consequences, not Julia.

The reality is that her lack of understanding of boundaries is what makes it a big issue for her and probably what allows Sandy to take advantage: No problem—Julia will cover, she's a dear.

Sexuality in the Workplace

Many ACOAs have been sexually abused as children. This is true for both men and women, although women are generally more aware of the experience. As a result, any hint of sexual harassment in the workplace causes a very powerful response. Any inappropriate gesture or remark will provoke either a panic or a battle response.

Although sexual gamesmanship is generally considered undesirable, the ACOA will go after the "perpetrator" with a cannon when a peashooter might have the desired effect. The other extreme of quitting or asking for a transfer may also be an overkill response from childhood.

Needless to say, the promise of promotion for sexual favors is, in and of itself, horrendous enough to warrant whatever power can be harnessed against it. Such "advances" confuse ACOAs, who always wonder if they are overreacting or minimizing when they are told, "Everybody does it! It's not such a big deal." The discussion here is about the obnoxious office Romeo who propositions everyone, rather than someone who pays a simple compliment—"How nice you look today."

Not only is there the early childhood trauma that surfaces in these instances, but also a lack of skill in knowing what to say or how to say it in order to get a point across without creating lifelong ill will.

Many EAP counselors who work with ACOAs report that they will tend to have high-risk affairs in the workplace. These involve, for example, the married boss. This kind of living on the edge is symptomatic of the ACOA's attraction to excitement, stress and chaos. It also plays into the attraction to someone who is unavailable, so that no real intimacy has to be established. What is established is the fantasy of "He will love me so much that he will leave his wife and we will ride off into the sunset and live happily ever after." Not to worry, though; he won't.

The problem that occurs here is that inevitably the boss gets bored and ends the affair; or belief in the fantasy puts pressure on the relationship and it ends; or the ACOA matures and becomes involved with someone available. And, as a result, the work environment goes sour.

This is the point at which help may be sought in the form of a complaint at being passed over or a request for transfer. Or the ACOA may be referred to the Employee Assistance Program or fired because of poor job performance.

Once again, the ACOA doesn't know what hit her but is certain the problem exists either wholly outside or wholly inside of herself.

Consideration must also be given to the ACOA who is gay or lesbian. The fear of being found out, the sense of being different, the sense of making yourself up because you don't know who you are—these are symptomatic of being ACOA and are also characteristic of being gay and closeted. These fears are, therefore, doubly powerful.

One of the significant distinctions that compounds the issue is that much of the fear that the ACOA experiences exists only in the emotional world and not in the real world. These fears may lead to certain self-defeating behaviors that create their own consequences but are, for the most part, ACOA-initiated.

For the gay person, the fear of being found out, the sense of being different, the need to manufacture a person because the real you would not be acceptable, exist in the real world. Corporate homophobia is a fact of life and is played out in a variety of subtle and not-so-subtle ways; the person who is gay and also an ACOA ends up extremely confused. *Which is my ACOA stuff? Which is my gay stuff? And who the hell am I?*

These distinctions need to be addressed by a counselor sensitive to both gay and ACOA issues because eventually the lie becomes confused with the truth and the result is disaster.

17

ACOAs
and Workaholism

Workaholism is a condition in which the workplace permeates the consciousness to such an extent that it is difficult to concentrate or think about anything other than work. It is different from enjoying your work in that it has more of the characteristics of an addiction. Work becomes a high, and withdrawal from it can cause nervousness, anxiety and depression. Family and friends are neglected and, although at first they encourage you and adjust, eventually they exclude you from their lives.

Working hard by active conscious choice is different from what is being discussed here. The concern here is for those who find themselves in a compulsive pattern that is not satisfying to them, who don't know how they got there or how to break out of the pattern.

Here is one ACOA's description of the workaholic situation:

When I wonder about how I became a workaholic, it is pretty clear that it was all part of a process. I didn't set out to be over-involved; it just happened. At work I feel loved, accepted, respected and trusted. These are all strong needs of mine. As these feelings grabbed me, I became more secure and developed a deep sense of loyalty. My trust in these feelings developed slowly over the past four years and nine months.

If I label my role here, I see myself as a family hero. There are several heroes here, and in some ways we work well together. We're committed to keeping everything running smoothly. We try to antici-pate all possible calamities and we fix the screwups. We do have problems working together, problems of control. I supervise someone who is also a strong family hero and she is the most difficult person of all to supervise.

Not all the feelings are good ones. I also feel frustration over poor communication, lack of planning, lack of direction and lack of clear expectations. I feel disappointed that others seem willing to be so pas-sive. I feel angry at myself when I react to their passivity by becom-ing more active and intense.

I know intellectually that if I were not here, it would all go on, that I don't make the difference, but I don't know how not to react. Because of the love and acceptance I feel, I am very committed to what goes on here. As long as I am here, I have to give it my absolute best.

The problem in all of this is the amount of energy it takes. When I am feeling frustrated or angry, I use up so much energy. I also do a number on myself—"You shouldn't feel this way; you should be grateful"—and that moves me nicely into guilt, which depletes me even more.

In the last four years, I've clearly become addicted to this job. I put the bulk of my time, energy, thoughts and emotions into this place. I tell the people I supervise that they and their families come first and then the job, but I don't practice this myself. I've let a lot go in these four years. I don't keep up friendships. I want to go out less and less. I've become more introverted and there's not much I talk about that isn't work-related. I'm boring to me. I've been a supervisor now for one year and, as a result, I feel more alone because my peer group is now much smaller. I'm less confident and less sure of myself. I've received positive feedback, but I don't really accept or believe it.

I feel panicky at times that I've made the wrong decision by becoming a supervisor. I've felt despair because I don't see a good future here and I'm scared because I don't know what else to do. I feel trapped. Like the alcoholic, I feel that everything is slipping away except my addiction to my job. My circle is getting smaller and tighter.

I reached a point where I saw only two alternatives. The first would be to quit; the other was to kill myself. That terrifies me because I don't know what else to do. Fortunately, I don't have such narrow vision that I don't know there are other alternatives—I just need to identify them.

One thing I really don't understand is how, after four years of doing well in my job, being promoted and getting good feedback, I still feel so unsure of my future and so lacking in confidence.

I realize the members of the family I work with are in various stages of their own recovery, but I feel I'm slipping backward. I don't know how any of this is coming across. I feel confused, but I am determined to get more comfortable. I do realize that only I can change how I feel. My first goal is to build up my confidence. I want to look at other alternatives and either find a way to become more comfortable here or make whatever change I need to make.

18

ACOAs
and Burnout

Workaholism is the first step toward burnout, and the ACOA is a natural candidate for burnout. Not knowing what is normal leads to overdoing and overproving. Not knowing limitations leads to saying no. Burnout is a condition that results when an individual gives more than he has to give. A person suffering from burnout feels there is nothing left.

Burnout is characterized by depression and inability to get out of bed in the morning; in loss of or extreme increase of appetite; agoraphobia; a variety of physical symptoms; and substance abuse. You can begin to address the issue of burnout by taking a good hard look at the following questions:

- How much have I taken on?
- How much of it is necessary?
- How much of it is unnecessary?
- What steps can I take to relieve myself of unnecessary responsibility? What steps can I take to relieve myself of responsibility which may not be necessary in the real world but only in the emotional world?

- How do I establish priorities?
- How do I balance a day?
- How do I prevent relapse?

Most of us burn out once. But for ACOAs, without intervention, the burnout pattern is to get sick, regroup and then head toward the next burnout.

This happens because it's the only way ACOAs know how to behave. With no understanding of or appreciation for moderation, they think that getting sick is the only way *not* to be in charge. The pattern is predictable.

ACOAs also suffer burnout because of deeper reasons. Part of the survival struggle that the ACOA carries into adulthood propels her toward burnout. It is hard for ACOAs to believe that they have succeeded at anything, that they have made it, and so they continue to play out historical issues.

A high-achieving ACOA shares the following feelings in a supervisory group. She has been hanging on to her anger at her parents even though they are no longer living. She has no idea at first that she is about to zero in on why she burns out when she "knows better"—*What's in it for you to stay angry? What is your gain?*

Her answer, profound and painful, makes it clear:

> *If I hang on to my anger at my parents, I don't have to risk death. If I'm angry, I don't have to risk being close. I don't have to risk growing up. If I grow up and become responsible for myself, I have to give up my search for nurture. I have to take care of myself. Taking care of myself means I will be all alone and if I am all alone, I will die.*
>
> *So I avoid that by holding on to my anger at my parents as the only route to freedom from them, but I end up locked inside myself.*

Owning up to the fact that I don't know how to take care of myself is very hard because I know so well how to take care of others.

I do and don't want to be responsible to and for myself. I want my independence, but I yearn for the nurturing. This is very painful to deal with so I try to reduce the risk of sharing this side of myself.

One of the ways in which I reduce the risk of being responsible is to take on many responsibilities. If I do that, then I don't have to face myself, and no one will know because I am superresponsible that that is the way I cover my fear. Being superresponsible to and for others will effectively hide the fact that I'm ignoring my obligation to myself.

This statement of the problem clearly demonstrates why asking the usual questions is not sufficient. In addition to the tools described earlier, it is imperative that you learn how to . . .

- recognize positive feedback
- acknowledge it
- let it in

Being offered greater responsibility is positive feedback. It may not be in your best interest to take on more, but that does not diminish or dismiss it as a "stroke." Sort things out. Be flattered (do it consciously, even if you can't feel it) that you are seen as being capable. Then make a decision based on what *you want* to do. The compliment of being offered a promotion does not mean you have to accept it.

At the first sign of stress, *slow down*. Learn to recognize your earliest stress symptoms. *Prevention* magazine published the list on the following page. Some items may be new to you; you may have others to add.

At the first sign of stress, *SLOW DOWN*. Yes—easy for me to say; almost as easy as *I told you* so.

Minor Symptoms That May Signal Stress

- Rashes
- More colds than normal
- Hives
- Memory slips
- Concentration slides
- Foot or finger tapping
- Teeth gnashing, grinding
- Awaking at 3 A.M. and being unable to fall back asleep
- Appetite disorders (eat too much or lose appetite)
- Diarrhea
- Heart palpitations
- Eyelid twitching
- Difficulty falling or staying asleep
- Minor back pain
- Sudden bursts of energy
- Increased sweating
- More minor accidents than normal
- Flatulence
- Frowning/wrinkled forehead
- Feelings of suspiciousness, worthlessness, inadequacy or rejection
- Anticipating the worst
- Cold, clammy hands
- Frequent bouts with flu
- Arthritic joint pain

- Nervousness before anything happens
- Not recognizing a personality shift and refusing to believe it when pointed out
- Cold hands or feet
- Halitosis
- Rapid heartbeat
- Racing thoughts
- Feeling trapped
- Anger, irritation
- Feeling that things are getting out of control
- Muscle aches
- Allergies
- Jaw pain
- Minor stomach discomfort
- Bloated, full feeling
- Constipation
- Facial tics, twitches
- Slight stutter
- Dry mouth
- Difficulty swallowing
- Nausea, vomiting
- Chronic fatigue
- Lack of interest in sex
- Gain/lose weight
- Menstrual distress
- Indecisiveness
- Frustration
- Anxiety, panic

Reprinted by permission of *Prevention Magazine*. ©1985 Rodale Inc. All rights reserved.

19

ACOAs
As Employees

Much of the inner struggle that ACOAs face in the workplace results from childhood myths. The myths had an effect on how they behaved and felt in the classroom during childhood; in adult life, the myths play themselves out in the work environment.

Myths are a part of a belief system. They substantiate our sense of who we are. The beliefs are internalized and are held onto both consciously and unconsciously. They are the result of childhood messages and, unless challenged, they are believed well into adult life. Once these myths are challenged, there is a sense of disbelief for ACOAs, followed by relief that the baggage no longer has to be carried around. But giving them up is not automatic. It requires hard work. Some popularly held myths include:

If I Don't Get Along with My Boss,
It Is My Fault

There is something wrong with me if I cannot make this relationship go right. There is something wrong with me if my boss doesn't treat me the way I ought to be treated. There is something wrong with me if I cannot relate to my boss.

Then again, maybe it doesn't mean there is something wrong with you. Maybe there is simply something wrong, or maybe there is something wrong with your boss.

The important question is, why, if you cannot relate to your boss and you have tried every way you know how, do you stay? What keeps you stuck? Why not consider working someplace else? The decision to leave a bad situation does not automatically mean you have failed. Recognizing the breakdown of your working relationship may mean that you are beginning to take better care of yourself.

There are many reasons why work situations might be undesirable. You may not get along with your boss and it may not have anything to do with a deficiency in either of you; it may come from philosophic differences that you both are unwilling to compromise. Seeking out organizations that are more in line with your thoughts may make for a healthier work environment for you.

It may also be that your supervisor reminds you too closely of that alcoholic parent whose approval you sought and could never achieve. You judge yourself because you think you should be able to handle it better now that you are in recovery. But why should you have to handle it? Why should you use all that energy to remain stable when you could be using it in ways that will enhance your growth? Leaving a work situation that is unhealthy for you is not the same as the *geographic cure* taken by alcoholics.

If I Am Not Productive, I Am Worthless

The worth of a person has nothing to do with productivity. You are worthy simply because you are. This is contrary to your early conditioning, so trying to prove your worth is automatic to you. As a result of therapy, a man I know divested himself of one aspect of his professional responsibilities. It took three people to replace him. He told me that as a child he learned that he simply could not trust his parents to be there for him. He had to take care of himself and they still put him down. They told him that he was no good, he was worthless, he was stupid, he was incompetent. He believed them but he couldn't trust them to help him find ways out of his struggle. So he relied on himself because he couldn't rely on anybody else. Although he couldn't believe in them, he believed their message. As a result, he didn't feel good about himself but continued to have to prove to himself that he was okay because he couldn't trust anybody else to do it.

If I'm Not Suited for the Job I'm Supposed to Be Suited for, There Is Something Wrong with Me

Other people have said you'd be an ideal teacher, or you really should be an administrator, or you really should take this promotion. But something in you says that's not where you want to be, that it doesn't feel right to you. Still, you believe the only reason it doesn't feel right is because there's something wrong with you. You've known for so long that other people know what's best for you, that what's going to feel good exists outside of you, that even if something inside tells you different, you discount it.

Sally was offered the job of head nurse. Everyone said she was ideal for the job, but when she thought about taking it she got sick to her stomach. She said to me, "I want to want the job I'm supposed to want. I just *don't* want it. But I should still go after it because I can't trust my own feelings."

You need to be able to allow yourself to trust your own judgment. Trust and go with it.

You can also make a mistake. Sometimes you are not sure that your fearful reaction is as much to be trusted as other people's opinions of what is best for you. It is hard to sort that out. One of the ways to sort it out is to take a chance. Either it will work out or it won't. There is nothing wrong with you if you decide that the change or promotion does not enhance you. You just need to decide in advance that you will not be stuck. Put the job on probation just as you are put on probation in it. It is hard for anyone to know in advance how a new job will work out. Why should you be any different? You can exhaust yourself trying to make the perfect decision before the fact and that simply isn't possible.

I personally prefer to make a decision, be it right or wrong, and learn from it, rather than be indecisive and let life happen to me.

I'm Afraid They Will Find Out That I Am Not Capable of Doing the Job

It really doesn't matter what your skill level is or what you're doing. If you don't continue to prove yourself, they will find out what you knew all along—that you fooled them, that you really don't know what you're doing.

This is apparent at the college level. The ACOA believes that acceptance to college was through a computer error; the As on your report card only put off the day of discovery. After all, you really don't know what you're doing, you really don't know what you're talking about. This helps propel you toward workaholism because you have to keep the pressure on yourself to keep them from finding you out.

I often wonder how employers in this sophisticated era can be so incompetent as to hire people who are not capable of doing the job for which they are hired—and how they make that error most often with you. Interesting paradox—your manipulative skills are so well developed that they hide your lack of skill on the job. Either your boss is fooled or he is not fooled. If he is fooled, he is foolish enough to continue to believe you are capable. If he is not fooled, he knew what you could do from the beginning.

It's a hard feeling to shake. Feeling incapable and being incapable are very different. Work on separating that out. The early tapes—the early messages you received from your family—address the feeling, but job performance addresses the capability more accurately.

I'm Afraid They Will Find Out That I'm Not Worthy of Having This Job

The sense of worth, or rather, lack of it, comes from the same thing that many ACOAs feel. They're going to find out what a disgusting person you are because you were responsible for whatever terrible things went on in your family. If you hadn't been born, everything would've been fine. Although other people may make mistakes, you *are* a mistake. You were told it often enough and now you believe it.

How stressful this is, particularly in a work situation where you are treated with respect and are valued. This will cause you to distance yourself from those very people who offer you the validation you crave. It creates an approach-avoidance conflict that is excruciating. The excitement of making a reality out of your childhood fantasy of getting your needs fulfilled is met head-on with terror that it is going to blow up in your face because you're unworthy.

If I Say No, I Will Be Replaced

So you don't say no. You believe that you are the one person they're not going to have any trouble replacing. At the very moment that you say no, someone will move into your job. You also don't say no because of a lack of knowledge of your limits.

I have clients who don't say no to things that are absolutely outrageous. A client of mine went to visit a relative who was three hundred miles away and dying. The boss called her and said, "Hey, we have a deadline to meet." She came back because she didn't know she had the right to say no.

The worst possible outcome of saying no—because what you are doing has priority—is that you will lose your job and that may not be the worst possible outcome.

Anything That Goes Wrong Is My Fault. Anything That Goes Right, of Course, Is the Result of Fate, Luck or Chance

Anyone who is unhappy is unhappy with me. This is an emotional response to something that happens in the real world. You know, for example, that the incorrect information in the report was not in your section. You know you were not responsible for it and yet you feel as if you were. You tell yourself that it is crazy for you to feel this way but you can't stop it. The question to ask yourself at this point is: When I was a child, did I get blamed for things that were not my fault? Did I get into trouble when I was nowhere near where the trouble happened? If your answer is yes then you know why emotionally you respond automatically as if you have to defend yourself.

A friend of mine called. "You won't believe this," she said.

"Try me," I replied.

"I just called my mother and she yelled at me for being over an hour late for lunch. I know I had no plans to meet her for lunch but—and here's the kicker—I felt guilty anyway. Does it ever stop?"

Hard to say—certainly being able to laugh about it helps.

Dismissing those things that go right as, "It was easy," or "Anyone could have done it," or "It goes with the territory," or "I just happened to be there" means that you maintain a low self-image. You feel bad about what goes badly regardless of your input, and you ignore what goes well, still regardless of your input. Sounds like a pretty stuck place to be.

I Should Be Able to Do Whatever Is Asked of Me

"Why would my employer ask me to do something unreasonable? Since I don't know what *reasonable* is, I get confused."

Maybe you shouldn't be able to do whatever is asked of you. It is very important for you to learn which requests are reasonable and which are not. The question is not whether or not you are able to fulfill the request, but whether it is an appropriate request. One main concern of most of my clients is how they can do less. How can I take on less? How can I make my life less stressful? In my supervisory group, a man under thirty years old had a heart attack that was stress-related. There is no reason for that if you can learn how to put things into perspective. Putting things into perspective can be taught—and can be learned.

Ability is not the key to whether or not you should do something. Nor is "If I don't do it, no one else will." That's one of the traps of your childhood. Is the request consistent with your job description and is it reasonable? That is all that needs to be considered. If you consider that and comply with the request anyway, then it is your conscious choice, which is different from a *should*.

I Shouldn't Have to Ask My Boss for What I Need

That sounds as though bosses should be clairvoyant simply to reduce your risk of not getting your needs met and having to deal with that. The rationale is "I would be invading my boss's space if I asked for what I need." So of course you don't ask. You take care of it yourself, whether it's little or big, whether it's within your domain or not.

One woman shared this observation, "When I ask my boss for what I need, I feel shame. . . .

"When I asked my mother for what I needed, she would fall apart, and I would feel terrible and end up not only not getting my need met but feeling ashamed. I had inflicted an additional burden on her. As a result, I would end up taking care of her, as well as having to meet my own needs."

Asking for help then becomes a very painful experience. Aside from the predictable difficulty of feeling unworthy of someone else's effort and the sense that I should be able to handle by myself whatever I think I need help with, the fact that my asking will do harm to someone else is what really scares me.

I Should Be Able to Fix It

"I should be able to fix anything and everything that goes wrong." After all, that was your history. You took care of everybody. It is what you know how to do best. "Don't worry, I'll. . . ." And what happens is that others will let you do it, will often take the credit for what you do, will take you for granted. Unless you get angry enough, you will continue to seek approval in this way. "No sweat, I'll get the . . . on the way to. . . . I'll lay out the money. . . . I was staying late anyway. . . . Yours doesn't work; take mine."

The Underachiever

Not all ACOAs are superresponsible superachievers who have been discredited. Many do not begin to approach their potential. They are held back not by choice, but as a response to their child-hood tapes. Many of the tapes are the same as for the superachievers, but responded to differently.

Sarah, although very capable, goes from one entry-level job to another. She is never satisfied, but that does not change the pattern.

"My mother is a workaholic. All my life people have told me I'm just like my mother and I hate that. I'm sure that's why I don't try to achieve. I'm terrified that if I did I would fulfill the prophecy and end up just like her."

Tom says, "All I ever heard was, 'You're a failure like your father. You'll never amount to anything.' I guess I believed it. Since it is inevitable that I will fail, why should I bother? After all, if I don't try, I can't fail."

That is only part of the risk of succeeding. For Tom the greater risk is that he will become an orphan, adrift and alone, cut off from his family. If Tom succeeds, it means violating his life script. It means his family members were liars and his life has been a lie.

If you are like Tom, you know that in order to continue to be a member of your family you have to play by their rules. That means you must fail. If you don't fail, you do not belong. Your bonding need is so great that the thought of going it alone and giving up that fantasy of getting your needs met is overwhelming.

Then you further judge yourself because you continue in patterns that are self-destructive, even though you know better. But the problem has nothing to do with knowing better. It has to do with a fear of abandonment.

In the workplace, some of that fear may come from wanting to be liked and accepted by peers. It is similar to the school-age child who, even though he knows the answers, doesn't raise his hand so the others won't think he is a nerd.

There are many who limit their achievement because they will not give their parents the satisfaction.

"They don't care about me. They only care about what I do. And that is only so they can brag to others about me. They never tell me." This self-defeating behavior comes out of anger at your parents.

"I go fast and then I stop dead in my tracks. I don't take the next step because I feel I will die if I do—or I'm taking the next step and I'm doing well and then I do something to sabotage myself."

This is a very powerful response to the childhood message, "You will never amount to anything."

The child within you believes that in going against this message, you are rejecting your parents. Rejecting them means you are all alone. The child in you is afraid that you cannot survive on your own, so it feels as though you are risking death if you continue to grow.

Another variation on this theme is, "All they ever do is nag me about how unsuccessful I am and how well everyone else is doing. I think I don't aspire more just to get back at them."

The reality goes deeper. There is a fear that if they didn't have this to complain about, there would be nothing for them to talk to you about. In fact, the parents do not want the child to succeed for their own unhealthy reasons, and she plays right into their script. It is bet-ter to be a loser than to be cut off from the family.

Trying harder, taking aptitude tests, faking it until they make it—these do not work in the long run for the people described here. Support groups and therapy are necessary, first to build a new self-concept and then to learn to behave in accordance with it. Those old messages need to be changed and new ones put in their place. That occurs gradually over time with lots of reinforcement and not without pain. The pain that is experienced happens at the point where the old tape of worthlessness is at odds with the new tape of worthiness. This may be exhausting and depressing.

Recognize ahead of time that this may happen and resolve to over-come it. You cannot allow the disease to win.

20

ACOAs
As Supervisors

The issues for the supervisor who is an ACOA are very similar to, if not the same as, the employee. They just play out somewhat differently. The way they play out also affects the ACOA's subordinates greatly.

These insecurities lead to management styles that may perpetuate the alcoholic family system. The behavior becomes alcoholic even if drugs are not present. The subordinates become codependent. You can create codependent responses in subordinates who come from functional families, but they will not be as profound as for those who come from dysfunctional families. ACOA supervisors will:

1. Demand Compliance

This is a boundary issue. They become ego-involved with their subordinates so they consider any poor performance a reflection on them.

2. Make Changes Overnight

Even though they are replacing someone who hasn't done anything for two years, and even though they probably have a grace period of three to six months before they are expected to make changes, they will push themselves to redesign an entire program within two weeks. Their need is to prove that their appointment was not a mistake so they put undue pressure on both themselves and their subordinates.

3. Want to Be Liked by Everyone

As a result, they will become overinvolved with their subordinates. They will encourage inappropriate self-disclosure and then find themselves in a terrible position when it comes time to rate job performance. The fear of rejection causes them to put off the appropriate confrontation or to handle it poorly. Things either wait until they get out of hand or little things get blown out of proportion. The need to reprimand causes great anxiety.

4. Give Away Their Ego to the Organization

This is another example of a boundary issue.

Jean is a middle-level manager with a small manufacturing company. She has been home with heart palpitations for the last two weeks, and her doctor recommends bed rest for two more. He can find nothing wrong with her heart. She went for a second opinion and the diagnosis was the same: stress reaction.

During the last quarter of last year, the company was in financial trouble. Cuts needed to be made and budgets adjusted to accommodate the difficulty. Jean, a very loyal employee, took those problems on as her own. The company difficulties became hers and the worry totally engulfed her. The company has passed the crisis but she now pays a personal price. Those who worked to solve the problems but did not become emotionally involved with them are now experiencing relief and personal satisfaction.

5. Keep Their Personal Feelings Under Control

Since ACOAs strongly believe that it is vital to keep their personal feelings under control, they keep a lid on them. This is a style that companies support. As a result, managers do not develop their own support systems and suppress their feelings; as I like to put it, they stuff their reactions. It is not unusual for physical symptoms to emerge, such as flushing, heart palpitations, tightness in the jaws and throat, ulcers and colitis.

6. Have a Need for Perfection

This need causes ACOAs to consider performance lacks, such as lateness, on the part of employees as a reflection on them. So they overreact. The subordinate needs to be held accountable for his behavior. Very often he is treated as if the behavior does not exist because the supervisor, internalizing the problem, believes that because he didn't come up with the right formula to fix it, the behavior is his fault.

Although they delegate responsibility, ACOA supervisors tend to be unable to let go and they over(micro)manage. They do not trust that others will do what they agreed to or will not do it well enough, or they back off completely as an overcompensation for their fear.

7. Become Enablers

They often feel responsible for the well-being and survival of their subordinates. As a result, they accommodate and cover up for poor performance. This sets their subordinates up to have unrealistic expectations, be manipulative and lower their job performance. It places an added burden on the rest of the work group.

The self-feelings of the worker and the self-feelings of the supervisor lead to certain management styles. These behaviors on the part of the supervisor and the reaction on the part of the worker are apt to reproduce the alcoholic family system.

Management Style	Codependent Response
Overcritical. Nothing is good enough. A flaw will always be found. Praise is withheld.	"I want her to like me. Next time, I'll be good enough."
Overdemanding. Swamps self with work. Swamps employees with work. Expects it done in unrealistic time.	"He wouldn't ask me to do it if he didn't think I could do it. I'll prove I'm worthy."
The promiser.	"This time she means it."
Workaholic or incompetent.	"I need to take care of him."
Demeaning. "You're paranoid. You're making a big deal out of nothing. How can you be so stupid?"	"If I had her pressures I'd probably react the same way. She wouldn't say it if there wasn't at least a grain of truth in it."
Laissez-faire.	"If I was important enough, he'd pay more attention to me. If I don't have full and complete instructions, I'll screw up."
Rescuing.	"She will understand my pressures and problems, and I don't have to worry if I let certain things go."

27

How the
Work Crisis Arises

21

How the Work Crisis Arises

In today's work environment change is the norm rather than the exception. Many who have adapted successfully to a work situation that has had some stability and predictability—either chaotic or peaceful—find themselves confronted with changes they did not anticipate or prepare for. When this occurs, many people who have functioned effectively and felt effective find themselves incapable of adapting to the change. They become anxious and respond in ways that are not in their self-interest. As a result they find themselves in emotional and/or job jeopardy. They are not aware of anything they can do to adapt effectively. They do not have the skills necessary to deal with what is happening. People in this position, if they are forced to implement change, will be in crisis.

Some people who have been effective in the work environment may suddenly find that, for no logical reason, they are no longer effective. No matter how hard they try, they are unable to understand why this is happening.

Some of the explanations that follow may help you to get a handle on the cause of the problem and help you find a way to deal with it.

Since the work life is critical to one's well-being, and since the workplace for many is a home away from home, it is important to understand the emotional significance of the workplace in order to understand the significance of a crisis in the workplace.

The way you perceive the workplace is directly connected to your self-perception. If the feedback you are given in the workplace is that you belong, have value and are important, you internalize the message *not* that your career is going well but that you are safe in life. When change occurs in the workplace, you do not experience it as "the job has changed" or "the career has to be reevaluated," but that you are unsafe and at risk in life. This dynamic is the direct result of your history. It will have occurred in similar circumstances in the past where there were peers and authority figures and a sense of needing to be dependent in order to belong. This would have been the dynamic in your family of origin or in your foster care family.

People spend a lot of energy trying either to duplicate early life experience or to ward it off. As a result, many find they seek out crisis-laden situations while others seek out situations where they feel very safe. The first person would be in personal crisis if he found himself in a supersafe environment, and the second would not be able to handle a chaotic environment. The switch for either would be profoundly painful.

The circumstances that follow are changes that, for many, precipitate a crisis in the workplace.

Promotion

One of the reasons why people are promoted is that they have the ability to interact with their fellow workers in a way that creates a minimum amount of conflict, and to read and respond to their fellow workers' needs. People will be rewarded for this ability because management believes that they can take on more responsibility. For some, those abilities are the result of career choice. For others, those behaviors come from a need to minimize conflict and always to be on top of things in order not to experience the painful dissonance of their childhood.

If you are made a supervisor and part of the criteria for advancement is based on those dynamics, you are put into conflict. The role of the supervisor is one that carries with it built-in dissonance with one's subordinates. People who are anxious about relating in this dissonant way will be thrown off balance. Pleasing your boss will now mean stressful relationships with your subordinates because the relationship has a built-in adversarial component.

For some, this level of responsibility is unmanageable. The playing out of history and the resulting disequilibrium cause the crisis. Upper management is now left with the question, "John Jones seemed so good—why didn't it work out when we promoted him?"

Many large companies offer educational experiences to deal with the transition from line-level worker to supervisory level, or supervisory level to upper management, but they do not address these dynamics. The focus in these programs is on helping the new supervisor to develop skills involved in motivating and evaluating employees and on disciplinary techniques, but most programs do not address the new supervisor's need for remedial help in managing the internal dissonance.

When you are promoted and now direct a team, you are in a parent position relative to your former coworkers. When others are now looking to you for evaluation, direction, approval or as a place to act out anger—and your need is to avoid conflict—several things may happen.

If a subordinate is dysfunctional and your family role is to take care, then you feel at risk if that person doesn't make it. If a team

reports to you and someone on that team is in a position of not making it, your history will make you feel the need to rescue. The need
to rescue will be automatic and will take precedence over how you
see yourself vis-a-vis the supervisory role. You will do everything you
can in order to allow that employee to continue to survive, which is
to say you will enable him, rather than demand that he produce.
Because of your own emotional needs, you are unable to allow yourself to find out if your employee, under pressure, can function without your protection.

Supervisory enabling is a common problem on the worksite.
Supervisors will take employees who are not capable of doing the job
under their wing and because of their own need will (1) rescue them
and give them special projects, (2) have others cover for them, and (3)
not tell management what is going on. The supervisor will continue in
this pattern because of his own need and will be powerless to do otherwise. A supervisor may have a team of ten with four dysfunctional
members whom he constantly rescues as a result of his own need.

A supervisor could have had tremendous rage at her own parent and
feel that if she does something to her subordinates that might provoke
them to anger, they would have the same rage toward her that she has
toward her parents. This creates a great deal of anxiety and gives the
subordinates a great amount of power. The supervisor will bend over
backward not to do anything to cause them anger or disapproval. In a
work setting, this dynamic makes it hard to enforce standards.

The typical enabling supervisor will yell and scream a warning, "I
will fire you" or "They will dock you," but every time limits are set,
the supervisor will back down. In relatively short order, subordinates
do not feel any pressure to perform.

Those who do perform become exploited by the workers who are
being enabled—for example, having to cover for an active alcoholic—and morale becomes low.

The crisis will surface if, for example, a company is bought out and efficiency experts are sent in and discover that the supervisor's work team is not producing up to standard. The supervisor is suddenly forced to change his style of managing based upon these investigations but is powerless to do so. This happens because it is not a work-related dynamic. He now has to face his rage at those people putting demands on him to "kill off" the people he is responsible for.

As long as production is not a company concern, the practice of enabling can perpetuate itself. When a higher level of management starts looking at how many people are required to do a particular task and then tells the supervisor that he should be running his unit with X number of people when he is running it with X + Y, a crisis is precipitated. He will discover that he cannot run it with X number because he "needs" to carry Y number of people. But his need is emotional, not professional, and he does not have to address it until he is challenged. The supervisor cannot produce by using the criteria demanded by the level over him. This will put the supervisor in crisis because he cannot emotionally eliminate his dead wood.

Change in the Job Role

If you have a role in the workplace, you are rewarded for performance related to that role. If that role changes, the criteria for reward change, and the changes cause dissonance.

For many people, a shift in role means a shift in responsibility and new responses to be learned. If your need is to perform perfectly and your need for acceptance is absolute, there will be great anxiety if your ability to be perfect is threatened. If you find a niche where the supervisor is supersupportive, then you don't have to be anxious. You have found a safe place where you are respected.

When the role is changed, the transition puts you at risk because you no longer feel safe. The transitional point is the crisis.

For many people there is also profound loss involved. When you have finally found a place of psychic comfort and learn that that place is going to be disrupted, the reaction goes deeper than that of going from one job to the next. The feeling of loss of the safe family is profound.

Change in the Authority Structure

When people have had a relationship with an authority figure in which they have felt safe, they develop certain fantasies around that relationship. They become somewhat rigid in the response patterns that work and they feel appreciated even if the appreciation is not stated in so many words. When there is a shift in supervisors and the new supervisor is more demanding, there is invariably the complaint, "I'm not appreciated anymore."

Even if the former relationship was silent, there was a sense of being valued. Now when the new supervisor has different criteria for approval or exhibits behaviors reminiscent of dysfunctional parent behaviors, the person is at risk. The person no longer feels safe and is back to the anxiety level he felt in childhood when he was not emotionally safe.

The individual may have become rigid in her behaviors and response pattern in order to ward off the anxiety. If the behaviors are no longer acceptable, it is difficult to give them up and behave in new ways.

If you have a supervisor who makes you feel safe, you will develop a profound loyalty. The loyalty also makes you feel comfortable and nurtured. As a result, you are at extreme risk if the supervisor leaves.

You then fantasize that the company is no longer safe. If they got rid of the supervisor, "What is to stop them from getting rid of me next?"

Change in the Organization Itself

Some people enter an organization and stay based on personal dynamics. If you enter an organization that is highly competitive and the criteria to survive is to beat out others and you thrive on that, then change in the organization means that the reason for entering no longer is the same as the reason for staying.

If you learned as a child to survive in this way and it has continued to work for you, you will not be able to utilize feedback around necessary behavior change in the new environment. If you need to be in a competitive, warlike mode to ward off your anxiety about being swallowed up and it is the only way you know how to be separate, you will be fine as long as the environment remains constant.

If the environment changes and there is an attempt toward order and harmonious interchange, you will not fit. It is too painful to be in an environment without contention. You need to fight in order to maintain your uniqueness.

An example of this is the labor organizer who is at the top of his form agitating for change but, when change occurs and he is charged with keeping the hard-fought-for harmony, he is very unhappy.

The reverse is also true. When you have entered a safe, nurturing, paternalistic environment, a change in the organization in which management becomes more structured or demanding brings up feelings of profound loss. You experience the loss of a safe family and loss of being able to allow the nurture and you feel rejected. If, for example, you're working for an airline and you have to work twice as many flights, or have fewer sick days, you may find that what you have been doing all along is not acceptable. You will then find your-self in crisis. You are back in your nonsupportive family of origin and not in the caring place you allowed yourself to need.

When organizations are fatter, you feel loved and safe; when they trim down and make demands, there is a feeling of vulnerability and fear of being abused. The response is personal and not professional. It is not possible for you to reason that the company's survival neces-sitates the change. You are only able to tune in to your own loss.

Many organizations, given adverse economic conditions, need to lay off employees. In many instances, people who are laid off are closely connected to people still at work. The people who remain are very much aware of the consequences to the people who are laid off, and that awareness directly affects their attitude at work.

Many organizations that have cared for their people attempt to address the issue of layoffs. They have outplacement programs and they help people do their résumés. However, some people cannot respond to the organization's effort to offer them practical ways of reintegrating economically.

These people are in crisis because of the loss of the family and early feelings of betrayal are opened up. They have no resources to combat the crisis. . . . There is a sense that it is the end of the world and, as a result, they become immobilized. Their first successful trust experi-ence may have been at work so they have no prior experience to call upon to help them through the crisis. They will be unable to cope.

The survivors can also become dysfunctional. The workplace feels like a wake. It's the guilt of the survivor. Some survivors become bit-ter and upset even though they previously felt comfortable and nur-tured. At the time they need to make the attitude switch, they are unable to look at the organizational survival needs. They see the organization as a person who threw out their friend. They also fear that they will be next. They can no longer afford to feel safe and nurtured, and, as a result, react in the workplace as they did in their dysfunctional childhood. The organization was "good parent" and is now "bad parent." They know no other way to respond. As a result, they become maladaptive.

Sometimes an organization will shift, and the shift will not be in the best interest of its workers. If the changes are to build, to sell or if the organization is being milked, some will notice and protect themselves careerwise. Others will notice but, in order to ward off the pain of loss and betrayal, will insist upon missing these cues and continue to be loyal despite the signals that suggest betrayal. They will stick it out to the end.

Change in Personal Life

A change can occur in your personal life that makes you feel unsafe and, as a result, you cannot perform effectively at work. People who struggle to have the perfect home life and the perfect work life feel that when something happens in their home life they are at risk in the workplace as well. The inability to be perfect at work causes such anxiety that it puts them in crisis.

Mary's job was to be the liaison between a major company and the public. She did it wonderfully well. As a child her role was to keep peace in the family. Her parents had a troubled marriage, and it was up to her to keep them together. Mary's husband left her without warning. Even though the marriage offered her little, she was devastated. She experienced herself as a failure at keeping things together. This resulted in her feeling like a fraud at work and she became immobilized.

The dynamic occurs when work and home life are similar. If they are different, the job performance may not suffer but there will be a projection on to fellow workers and supervisors of, for example, rejecting behaviors.

John felt marginal as a child—he never felt that he really belonged. He was under fire at work, which brought up the early feelings and, as a result, he became aggressive and defensive in the work environment and put himself further at risk.

Frustration of Career Goals

If you have an inordinate need to be appreciated or acknowledged because you were so unappreciated or were not acknowledged as a child, you will look for ways to gain that appreciation and acknowledgment as an adult. The workplace can be an ideal place for you to meet these needs.

If your supervisor is encouraging and supportive, there is the expectation that the support will translate into support for your advancement as a token of the appreciation. When the fantasy is not realized, then you question the appreciation. *Was it fraudulent? He never meant it. She was lying to me.*

If the positive things the supervisor says are translated in a way that you think you can trust and then the supervisor does not support an effort toward promotion, your trust is violated and you have a sense of betrayal.

If your family role was to take care of everybody, but they were so dysfunctional that you could not do that and you had to make up for them, then you will find in the work environment that you must be perfect to make up for the imperfections of others. When there is an offer of promotion, it causes a crisis because you feel you are abandoning this family of failures. You need to be the savior. As a result it is not unusual to sabotage the promotion. You may screw up tests, not show up for interviews and the like. Since this is unconscious behavior, you will be flabbergasted when the promotion does not come through.

If your career goal is thwarted and career is your only way of feeling potent, if ambition is a reaction to deep feelings of impotence, then a crisis in upward mobility can result in impotence in intimate relations. If this feeling comes from lack of early nurture and you regress, you will not be capable of feeling a bond with your present family. As a result, you cannot use any attempts on the part of the family to offer nurturance. You simply cannot respond. The family will feel rejected at a time when they believe they are most needed. This will also put the family in crisis and compound the dysfunction.

Some who have internalized messages of not being good enough, but who still strive to achieve, will sabotage success, create crisis where it did not exist before and maintain symbols of not having made it even if they have. An example is a man who develops a good business but contracts with services that don't come through consistently, so he is always in a struggle. It's like living on the edge. It's the only way he can be faithful to his family and to himself.

Difficulty with Peer Relationships

If you have a certain way of belonging with peers and that role shifts, the shift can create a crisis. If you are considered a strong team member and as a result are given more responsibility, you feel at risk if your need is to do well but not stand out. If the additional responsibility causes a shift in your peer relationships and you become more visible, you will then fear disapproval and be anxious because you are not sure how to respond.

If you are an advisor to your peers and a new person who threatens that role comes on the scene, the same anxiety results.

SECTION TWO

Developing
Healthy Patterns

The problem has been stated. The complexities have been exposed. The next question is: "What can be done about it?" Or, as the typical ACOA would say, "Is there any hope?"

The answer is simple—yes. There is hope. And yes—there is a great deal that can be done about it.

This section of the book contains the *how-to* of unhooking from the past and living in the present, all the while being mindful of the future.

22

Getting Through the Work Crisis

This section is designed to get you through the crisis so that you will not sabotage yourself when you are going through it. It will help you in three ways:

1. You *won't* have the additional problems you created to deal with, as well as adjusting to the external change.
2. You *will* be able to make rational decisions as to what you want to do in your work life, in both the short run and long run.
3. You *will* be able to see that it is a *work* crisis, not something else.

The very first step is to sort out the problem. You need to recognize what the work problem is and what the emotional block is. This is difficult to do because when the crisis happens, it is so all-consuming that there is no energy left to see that you are responding irrationally. Even if you cannot see how irrational you are, you may be able to experience your unmanageability. If you can see your reactions and they are different from your former reactions, you can use that as an indicator of crisis. If you are beginning to act in ways that are alien to a prior successful pattern and if a part of you is fully locked into that way of reacting, that is another indicator. If you experience pain or anxiety or rage, or are acting out bitterness or resentment, or if you start drinking a lot and that pattern began at the same time that something happened at work, those are also indicators.

At that point, something somewhere has to alert you and say, "Watch out!"—because you no longer have any options that help you protect yourself and act in your *economic* self-interest. Those signals are tough to catch because you're not looking for them. If you don't look in the mirror, you don't know that your nose is red. If there is no part of you that can sort this out and identify this pattern, there is no way to monitor it.

You may be getting external cues that indicate something is wrong. They may come in the form of feedback from other people. If people always said certain things about you and they continue to give the same message, then nothing has changed. But if people who used to see you one way are giving you feedback indicating a change, that's the time to give some credence to that feedback. It is the time to wonder if you have a handle on your reactions. You then need to begin to think about protecting yourself. Chances are you will not feel motivated to change. You will feel completely and totally justified in your reactions. You will want to fully protect your present style because not to do so would be very painful. You will therefore resist experiencing that level of pain.

All you need do at this point is acknowledge that there is a work crisis and that you are resisting recognition of it. Step 1 of the AA program applies here: *I am powerless over my reaction to the work crisis and my life has become unmanageable.*

Allow Another Viewpoint to Exist

Allowing another viewpoint to exist means allowing another perception to have possibilities. This is very difficult to do when you are reacting to deep emotional pain.

You have to know yourself in order to know how to manage this step because different people do it differently. It is a step in which you are very vulnerable and you have to be ready to be good to yourself. You have to expect pain but allow yourself to exist in the current world, separate from your regressed state, which is a powerful reaction to a painful time.

If you don't react well to feedback from other people but are able to manage a more distant feedback, you might attempt a visit to a religious organization or consult with someone who represents a religious persuasion. Allow the input to come from a source that is as consistent in its position as possible.

If you respond well to self-help groups, there are many that you can join in order to begin directing your energies toward looking at another perspective.

You are fragile and you need to receive input in the way that is most palatable to you. You need input to be presented in the way that is least emotionally loaded for you. For some people, talking to friends and leaning on people becomes the way. This works for people who are capable of being somewhat dependent. For some people, going to a person who represents a religious organization is more tolerable. It doesn't mean one way is any better than the other. The way you choose is the way that works best for you.

There are people who, faced with a work crisis, will develop a profound connection with a rigid ideology as a way to cope. That is another way to do it. It is a way not to feel the psychic pain and to feel bonded. The bonding with the ideology makes the person feel complete. The result is that you are less fully invested at work. The energy that was previously invested at work is invested in a place that gives nurturance and comfort. Your need to react to the work-place in a better way can be easier because you have a place where you can feel connected.

The point is that when you are faced with a work crisis, it is impor-tant for you to acknowledge that you need to distance a little from the situation at work in order to see it for what it really is, and you need to find another place to be connected to or another idea to feel connected with.

If your need for meaning was fully satisfied at work, there may be no other place you can see that has any meaning. You may have to test out one of the options offered here as a leap of faith. If something else can become significant, then you can have some free energy to look at work more realistically. There is then movement away from defining yourself as your work. It can mean relating to family or to an association differently. It is similar to the recommendation of ninety meetings in ninety days for the newly sober person so that he can be connected with something other than alcohol. You take the cotton out of your ears and put it in your mouth. Step 2 of the AA program applies here: *[We] came to believe that a Power greater than ourselves could restore us to sanity.*

Change Your Responses at Work

Once you have completed the second step and have developed some meaning in life outside of the work environment, you need to begin to change your behavior in very simple ways. Changing your behavior at work does not mean correcting it. It does not mean changing it radically. It simply means to begin to react more neutrally at work. If you are capable of doing it, it may mean behaving the way you did before you were in crisis. If you were functional beforehand and you can return to that and behave that way, you have accomplished a great deal. If the wound is still pretty deep and, as you begin to look at work the situation is just beginning to clear up, you may only be able to be neutral. You may have to be able to stay neutral before you can once again live effectively at work. In order to neutralize the situation, you need to look around, get the picture, talk to people outside of work about what you are seeing. You need to connect with people with whom you can talk about what you are seeing, so that you can understand what is going on in work terms instead of emotional terms. You have to be able to take a look at the work environment in a way that has to do with your career and your survival, not your feelings. You are, in effect, relearning how to connect with work. You are learning how to do it in a way that has to do with career and money—not with emotional need.

If you are a supervisor who is enraged at upper management and are expressing your anger by telling your subordinates how lousy the company is because you feel pained about needing to shift the rules, you need to stop doing that. You are going to want to just be neutral about things—not to be fully effective but just to be neutral. Stop complaining to upper management and stop demeaning the workplace to subordinates.

Stop doing things to invite a fight. Stop doing things that would suggest personal rage at what has happened. Simply stop that behavior. If you're not handing in your work to get even—or you're not producing as well to get even—or you are coming in late to get even—or you're terribly upset a lot and have a tight pain in your stomach—interrupt that kind of behavior. That behavior does not serve your best career interest. You don't have to feel differently. Just behave differently. Try to keep work at work.

If you are feeling physical symptoms like stomach cramps, headaches or nausea, try to develop strategies to manage these symptoms, for example, relaxation strategies, exercise—things to minimize the new behavior that is related to the work crisis. Recognize that acting out will only sabotage you in the future and make the crisis worse. If you stop complaining, if you stop being hostile, that does not mean you now agree with policy. It just means you are going to act in the way that is in your best interest.

You are intentionally establishing a neutral zone. You are not signing a peace treaty. You create the neutral zone so you won't do something that will cause you to pay dues in the here-and-now, and you maintain the zone until you can reframe your understanding of what happened at work.

It might be that as you take a second look at your work situation, you will find new options emerging.

You may decide that this company is not for you. Your best interest may be served in starting to write a new résumé. You may consider taking early retirement. If your decision is based on input from other people and on examining what's going on in your career, then just pulling back and making a decision doesn't mean you have to take action. You may decide to hang in and ride out the storm. It simply means you are looking at what makes the most sense in terms of what you need.

Seeing it in these terms is different from the way you saw the workplace in the beginning. In the first place you saw work as your family. If you decide that leaving your family is acting in your best interest, a basic need is violated: to stay connected with your family.

The workplace should not be your home away from home. In some ways you may, as a result of the crisis, be developing a new skill. It may be very painful because you may feel disloyal. You may feel you don't deserve to act in your own interest. Those feelings will come up now. Be ready for them. It may not be possible to take action at a time when you are dealing with such a painful experience. At this point, all you need do is just examine what action would be in your best career interest.

Look at the situation with someone who can help you do it in an objective way. It is too emotionally loaded for you to do it by yourself. If you have friends who are objective, they can be very useful at this time. Do not pick friends who are (1) as angry as you are and will direct you to do something for their rage, or (2) who clearly identify with you because they have a similar history and may guide you to act out their fantasies. These friends may not be able to be objective because they care too much about you and what you're going through to see things clearly.

This is the time to take an objective look and incorporate objective people. If you have people in your life who are objective and whose career perception is clear, they may be able to help.

It may be the time to see a professional who can offer an objective point of view. If you choose to go to a professional, be sure the professional you go to is one who will be reality-oriented and will help you work on your current situation. The professional for this time is someone who is going to help see the decisions you need to make around the workplace. She may help you link here-and-now and the there-and-then in order to help you focus on the workplace. Her help will not be focused on your history as it relates to the workplace, but to your current situation. At another time you may want to focus differently, but for now, in the crisis, this is the appropriate focus.

As you look at the workplace more objectively and with the help of someone objective, you can anticipate some pain, some automatic rejection of ideas and some denial. Looking at the situation more objectively brings you another step further away from the emotional need that existed initially. It is important not to judge yourself because it is so hard for you to see the situation objectively. If you could have looked at it objectively from the beginning, you would have. If your early life experience and those emotions had not interfered, you probably would not be in a crisis this severe.

Take your time. If you've been able to maintain a functional mode, you now have time. As a result of this process you can now look at action options. You are now not only looking objectively, but a little more deeply. *What does this mean for me here? Is this the place where I want to continue to work? Is this the place where I need to be? Looking objectively, what are my goals? Am I better off leaving or am I better off staying? Do I want to maintain the role that I had prior to the crisis? Was that role good for me? Are there ways for me to modify my role?* There are many options when the pressure is off.

If you now find it desirable to invest some energy outside the workplace, you may decide to invest less energy at work. You may decide not to quit but to shift your energy a little. Looking at goals gives you a chance to explore the whole picture and lets you see objectively what it was like before. When you were in crisis, you were facing the pit that you avoided all your life. Now you're in a position to see what you did in order to adapt.

The crisis does not have to be seen only as an enemy. It can also be seen as an opportunity. You may have been stuck and can now get unstuck.

The initial goals you should identify are short-term goals. But looking at short-term goals can also afford you an opportunity to look at your long-term goals and how the two relate. If you are the adult child of an alcoholic, chances are you have never really looked at long-term goals or known how to develop a long-term plan. So one of your short-term goals might be to learn how to develop long-term goals.

Once you have examined your goals, you won't feel obligated to make a change. As long as you're functional at work, you still have the luxury of maintaining your neutral stance while you explore your options. You may decide to stay put for a year and maintain your *status quo*. You may not want to make a major decision for that period of time. In effect, you have achieved a goal for a year. You can be free to enjoy other things. Along the way you may have many questions, but you've done what you need to do for now. You will live crisis-free.

Recognize that living crisis-free may in itself require an adjustment on your part.

If your life is crisis-oriented and that is how you live your life, that is a crisis with a small c. If you continue to have crisis as you have known it before, that is a part of who you are. The Crisis—with a big C—that we are talking about is a reaction to an event that causes you to behave uncharacteristically and self-destructively. If having a crisis is the norm for you, then *not* having a crisis would be a crisis. If functioning at work is your norm or having a certain role at work is your norm and that gets shifted, then the crisis is related to that. And that's a Crisis with a big C.

This distinction is something you may begin to filter out in going through this process. The two kinds of crises may feel somewhat the same inside but in reality they are different. We usually use the term *crisis* to mean being in situations where we feel anxiety or a sense of imminent danger. But in this context, we are talking about something different. The crisis in the workplace results from an event that causes an uncharacteristic set of behaviors or feelings. It is not necessarily a crisis that makes the adrenaline start to flow.

There are a lot of people whose lives are a mess but who do well at work. There are a lot of people who are continually in difficulty at work. They constantly act out at work in ways to ward off early pain. They are always late or in some difficulty with authority figures. For some, these dysfunctional patterns are the norm. If you behave regularly in this way, you will discover that interrupting the pattern has a different flavor. In that event, you might need to look at what in your psychological makeup is causing you to behave this way and emphasize this aspect, rather than the particular work crisis of the moment.

Recognizing Your Work Style

Here is another way of looking at the meaning of crisis in the workplace. You are reading this and maybe wondering, *Where do I fit? I always have crises at work. Why don't I identify with what is being said?*

It might be that, affected by your childhood, your style or the way you relate to your current work environment makes you crisis-prone and that is your norm. It is important that you understand how this section relates to you as well. You may be constantly in pain about work. You may be always in conflict with your boss. You may keep losing jobs and not understand why. The job loss does not relate to an inability to do the work but to an inability to relate to others. If you can't do the work because of lack of skill, you may be able to learn to do the work by getting training. If you are unable to relate at work but have the skill, then there's something else going on. If these problems are true for you, you may be crisis-prone at work. Your situation is different from that of the person who doesn't usually feel appreciated but finds a way to behave at work that is appreciated. When one is feeling functional at work and then the crisis hits, it is not the same as if you . . .

- constantly feel unappreciated and angry and act out
- constantly feel the boss is out to get you, no matter who the boss is
- constantly walk around with the feeling that if you haven't done everything perfectly, something terrible will happen
- constantly feel at risk
- constantly quit jobs because you feel unsafe

This situation may not be a work crisis. It may be a personal crisis that plays itself out at work. You have to take a look at the patterns and the way in which you play out your internal problems at work. You may have to think back on each time you insisted that this boss was lousy or that boss was lousy or this organization stinks or that organization stinks. It may make sense for you to sit down and see if there are any patterns to your actions. If there are, ask yourself whether or not something you are doing is the cause. It may be your attitude or your choice of employment. You don't have to be angry at yourself if you find that to be the case. It means that it may be worth your while to sit down in a safe, quiet place and give it some thought.

The remediation process that has been described here is not necessarily appropriate for you if you fall into this latter category. If you do, you might want to take a look at the myths and other areas discussed in other parts of this book in order to more fully identify what it is that you are playing out at work.

For most of you, both of these aspects will have validity at one time or another.

As long as the workplace has the same stability for you that it has always had, this book may not be useful to you because you have succeeded in warding off the pain from the past and feel safe and functional. The crises we have talked about remedying are those that are caused by circumstances out of your control and those that, because of your history, you lack the tools to respond to appropriately. This section is designed to help you develop those tools.

One caution: Don't rush to act on an idea or make a change you believe is needed unless your job is at imminent risk.

If the need to change is not immediate, chances are that whatever decisions you make should be held up or slowed down for careful planning. It will take a while for everything to quiet down so that you can make a decision you are certain will not backfire. Let the dust settle.

Start to look at new career options in a realistic way. Read about changing jobs. Give yourself time. The crisis in the workplace has all the power of a trauma and you need time to heal from a trauma. Exploring new career options requires different skills and thought patterns, different modes of operation, different affiliations. The skills needed to get through the crisis are not the same as the skills needed to explore new career options. You need time to learn those skills, if the workplace gives you time to plan.

Don't tell anyone at work that you're thinking of leaving. Keep that outside of the worksite. The decision to leave does not mean that you have failed where you are. It just means that you may need to make a decision to leave.

You may decide you can advance your career where you are. Give yourself time to be where you are. Then look carefully at what would serve your interest in that direction. You may decide that where you are, now that you are adjusting, is precisely where you want to be.

You may want to look at early retirement. You may want to go back to school. You may want to do something entirely different.

All things are possible when you've passed the crisis. Working it through not only helps you survive in the moment but can ultimately be enriching. As the AA program tells you—one day at a time, one step at a time. It gets better.

23

Changing Jobs

ACOAs *do not accept change easily.* Change, regardless of its nature, involves loss. The sense of self is tentative and, for many, the personal identity and the work identity are one and the same, so any change in the workplace is disruptive. It involves the loss of self as it has been understood by the ACOA. Many find themselves in tears when things are going well and devastated when things are going poorly. Identification with occupation is not exclusive to ACOAs, but the exaggerated reaction to change is relevant.

Leaving a job is stressful to the ACOA because leaving is a sign of disloyalty, so the ACOA will experience guilt.

ACOAs believe that former colleagues . . .

- will be angry with them
- won't like them anymore
- will punish them

They also believe that . . .

- the new colleagues will reject them, so they will be alone in a hostile environment. If the ACOA takes care of himself, he believes something terrible will happen to others.

- those who were under their protection will be thrown to the wolves.

It's called survivor guilt.

For many, the leaving is more difficult than the new start. That is not only because of the struggles involved in leaving, but also because focusing on the leaving serves as a smokescreen to avoid the fears involved in the change, including (1) fear of success and (2) fear of failure.

Much has been written about the female fear of success (nice girls don't) and the male fear of failure (if you're a man, you will succeed), and those culturally defined fears exist for the ACOA as well. In and of themselves, the messages "You'll never get a man" or "The world will know you're a wimp" can cause you great anxiety.

However, for the ACOA, the underlying message, "You're not worthy," and the unconscious belief in that message cause panic when the ACOA attempts change.

The decision to change jobs is excruciating for an ACOA because the ACOA lacks decision-making skills. The ACOA has no frame of reference for making a careful, thought-out decision without help.

It is not unusual for an ACOA to get stuck in trying to make a decision. This comes from forward and backward projection and an inability or lack of understanding of necessary steps in the moment.

Since leaving is so hard, it has to be the perfect job. It has to be the right location, the right title, the right job description, the right salary, the right perks, the right opportunity for advancement, the right assistance—in short, everything. Otherwise, why bother? The agonizing over leaving means that the new job is a lifelong commitment. The idea that the company might change, that you might change or that what is ideal for you today may not be ideal tomorrow is too complicated a notion to enter the picture.

Changing jobs involves learning, and learning involves risk. This brings up the childhood fears, "If I take a risk and it's a mistake, my parents will humiliate me, mock me and make fun of me to their friends." The memory of that torture is excruciating.

In general, people look for new jobs because they are unsatisfied where they are, a growth opportunity presents itself, it is time to move on for one's own development, or circumstances intervene.

As a result of the ACOA's decision-making problems, job changes will often happen to her, rather than result from the ACOA making the decision. Whether the decision to change jobs is her own or someone else's idea, the ACOA is prone to make impulsive decisions and live with the results of those impulses.

ACOAs look for a new job when the present situation becomes intolerable. Dissatisfaction is generally rationalized or dismissed or blamed on self. Subsequently, the discomfort builds until the situation is intolerable. Then the ACOA must find another job or he will create additional problems for himself or get fired. The result is that the search is made with great urgency, and a new position becomes more the luck of the draw than a carefully selected choice. This rapid choice is a good way for setting up the same situation all over again.

Even though the ACOA complains that she is under-appreciated and underutilized, she does not meet growth opportunities with enthusiasm and an inner self-validation. The ACOA meets them with fear of discovery on the one hand and, on the other, the suspicion that any growth opportunity is not all that it appears to be. Since most new opportunities are not all they're purported to be, looking at the negative side helps to allay the inadequacy fears. It is a sign of growth for the ACOA to address concerns directly and discuss terms. It is more usual to stuff concerns, put off the decision, panic that someone else will be offered the job and end up accepting the job on the employer's terms. Losing the opportunity as the result of avoidance is an alternate possibility and leads to an initial sense of relief. Then the fantasy of *if only* sets in.

ACOAs rarely move on solely because it is time to go further. This comes from an inability to generalize skills. "I may do fine where I am, but could I make it somewhere else?" Jobs are not looked on as opportunities to demonstrate particular skills but as self-definition.

Moving on because it is time is a carefully thought-out and calculated decision. It involves preparation, planning and deliberate, systematic action. This is contrary to the operational mode of the ACOA, who operates best under pressure and in crisis.

ACOAs change jobs when circumstances intervene. Getting fired brings the same devastation for ACOAs as it does for others. Rejection—regardless of whether the job was worth having—brings up insecurities and people respond with either depression, which debilitates, or anger, which energizes. ACOAs are less prone than others to be able to use anger on their own behalf. It has been such a destructive force in the past that it is hard to harness it and make it useful. The knowledge of how to use anger and the freedom to see anger as being creative are not available to the ACOA.

Other circumstances, such as company moves, are managed extremely well by ACOAs. They are calm in the crisis and are able to do what needs to be done. Where others may fall apart in crisis and not be able to think clearly, ACOAs become energized and think clearly. This is one benefit of the legacy of living from crisis to crisis in childhood.

24

Developing Healthy
Workplace Relationships

I would encourage you to begin thinking in terms of how to make
things different. You can dwell forever on the pain. It is important
to take a very good look at your issues, bring them out, chew them
up, spit them out, know that they'll come up again from time to time
and go on. You need to dwell on how you're going to make things different, what you're going to do to feel different in practical kinds of
ways. What follows is a practical list.

Know Your Performance Style

Either accept it and work with it, or work to change it.

Many of you learned to do things under pressure because that was
your life experience. You went from crisis to crisis. Nobody taught
you how to do things systematically. Nobody said, "You need to
spend an hour a night on your homework." So when you were in
school, for example, if you got your paper in at all, you did it the
night before. And now you have a deadline at work; even if you have
had plenty of lead time, you probably do the job the night before.

Then you come down on yourself, thinking there's something wrong with you because you always leave things until the last minute.

Leaving things until the last minute may be the way you work best. So rather than decide there's something wrong with you, recognize that this is the way you perform. Accept it!

If you have a history of getting things done when they're supposed to be done, don't automatically decide that you're doing it the wrong way. Know your performance style. It is important to know that about yourself. Different people operate differently, and your early experiences may have taught you to operate best under pressure. It may have become your performance style. Concern yourself with it only if it's not working for you. Don't fix what's working. "If it ain't broke, don't fix it."

Be Aware of Your Priorities and Live by Them

Not rigidly, but mindfully. ACOAs tend to give everything equal priority. Getting the wash done has the same priority as, say, filing your income tax. Life consists of many chores, obligations and projects. If each one has equal priority, it is very easy to become overwhelmed by all of them. Not everything has to be done immediately, but some things do. Not everything has to be completed immediately, but rather just held to manageable levels. If prioritizing is one of your difficult areas, you may need help with it.

The first thing you need to do is make a list of the things you have to do and give them a 1, 2 or 3 priority. If you have trouble doing this, ask your boss what needs to be done and when.

If you have time when you have completed the 1s, then do some of the 2s. Make this list every day. It will help to give you a handle on things. Otherwise, it is too easy to feel overwhelmed and to panic. Those feelings take a lot of energy and will drain you to the point where you are only able to accomplish very little, and that feeds the panic.

Discover Your Limitations and Live Realistically Within Them

You cannot do everything. We all have limitations. It is important to know that recognizing your limitations is not a way to put yourself down. Rather, it is a way to set realistic parameters to your work life. Become aware of your assets and respect them. You may not be able to feel good about them but you can be cognizant of them.

Be sure of your job description. It should be in writing. That way, you can know what your employer expects of you, and you can determine what is reasonable to expect of yourself. If the demands on you are far different from your job description, it is important for you to find out what that means.

With a sense of your limitations, both personal and in terms of your job, you can then do some realistic goal setting. You can then define some parameters and become more secure in your work life. You can determine your direction and begin to develop a systematic way to get there.

Practice a Stress-Reducing Discipline Daily

This is absolutely essential.

Since so many of you are drawn to high-stress occupations, it is very important to find ways of managing stress. A relaxation technique such as meditation or self-hypnosis, practiced on a daily basis, should become part of your lifestyle. If you don't practice it on a daily basis and it does not become a habit, you will not be able to draw on it when you need it.

Not only is this useful for reducing stress, it will help you to be more creative. Ideas that have no room to surface in a flooded mind or in a mind that is being outer-directed can come to the fore during meditation.

Many of the stress-related illnesses that you are prone to can be minimized, if not avoided entirely.

Separate the Being from the Doing

It's a complicated idea. What happens is that when someone criticizes your work, you take it as a criticism of yourself.

A counselor came in to see me, devastated because a woman said, "I am leaving your therapy group because I can get the same stuff from Al-Anon." The counselor began by defending himself. "You know," he said, "I've been a therapist for ten years and this hasn't happened to me before. I know I'm competent."

These are his words but not his feelings. He didn't react to her in terms of his competence. If he had reacted to her in terms of his competence, then he could have explored with her what it was about the group experience that she found lacking and learn from it.

What he reacted to instead was from an earlier time. What he heard was his father saying, "You'll never amount to anything." We had to address what went on in his self-esteem first in order for him to learn and change in the doing. When he recognized that the tape he was playing in his head was old and not accurate, he could then separate from it and look at the criticism in a new light. This happens over and over. Be careful, when someone criticizes you for what you do, that you take a look at it in terms of what you have done, not in terms of who you are. And if they criticize you in terms of who you are, then it is important for you to assess carefully whether or not this is a work situation that is beneficial for you to be in. None of us needs to be in a situation where our person is being judged.

Build In Time for Yourself

It is essential for you to have elements in your life other than work. Family, friends, hobbies and the like need to be part of your life.

If work is your whole life and the only place where your needs are met, you put yourself at risk. The loss of a job, a new boss who is difficult to work with or job dissatisfaction will be far more devastating than if you have other interests. Your entire identity should not be defined by your occupation. Loss of job need not be equated with loss of self if you take proper safeguards.

Building in time for yourself can also mean creating "nonproductive" time. Taking a bath, reading a novel, going for a walk, listening to music, riding a bike—these all fall into that category. Build this time in on a daily basis. Put it in ink on your daily calendar and be as conscientious to the self-commitment as you are to your commitment to others.

Learn What Is Appropriate and What Is Inappropriate to Share in the Work Setting

Though you feel close to others whom you work with, this does not mean that it is appropriate to tell them personal things. ACOAs, because of the boundary issues, tend to confuse this. An employer who comes to me for supervision asked my assessment of someone she had just interviewed: "You know, I really want to hire her, but during our interview she said, 'If I appear a little nervous it's because I just came from my doctor and he says I may have herpes.'"

That information was inappropriate to share with a potential employer. It started the employer questioning what the potential employee is going to share and what she is not going to share on the job. "I'm going to be sending this individual into schools. She's going to be developing relationships in those schools, and I'm concerned about what she will say."

It is not a good idea to share your fears and concerns with your employer. No matter how good the relationship is, your employer has got to be concerned about your job performance if you tell her how panicked you are that you won't be able to make it financially after the divorce, how you have had three sleepless nights in a row because your son comes in very late and very drunk. Your employer may care about you and your well-being, but that is not the relationship where disclosure of this nature is in your best interest.

Learn to Leave the Fantasy out of the Workplace. Learn How to Realistically Assess What Is Happening

It goes something like this: Because it's very easy for you, you get caught up in the fantasy. You need to assess realistically when your boss says, "I know I didn't give you the raise I promised, but in six months things are really gonna change," or, "I know the office is not what it's supposed to be, but when we expand. . . ." Be really careful about how easily you get sucked into this kind of stuff. "I am asking you now to take on this additional responsibility but it's not perma-nent." Watch it. Watch it.

Wishing doesn't make it so. It didn't when you were a child and it doesn't now. The difference is that as a child you had few options. As an adult you're in a different position. You can set a deadline for yourself. You can discover what control you have over seeing that desired changes occur. Then you live in the real world and take charge of yourself regardless of what flights of fancy are going on around you.

Don't Guess. Check Things Out

Guessing is one of the things you learned to do best as a child. You never learned to check things out; you never learned to ask. You never learned to question. But you really need to check things out. Things may not be as they appear because you're seeing them only from your personal frame of reference, so it's very important to ask if you're not sure. If you decide that somebody is angry with you, ask why. It may be important for you to know. And who knows? It might not even have anything to do with you.

A man who came to see me was very disturbed because someone was no longer saying hello to him in the morning. He couldn't figure out what he had done to offend this person and didn't know how to handle it. "What do I do about it? Do I confront him? Do I ignore him? Do I let it go? I'm lost and I don't want to make things worse."

"Are you the only one he's not saying good morning to?" I asked. He thought for a minute and then said, "Come to think of it, he's not greeting anybody."

The possibility is very strong that it may not have to do with you. It may have to do with him. Checking things out quite often takes the sting out of them. It helps you to begin to look at things realistically. Workplace rumors need to be checked out. Somehow, the walls have ears, but quite often the ears are clogged.

Mary, after a week of near desperation, finally went to her boss with a rumor she had heard. "I hear through the grapevine that you are looking to replace me and I thought I was doing a good job." She struggled to hold back the tears.

"I was hoping to save this announcement for the staff meeting and surprise you," he replied. "Your promotion has come through. Congratulations."

Before you approach your boss or coworkers, it is a good idea to check things out with a person or support group who cares about your best interest. You may need help in determining the appropriateness and style of presentation.

Although different circumstances may call for different strategies, the principle remains the same. Check things out. Don't guess.

Overreaction Is Historical.
Learn to Separate the History from the Moment

If you find that something is really making you nuts, it probably doesn't have to do with the given situation. It probably relates back to something that happened in your childhood, and the person in question has become someone else to you. It is important, before you act or react on the basis of that, to figure out who that person is.

June's boss called her and said, "I need to see you. I have some bad news."

June panicked. "Oh, my God! What have I done? What is going to happen to me? How can I cover myself? The panic was overwhelming. By the time I got to his office I was a basket case. He took one look at me and realized he had alarmed me. 'I'm sorry,' he said. 'The problem has nothing to do with you. I just need your input on how to explain to the staff that I'm not going to be able to offer the salary increases that I had projected.'" Her overreaction was a direct result of her childhood. Anything that went wrong became her responsibility to fix, regardless of whether she had any part in its going wrong or whether she had any idea of how to fix it.

25

Finding the Right Job for You

Part of your growth may involve realizing that the job you hold may not be the right job for you. It is important to recognize that changing jobs involves a process. It is the same process for everyone, regardless of whether or not they grew up in a dysfunctional family. There are four steps in the process that ACOAs may not be aware of:

1. Prepare an up-to-date résumé, whether or not you are satisfied with your present employment. This will give you an opportunity to explore whatever may come along and interest you— even tangentially. If you do not know how to prepare a résumé, pick up a book on the subject and follow those guidelines. Nobody automatically knows how to do it until they have done it the first time. Have someone you trust look it over for typos or additional thoughts.
2. Take an interest inventory to see where your interests lie.
3. Take some aptitude tests and see where your potential lies.
4. Take a personality profile to find out your interactive style.

You may or may not be suited for the work you are doing and may be very confused as to what to do about it. Defining yourself by the opinions of others and trying to accept them as your own is most perplexing.

Taking stock of yourself in the ways listed above will give you an objective assessment of your ideal work profile and then you can explore the options. There are some good books on this subject. *What Color Is Your Parachute?* by Richard Nelson Bolles (Ten Speed Press) is among the most readable.

Learn about the process of job change and try to set up an orderly system for yourself—step-by-step—with a reasonable time frame.

You may feel that others have the edge when it comes to parenting and intimate relationships because they may have had good role models, but in the marketplace, as uneasy and insecure as you feel, you have the better survival skills. Those skills are a great leveler.

26

ACOAs As Counseling Professionals

ACOAs make fine counseling professionals. Indeed, many ACOAs, as we have seen, are involved in the field. This discussion does not relate to inadequacy on their part but rather the pitfalls many experience at work as counselors. It relates to their self-feelings and how they get in the way of feeling good about the job they do.

Adult children of alcoholics have very well-developed gut responses. This is a survival skill they learn as children. Words are not as meaningful to them as they are to other people. They can get their clues not only from the words but from a variety of other sources. They are able to gain a sense of what their client is feeling and where their client is at without going into lengthy descriptions, which very often get in the way of knowing what is really going on. Since these gut reactions are so basic as to be almost instinctual, it is difficult to explain how you know. Counseling is one area where identification with childhood trauma can add to one's expertise—unfortunate, but true.

Children of Alcoholics Very Often
See Themselves As Frauds

It is not unusual for the ACOA counselor to believe that she is a fraud. It has far more to do with self-feelings than with performance.

Someone I supervise came to me with this issue not too long ago. "How can I help my clients build their self-esteem if I struggle with that myself?" he said.

The idea that unless all of your personal issues are resolved, you are counseling under false pretenses would mean that no one would be qualified to be a counselor. If your client's issue is your own *current* struggle, you may need to refer him to someone else. Counselors need to be human, and not being finished is a part of being human.

Most of us, from time to time, when faced with new situations that involve the demonstration of confidence, feel like little kids playing grown-up. It is that child within us that has the performance anxiety.

The fear of the ACOA is deeper, and each workplace job performance assessment brings it up all over again. "How long will it be until they discover I've been fooling them into believing that I know what I'm doing?" This leaves the ACOA in a continual state of stress.

Adult Children of Alcoholics Tend to
Overidentify with and Become Overinvested
in Their Clients

This is a boundary issue that relates directly back to childhood. It was impossible to know where your needs and feelings ended and someone else's began. It was impossible to know who was the parent and who was the child. To what degree were you supposed to make it right for everyone else? How could you know what was your problem and what was somebody else's? It's very easy to become overly concerned with your clients as well.

It is not to the client's benefit to bring concerns about her home with you night after night. It does not improve your skill as a counselor not to be able to leave your clients behind. The client will not know the difference, but you will propel yourself toward burnout. You are not your client. Your client's growth is not a measure of your personal growth. The parameters need to be made clear, and one of the ways to make them clear is to work with the client during the time that you are working with the client and let that be that. If supervision is necessary, that is something else again, but supervision is formally structured. When you leave your place of work, you leave it. You may have to fight your mind for a while in order to accomplish this, but it may be the difference between your remaining in the field and your getting burned out. Taking your work home with you does not make you a better counselor.

The discussion in a supervision group was on working with families in which a family member has committed suicide. As the discussion went on, one of the clinicians in the group looked more and more depressed. When I asked him what was going on with him, he said, "The discussion is getting to me. This is a very serious problem area for me. I find that I take on my clients' issues like lint and I am unable to pick them off. I know how to be different. I know the professional discipline that it takes. I know the principles of detachment. I know *how* to replace one thought with another. I know that I am not all-powerful and cannot fix everything for everybody. None of that knowledge seems to do me any good. What do you suppose this means?"

"It's certainly a boundary issue for you," I said. "Your parents never respected your boundaries. They constantly humiliated you in public.

They took credit for whatever you did that was good and wonderful. They never let you be separate from them. They never let you develop and separate yourself as a person. I suspect that this is a reason why you're going to be the opposite of your parents. You are so angry at your parents and so critical of your parents that whatever they say, whatever they do, however they behave, there is a red flag saying, 'I will behave the opposite way.' Since they were always angry, you never allow yourself to be angry. Since they were always out of control, you always need to maintain control.

"I suspect they also had no compassion for other human beings. They certainly had no compassion or sensitivity toward what you were feeling, and certainly did not spend time and demonstrate concern for what was going on with you. Here again, you have decided to be the opposite of them. In so doing you have become over-involved. You are too caring."

It is the extremes with which we must concern ourselves. Because your parents were not caring does not mean that you need to be all-consumed with caring. It does mean that you have to move a little bit more toward their position. The ideal for both you and your parents is to be more centered. The reality is that for your own growth, you need, in some ways, to be more like them.

ACOAs Need to Have Everyone Like Them. They Seek Approval Not Only from Their Supervisors and Peers, but Also from Those They Serve

This is another area that can become burdensome for you. Clients will simply not like you all the time. It is part of your responsibility to do and say things that they do not like. They cannot separate your words from your person, and they will get angry at you. This goes with the territory. You need to be very careful not to carry this response around with you. The important thing is that your clients hear and do the things that are to their benefit. The important thing is the positive movement toward growth.

A client of mine called me from a rehab center. She was very angry with me. She said, "You told me I would not have a great deal of difficulty with withdrawal and I had a terrible time." My response was, "That was because I didn't realize what bad shape you were in."

She began to laugh. I did not have to take on her anger. I did not have to defend myself. I was able to effect her getting the help that she requires. That is my job. That is my goal. If she needs someone to blame when she is angry, so be it. The blaming will not last long. It will stop when she begins to feel better. But her interests are my interests. It's very hard to separate that out if you are looking for your client's approval.

I suggest that if you need to seek approval—and we all do to one degree or another—you seek it from people who are in at least as good shape as you are. If your clients are in at least as good shape as you are, you may want to reconsider what you are doing for a living.

Adult Children of Alcoholics Avoid Conflict

It is certainly understandable that if you grew up in a home where there was always conflict and never resolution, you would back away from it. If you grew up in a home where you were afraid, when anger was expressed, that either you would be hurt or that someone else would be hurt or that you would be invisible or that someone else would be rejected, it is not difficult to see why you would discourage this kind of behavior.

An aspect that you have to look at critically is whether or not you yourself know how to resolve conflict. It is absolutely essential, not only in your personal life but in your work life, that you develop the necessary tools to deal with working through and resolving conflict.

Adult Children of Alcoholics Have Difficulty Making Referrals

The difficulty in making referrals comes from fear of being found out. If you make a referral, the fear is that others will discover that you are incompetent. They will learn that you could not work with this client, that you did not have the necessary skills to work with this client. You don't want people to know your limitations. The reality is that we all have limitations, and the idea is not to try to hide them but to recognize them. In recognizing that there are others who are more skilled with certain clients than we are, we better serve our clients. We cannot be specialists in all areas. We cannot relate to all the people who come to see us. It is not possible nor is it desirable. "I cannot help you, but I can help you find somebody who can" is a statement of competence.

ACOAs Are Impatient with Stuck Clients

This results from self-judgment, in part, and also a judgment of the client. The self-judgment is, "If I were a better clinician, my client would not get stuck. Therefore, the inability of my client to move at this time is a negative reflection on me."

The other part of it is a countertransference issue with your client. "I was where you are and I got through it, I got by it, I did what I had to do. Why can't you?"

There may be two realities here. One may be that your client only looks stuck. Sometimes people need time to consolidate their learning. Sometimes people need to take a breather before they move on and make new decisions. Sometimes clients remain stuck so that they don't have to make the change that is so terrifying to them.

The other aspect is that there may be something you could be doing for your client that you are not doing. Believing that it is an inadequacy in you that causes your client to be stuck will get in the way of your asking a supervisor or a fellow counselor for some thoughts on what they would do if they were in this position.

"My client is stuck" and "I must fix" are not equivalent statements.

Many Look for a Treatment Road Map

Many want to know before they begin with a client just exactly what to do, how to take it, where to take it, how long it will take, what the best approach to take is, what one should not do and so on. It's not unusual to get this request for guidance. Essentially it's asking for a road map through treatment. It's not a whole lot different from the road map that many ACOAs want for their lives. "Tell me what to do. Tell me how to handle myself. Tell me if I am doing the right thing. Tell me if I am doing the wrong thing. Is this a good decision to make? Is this a poor decision to make?" This difficulty and this need for structure, order and direction are legacies from childhood. Because there was no foundation on which to build, there is a great deal of insecurity left in deciding what the correct road to take is.

Those of us who train counselors would be disrespectful in giving you a treatment road map. There is no treatment road map just as there is no life road map. There are the things that work and the things that don't work. There are the things one tries out that work successfully, and there are things one tests that don't work out so successfully. It is important to be able to help your client discover options and alternatives, to help your client be aware of the possible consequences of exploring each one of these options and alternatives. If this is what you are truly asking, if this is what you are really looking for, it is different from looking for a road map. It is saying, "What are the different courses this treatment could take? What are the possibilities that I need to be mindful of before I begin? What are my goals and what are my client's goals?" Those are legitimate questions. Those are important questions. Those questions may need to be asked.

ACOAs Who Are Clinicians Are Poor Stress Managers

Being stressed has been the natural order of things. You grew up in a stress-filled household. It was what you knew. It was the way you felt all the time. As a result, when you are stressed in the workplace, you are not necessarily aware of it. Working with clients is a very difficult, highly stressful situation. You do not have an opportunity to relax; you do not have an opportunity to give anyone less than your full attention. If you are relaxing or if you are giving your client less than your full attention, you are not doing your job. Therefore, by definition, you are in a highly stressful situation. This isn't to say that it cannot be really satisfying—maybe you prefer to work this way. What it does say is that it is important for you to recognize that this stress must be managed. It is important for you to recognize that you must take relief from the stress. It is important that you develop the means to do so.

ACOAs Who Are Clinicians Deny Their Own Countertransference

Countertransference somehow is a dirty word. Clinicians are not supposed to countertransfer. Clients are supposed to transfer but clinicians are not supposed to countertransfer. Therefore, a clinician who has a countertransference reaction to a client is less than perfect. So since ACOAs who are clinicians feel they have to be perfect, they will tend to deny their own countertransference. It is not possible for you not to be drawn to a child you would like to take home. It is not possible for you not to be furious at someone who behaves like someone in your life who abused you. It is sometimes not possible for you not to be sexually drawn to a client. This is simply the way it is. Admitting it to yourself means that you can get a handle on it. Sometimes it's not serious. Sometimes your awareness of your response to this client means it will not get in your way.

Sometimes a reaction is so powerful that it becomes necessary for you to refer that client to somebody else. This is not a reflection on you. If it happens consistently, you may want to take a good look at the matter. It is not useful for you to deny it. The transference of the client to the counselor is a very useful one for the ACOA. It is not harmful for the clinician to be proud of the client's growth and progress. This pride is certainly a parental pride. It feels good and it is not at all harmful to the client. If it goes much further than that, you need to be careful. I know I had to stop seeing young children. My countertransference reaction to them was too great. I wanted to bring all of them home with me. I wanted to take care of them. They had in fact become mine. This was not useful or beneficial to them, nor was it useful or beneficial to me.

ACOAs Who Are Clinicians
Have Difficulty Limiting Their Caseloads

You are the one in the agency who will take on that additional case. You are the one they can always be sure will take one more. This has to do with your inability to say no. This has to do with your not recognizing when you are being exploited.

It is very important that you recognize just how many clients it is appropriate for you to handle and at what point it is a good idea for you to say no. Check around. Don't do this within your own agency; if you are being exploited there is a very good chance that others are being exploited, too. Check with people who work in other places and feel comfortable with their workload. See if they are carrying as many clients as you are. See how their case management is worked out. Where in your day is time built in for the paperwork that piles up way over your head? Where is time built in for you to return phone calls? This is all part of your job description. If you are seeing clients from the minute you walk in until the minute you leave and then have to do this work on your own, your caseload is inappropriate. It is exploitive. You must take steps to balance the situation.

This may be a good opportunity to check and find out if you are propelling yourself toward burnout. The counselor who does not take careful precautions will not last. Balance is the goal.

The Balance/Burnout Checklist for Counselors

Emotional Health

1. How much time do you spend worrying about your clients and their problems?
2. Are there moments when you believe your work situation is

hopeless and that you cannot help anyone?

3. Do you have strong mood swings and feelings about your clients? Your work? Your own family and friends?

4. How often do you blame the administration, your colleagues or your clients for your own bad feelings?

5. Would your life be fine if only staff and clients behaved differently?

6. How often do you feel lonely? When you're with others—or by yourself?

7. Do you ever question your own sanity? Lose control?

8. When does your own behavior make you feel ashamed?

9. Are you often fearful?

10. Is work more important than your family and/or social life?

11. How do you control your anger and frustration?

12. What makes you feel responsible for the behavior of others?

13. Do you feel guilty about your work some of the time?

14. Do you feel overwhelmed by your working responsibilities?

15. Are you becoming more sensitive to and more critical of others at home and at work?

Physical Health

1. How are your sleeping habits being affected? Do you toss and turn? Escape by sleeping long hours?

2. What physical symptoms of illness in yourself have you noticed? Headaches? Nausea? "Knot" in the stomach? Exhaustion? Agitation? Backaches? Pains in the neck?

3. How have your eating habits changed?

4. Have you been involved in physical violence in your home or with friends?

5. How has your sexual life changed?

Social Health

1. How is your concentration on your work affecting your daily life? Are you working overtime? Not spending time with family and friends? Not taking time for recreation?
2. Do you spend much of your time reacting to crises and feeling your life is not your own?
3. Has life become so very serious that you have lost your sense of humor?
4. Do you find yourself forgetting things? Losing things? Having minor accidents?
5. Do you spend your free time during the working day talking about clients?
6. Do you have your clients check in with you regularly so that you may monitor their behavior?
7. How do you overprotect your clients?
8. What responsibilities have you given up in your family so that you may continue to concentrate on work?
9. How have you let work interfere with social plans?
10. Do you ever feel unappreciated at work?
11. Do you sometimes think your clients cannot survive without your good advice?
12. How do you let clients affect your own feelings? Your behavior?
13. Do you ever threaten clients or intimidate them in confrontations? Are you ever sarcastic?

Reprinted from the Hazelden publication entitled, *Manual for the Family Program for Professionals*.

27

Thoughts for Employee Assistance Programs

An employee assistance program (EAP) is an ideal route to draw ACOAs into the treatment they need. Because people spend a large portion of their lives in the workplace, it is here, surrounded by colleagues who do not necessarily have the personal investment in the working relationship, that ACOA behavior can be perceived and addressed—for the good of both the individual and the company. There are no losers when the ACOA gets the care he needs and deserves.

For the individual, this care can often serve as the deterrent from progressing into alcoholism or other forms of substance abuse.

As Cindy tells us:

Five years ago, frightened by my own increased drinking, worried about the impact of alcoholism on another generation and supported by therapy, I made a decision to stop drinking and to face the personal and family problems related to multigenerational alcoholism that I had avoided and denied. The decision to take charge of my life and then to fulfill the Serenity Prayer has increasingly contributed to an understanding of my motivations, and therefore a lessening of the necessity for me to work out my unresolved conflicts through the work itself.

It can help to quiet what Mark called "the inner voice of failure" that sabotages the personal as well as the professional life.

Michael, the manager of an EAP for a large high-tech research company, describes the benefits for the company as well as for the individual:

> *In almost every case, adult children of alcoholics respond well to counseling. . . . The degree of isolation, support systems, etcetera, determines the length of treatment. The prognosis for these clients is excellent once they are treated.*

In other words, when you begin to address the issues of the ACOA in the workplace, you begin to address the billions of dollars lost through poor job performance, lost sales, on-the-job accidents, absence from work, medical costs, and the costs of hiring and training new personnel.

But it was the religious counselor who most poignantly described the benefits of ACOA treatment:

> *God made you. It's okay to be you. It's even okay to love your-self. In fact, the more you can love yourself, the easier it is for you to help others.*

This ideal exists in all relationships. It is a workplace goal as well as a personal goal. It is a direction for us all to follow.

Some companies are in a position to offer an educational series to their employees. The components of an educational series on and for adult children of alcoholics could be the following.

Week One: An Overview—
Adult Children of Alcoholics

The first week is designed to include general information pertaining to ACOAs. This seminar introduces the education series and describes the content and focus of the seven following weeks.

Objectives

Participants will learn of the cost of alcoholism and related problems to their company.

Participants will become familiar with the research, literature and experiences of the largest population of people affected by alcoholism.

Participants may identify themselves as belonging to this population.

Participants will have the opportunity to ask questions and receive clarification on individual problems and concerns, and to assess whether the education will be of further help.

Week Two: The Childhood Experience

This seminar introduces the "family disease" concept. The interpersonal dynamics of the alcoholic family are explained. The leader discusses early perceptions of reality and the coping mechanisms children of alcoholics developed for survival.

Objectives

Participants will become aware of the progressive processes of the family disease.

Participants will become aware of how these family dynamics can be replayed in the workplace.

Participants will become familiar with how a functional family system deals with problem-solving, expression of emotions and communication.

Week Three: Adaptation to Alcoholism

This seminar focuses on the roles assumed by family members, and how these roles are both functional and dysfunctional in childhood and adulthood. This lecture stresses the need for ACOAs to identify how roles serve as a protective defense from emotional turmoil, as well as provide the ACOA with a sense of self based on what they do versus who they are and how they feel. This seminar includes a discussion on conditional versus unconditional love.

Objectives

Participants will become familiar with various roles assumed in alcoholic families and identify how various roles serve in maintaining survival, reducing stress and creating a sense of stability for the ACOA.

Participants will discuss the strengths and weaknesses implied in various roles, what the advantages and disadvantages were, and what emotions the roles repressed.

Participants will identify how the alcoholic and codependent parents responded conditionally to various role behaviors versus responding unconditionally to the whole child.

Week Four: Adult Traits and Characteristics

This seminar focuses on a discussion of adult traits and characteristics as determined by researchers. It addresses problems experienced by ACOAs and how these problems have roots in the family history of alcoholism. The messages and distorted perceptions internalized throughout childhood in an alcoholic environment are examined.

Objectives

Participants will become aware of the manifestations of the employee's isolation in the workplace.

Participants will learn how these internalized overt or covert messages interfere with the employee's present functioning.

Participants will develop strategies toward change.

Week Five: Self-Help for ACOAs

This seminar uses a broad-based definition of self-help to assist the ACOA in utilizing resources to aid in recovery. The traditional programs of self-help such as AA, Al-Anon and ACOA are discussed. The participants are also exposed to the help available through education and various community resources. Various forms of therapy are discussed.

Objectives

Participants will become aware of available recovery programs.

Participants will utilize a variety of resources to help with various needs.

Week Six: Intimacy

This seminar will, through lecture, film, discussion and group exercises, show how living with alcoholism can interfere with the ability to experience intimacy. The goal of this seminar is to define intimacy and discuss the components of healthy relationships.

Objective

Participants will discover how problems of intimacy can affect workplace behavior.

Week Seven: The Recovery Process

This seminar focuses on the recovery process. Needs and problems encountered during various stages of recovery are discussed. The behavioral, cognitive and emotional changes experienced in recovery, and how change occurs, are highlighted.

Objective

Participants will learn to understand recovery as a process.

ACOA Warning Signs: A Checklist for EAPs

Just as it takes time to get to know someone, it takes time to perceive the effects of an undiagnosed ACOA on the job. Here are some of the most important manifestations of ACOAs creating difficulties for themselves on the job:

- Procrastination
- Perfectionism
- Indecisiveness
- Impulsiveness in decision making
- Inconsistent productivity
- Too many questions
- No questions at all
- Difficulty in accepting compliments
- Constant approval-seeking
- Often working very late
- High absenteeism
- Overinvolvement with other employees' personal problems
- Apparent disregard for other employees' feelings
- Assuming responsibility for other people's mistakes
- Lack of initiative
- Frequent emotional outbursts
- No display of emotions at all
- Too much discussion of personal life
- No apparent life outside of work

The reader will see that many of the items on this list form pairs. The ACOA will often flip-flop from one extreme to the other—productivity is a case in point.

But it's important to note that these manifestations vary, depending on the nature of the workplace, and that this list is incomplete. Further research is required to determine whether ACOAs create stress on the job, how they respond to it when it does occur, and what effect this has on their fellow employees.

Crisis Counseling for ACOAs: A Checklist for EAPs

1. *Referred for job performance problems.*

   Look first for signs of substance abuse.

2. *Absenteeism due to illness.*

   Check for burnout or substance abuse.

3. *Problems with peers and supervisors.*

   Look for playing out of alcoholic family system.

4. *Problems with family.*

   Look for substance abuse or other compulsive behaviors in
   self, spouse or children.

   Look for lack of understanding of how to solve the problem.

5. *Problems with intimacy.*

   Look for fears of abandonment.

   Look for substance abuse in lover.

   Look for lover within the organization and the relationship
   going bad.

28

Conclusion

The legacy of childhood clearly demonstrates itself in the work-place. This is true for everyone regardless of their background. Your history can either work for you or against you. You can decide to change or adapt. Once you have insight, you have choices.

Clinical practice clearly shows that ACOAs respond very quickly to treatment. They are eager for help and make very good use of tools gained in the counseling process.

In the substance-abuse field, we talk in terms of prevention, intervention and treatment.

Prevention lies in education. "I feel this way because of part of my childhood experience. I behave this way because of part of my child-hood experience."

Intervention lies in breaking the cycle. "I need to make changes because what I'm doing and feeling is not working for me."

Treatment is the development of new messages:

I am a person of worth.
I can demonstrate it.
I can feel it.

I can make choices.
I can work for you and not lose me.
I can grow with the organization and not leave me behind.
I will take me with me.

The EAP counselor who works with the ACOA participates in an exciting growth process. The shift from me (the object) to I (the subject) creates an energy that can be productive for all concerned.

The value of the ACOA in the workplace gets clearer and clearer. Recognition of the signs of ACOA issues as they surface, and responding quickly and appropriately to them, will, in both the long and short run, result in maintaining superior workers and greatly reduce the losses due to burnout, physical problems, substance abuse and impulsive job changes. It is in the economic best interest of companies to be responsive. It is to the advantage of all—not just ACOAs, but their colleagues as well—to address these issues as they arise and not wait until they reach bitter fruition. The workplace itself will become a more productive and healthier environment.

SUGGESTED READING

This list is by no means complete, but it is a good place to get started.

Bradshaw, John. *Healing the Shame That Binds You*. Deerfield Beach, FL: Health Communications, Inc., 1988.

Toxic shame is the core problem in our compulsions, codependencies, addictions and drive to superachieve. The variety of healing techniques given here can help you release the shame that binds you.

Harris, Dr. Thomas A. *I'm OK—You're OK*. New York: Harper & Row, 1967.

This book discusses social and developmental aspects of human behavior, based on transactional analysis.

Middelton-Moz, Jane and Lorie Dwinell. *After the Tears*. Deerfield Beach, FL: Health Communications, Inc., 1986.

Grief and loss reflect the family legacy of alcoholism. Children from these homes suffer long-term depression and erosion of their sense of self-worth. With the aid of this book, you can reclaim the personal losses of childhood.

Miller, Alice. *The Drama of the Gifted Child*. New York: Basic Books, 1996.

Gifted (sensitive, alert) children recognize at a very early age their parents' needs, and adapt to them. This childhood "drama" can result in the destruction of the ability to experience authentic feelings in adulthood, especially feelings of sadness. This book has helped many readers to discover within themselves the little child they once were and to regain the capacity for genuine feelings that are a source of natural vitality.

Paul, Jordan and Margaret Paul. *Do I Have to Give Up Me to Be Loved by You?* Minneapolis: CompCare, 1984.

Enables couples to learn to work through conflict in ways that create more love and intimacy, not less. This book talks about fears and false beliefs which are obstacles to loving feelings, and provides exercises for couples so that they can explore their feelings together.

Peck, M. Scott. *The Road Less Traveled*. New York: Simon & Schuster, 1978.

Provides step-by-step guidelines to help the reader along the difficult path to psychological and spiritual growth.

Pietsch, William V. *Human Be-Ing. How to Have a Creative Relationship Instead of a Power Struggle*. New York: Signet, 1974.

A readable and practical handbook about improving relationships.

Vale Allen, Charlotte. *Daddy's Girl*. New York: Berkeley Books, 1980.

A true story from a woman who survived her father's abuse, she tells how this trauma effected her and the people close to her.

Whitfield, Charles L., M.D. *Healing the Child Within.* Deerfield Beach, FL: Health Communications, Inc., 1989.

If your inner child is buried beneath layers of guilt, resentment, shame and isolation, you'll find here a road map from discovery to recovery that will enable you to gently heal your child within, reclaim a vital sense of spirituality and create the gift of personal freedom in your life.

Woititz, Janet G. *Marriage on the Rocks.* Deerfield Beach, FL: Health Communications, Inc., 1979.

What is a person to do when his or her spouse drinks too much? When the marriage is "on the rocks?" Here is sensitive, thoughtful, compassionate advice for the person who lives with and loves an alcoholic spouse. Here are tools for change.

Woititz, Janet G. *Healing Your Sexual Self.* Deerfield Beach, FL: Health Communications, Inc., 1987.

Whether your experiences were what is conventionally described as sexual abuse or the more subtle forms described here, you can break through the aftermath of sexual abuse and enter into healthy relationships. Survivors are shown here how to recognize what went wrong and to deal effectively with the many psychological manifestations of trauma.

Woititz, Janet G. and Alan Garner. *Life Skills for Adult Children.* Deerfield Beach, FL: Health Communications, Inc., 1990.

If you have difficulty asking for what you want, solving problems, handling criticism, or saying no and sticking to it, the lessons and exercises in this book will help you learn how to stand up for yourself without losing your temper, make a decision without second guessing yourself, avoid feeling worthless when someone criticizes you and feel confident instead of apprehensive about saying "no." These and other new skills you'll learn here will improve your self-image and make your complex adult life easier.

NOTES

"Employee Assistance Programs: Blending Performance-Oriented and Humanitarian Ideologies to Assist Emotionally Disturbed Employees." *Research in Community and Mental Health*, 1984, Vol. 4, pp. 245–259.

Podolsky, Doug M. "RTI Report: Economic Costs of Alcohol Abuse and Alcoholism." *Alcohol Health and Research World*, Winter 1984/1985, pp. 34–35.

"A Retrospective Study of Similarities and Differences Between Men and Women Employees in a Job-Based Alcoholism Program: 1976/1977." *Journal of Drug Issues*, 1981, Vol. 11, pp. 233–262.

Shealey, Tom. "Your Secret Signals." *Prevention*, September 1985, Vol. 37, no. 9, pp. 68–72.

Sonnenstuhl, William J. "Understanding EAP Self-Referral: Toward a Social Network Approach." *Contemporary Drug Problems*, Summer 1982, pp. 269–293.

413

Steele, Paul D., and Robert L. Hubbard. "Management Styles, Perceptions of Substance Abuse and Employee Assistance Programs in Organizations." *The Journal of Applied Behavioral Science*, 1985, Vol. 21, no. 3, pp. 271–286.

Trice, Harrison M. "Employee Assistance Programs: Where Do We Stand in 1983?" *Journal of Psychiatric Treatment and Evaluation*, 1983, Vol. 5, pp. 521–552.

Trice, Harrison M., and Janice M. Beyer. "A Data-Based Examination of Selection Bias in the Evaluation of Job-Based Alcoholism Programs." *Alcoholism: Clinical and Experimental Research*, Fall 1981, Vol. 5, no. 4, pp. 489–496.

"Work-Related Outcomes of the Constructive Confrontation Strategy in a Job-Based Alcoholism Program." *Journal of Studies on Alcohol*, September 1984, Vol. 45, no. 5, pp. 393–404.

ABOUT THE AUTHOR

Janet Geringer Woititz, Ed.D., was the founder and president of the Institute for Counseling and Training in West Caldwell, New Jersey, which specialized in working with dysfunctional families and individuals. She was the author of the bestselling *Adult Children of Alcoholics* and *Struggle for Intimacy* as well as *Marriage on the Rocks*, *Healing Your Sexual Self* and *The Self-Sabotage Syndrome: Adult Children in the Workplace*. Her books are also available as tapes.

NOTES

NOTES

NOTES

From Janet Woititz

From Edward Bear

The Dark Night
of Recovery

Conversations from
the Bottom of the Bottle

Edward Bear

Code #6536 • Paperback • $9.95

The Dark Night of Recovery is for anyone—
recovering or otherwise—who has ever
struggled or felt lost and alone.

From John Bradshaw

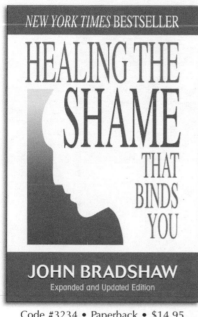

Healing The Shame That Binds You is a book about naming and healing an elusive and life-destroying monster called toxic shame.

Code #3234 • Paperback • $14.95

Bradshaw shows you ways to escape the tyranny of family-reinforced behavior traps and demonstrates how to make conscious choices that will transform your life.

Code #4274 • Paperback • $13.95

From Robert J. Ackerman

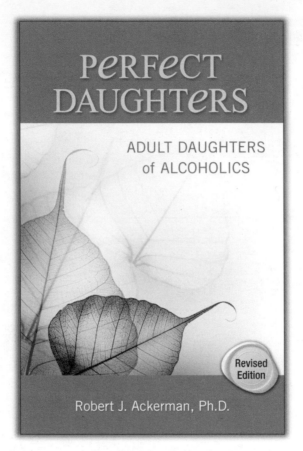

Code #9527 • Paperback • $14.95

This edition contains updated information throughout the text and completely new material, including chapters on eating disorders and abuse, as well as letters from perfect daughters in various stages of recovery.